Also by Tom Ringley:

Rodeo Time in Sheridan Wyo
A History of the Sheridan Wyo Rodeo

A History
of the
HF Bar Ranch

TOM RINGLEY

Cover Design: Antelope Design
Drawing by Jim Jackson
Photo by Lily Bliss

www.pronghornpress.org

*To all the stewards of HF Bar Ranch
Family, Dudes and Staff alike,
Past present and future.*

Dudes

Don't misunderstand the term "dude." It's a legitimate hundred percent American term in Wyoming nomenclature—and means any visitor from "outside," just as "savage" means the rancher, his cowboys, and all the rest of his business associates— which is to say his "outfit."

—"Rope Your Own," by the Head Wrangler—*Sunset Magazine* 1926

...a dude, in western parlance, is any visitor from the "outside" who pays to stay on a ranch or hires a local inhabitant to guide or cook for him. An easterner or a westerner, all are the same to the cow-puncher—so long as one is city bred, he's a dude...

—*Sunset Magazine,* June 1930

...A dude...is anyone whom Mr. Horton puts on an old horse and makes believe he is a red blooded American...

—Henry Platt as reported in *The Sheridan Press,* 1926

Forward

I'd love to have a nickel for every person who has ever told me they wanted to come live on the HF Bar Ranch as one of our animals. It's a very common request. First, I think that it is about "care." Our number one concern is that everyone feels comfortable and cared for here. And then, I think it is because the Ranch is about "equality." Once you enter the gate, no matter what walk of life you claim, all of us are on equal footing. One of us always knows an answer to something that none of the rest of us knows. People have mentioned to me, numerous times, that there must be some "magic" here because, from the time they arrive until they leave, they experience a part of themselves that immediately feels good, forgets their "problems" for a while and allows them to behave like the child inside them would want them to.

In the following pages, you will read about the glorious and, oftentimes, rakish history of the HF Bar Guest Ranch. The stories of the people who have been a part of this grand old Ranch reverberate over and over again the timelessness of the place. There aren't enough pages, really, to cover all that has gone on since the first person passed through the Ranch gate, but Tom Ringley has captured so very much of it!

Books like this make you reflect on what you've done with your life. It is, after all, a history book. I'd like to think that what started out to be a memorial to Jack Horton's life has turned into a life's work for me. With the help of many people—and they all know who they are—I believe a unique place has been reincarnated over these past several years into not just a "Western dude" experience but, rather, an educational and, often, life transforming place of healing and inquisitiveness whose very nature causes people to, somehow, improve or reinventory the way they live. Sure, people come for the horses and the fish, but, most of all, they gather for the splendor of the place. All worlds seem to come together at the H F Bar. Just cast an eye at that amazing sky on your way back to your cabin at night. Rarely is there a night that you don't see a shooting star.

This same magical attraction to the HF Bar Ranch led Tom Ringley to undertake this immense story-telling project. It was a labor of love and understanding which is apparent in the sensitive, objective and honest treatment he has presented. Tom's insight and fervor for the subject was unflinching. We are grateful to him for "getting it down" for us and for those who will follow in the years ahead. Surely, you will hear the wind rippling through the ponderosa pines as you turn the pages.

Margi Schroth
HF Bar Ranch
2006

Table of Contents

Part 11

A Joint Venture...59
The Hortons and Gorrells
1911-1930

Chapter 4 HF Bar Beginning...61

Chapter 5 The Twenties...100

Part III

Truly the Horton Place...161
1930-1948

Chapter 6 The Thirties...163

Saddlestring

Introduction

In 1911, near the small town of Buffalo, Wyoming, an ex-Iowa farm boy turned sheepherder, Frank O. "Skipper" Horton and his brother-in-law, Warren Gorrell, a Chicago financier, made an important discovery. Quite by accident, they chanced upon a small acreage at the foot of the Big Horn Mountains near where two creeks, the North and South Forks of Rock Creek, converge. A gruesome tragedy made it possible for Skipper Horton and Warren Gorrell to acquire the land and establish the famous HF Bar Ranch.

The compelling story of the HF Bar Ranch, which was originally established as a resort and working ranch, and how it has evolved over ninety-four years to become one of the oldest and most successful dude ranches in the nation has never been told. I am privileged to be able to tell the complete story.

I am no stranger to the subject. My interest in HF Bar stems from a longtime connection. My uncle, Dean Thomas, worked there for fifty-six years. I worked there, as well, for several summers in my high school and college years and later was, and still am, a frequent visitor. Jamie Ringley, my son, who made his first visit to HF Bar when he was less than a year old, has made the HF Bar his career and has worked there for over twenty years.

I have always harbored a thought that the history of HF Bar

should be recorded. But it wasn't until late in life that I found the wherewithal to do something about it. I realized that I should take the project on after I published a modest history book titled *Rodeo Time In Sheridan Wyo.*

It was while working on *Rodeo Time* that I experienced the thrill of discovery through research. It is truly a "eureka" moment to unexpectedly find, in an old dusty box, a letter that illuminates a mystery, the unexplained or the unknown. I also learned how satisfying it can be to compile and organize material in a way that completely informs the reader about a subject which has perhaps been treated before, but only in a sketchy, piecemeal, error ridden fashion. It is pleasing to fill in the gaps, shore up the facts, and set the record straight—and by doing so add to the body of western history.

With my newly acquired penchant, I approached Margi Schroth, the owner of HF Bar Ranch, and proposed that I write the story of the HF Bar Ranch. Was she interested? Margi replied that she sure was and added, "There is quite a story to be told." Margi was right about that!

I hope I have treated the story appropriately. It is so much more complex than I'd imagined. Margi gave me unfettered access to the old dusty safe in the back of the ranch office where I uncovered material which had not seen the light of day since it was placed there so many years ago. In addition to material about the ranch itself, I discovered a mother lode of information about generations of HF Bar people, primarily involved family members. The information not only gave me insight into how interesting they all were, but also how human. In treating this sensitive material, I have attempted to be as objective and fair as possible in order to tell the real story. Any conclusions or inferences that are drawn are strictly my own and for them I take full responsibility.

It was very difficult to decide who should be mentioned in the story. Besides involved ranch family, there have been literally thousands of guests and employees that have passed through the main

gate of HF Bar to work, relax and play. In the end, I had to use the information available and "go with what I know." My choices leaned toward those whose mention I thought would further the HF Bar story in some way. Those not mentioned are, nonetheless, a very important part of the HF Bar Ranch history

Literally everything that has ever been written about the HF Bar Ranch attributes its establishment to one Frank O. "Skipper" Horton. For whatever reason, his co-founder, Warren Gorrell and his wife Demia, disappeared from the radar screen and have rarely, if ever, received mention in any documentation about the HF Bar Ranch. Hopefully, I have corrected this historical oversight.

The history of HF Bar must begin with the introduction of the Horton family and Skipper. Warren and Demia Gorrell will enter stage on cue.

Tom Ringley
Big Horn, Wyoming
2006

Saddlestring

Part 1

Before HF Bar

Chapter 1

The Hortons

Skipper was a tenth generation Horton, but we begin this story with his father, Charles Cummins Horton, who was born in Goshen, Orange County, New York on January 13, 1839. Charles moved to Muscatine, Iowa, with his parents in the 1840s and had three siblings; brothers, James Lisle and Edwin Webb, and sister, Sarah Lisle.

The obituary of Skipper's father was published one day after his death on April 21, 1916, and provides some insight into the man:

Charles Cummins Horton was a native of New York State, having been born at Goshen, Orange County, Jan. 13, 1839, a son of Dr. James S. and Mary Gamble Cummins Horton. That young Horton came of "fighting blood," and possibly was predestined to become a commander on the field of battle, is indicated from the fact that he sprang from Revolutionary stock on both sides, his great-grandfather, Capt. Jonathan Horton, serving throughout the Revolutionary War as well as a maternal grandsire, Archibald Gamble, who was an engineer on the staff of General Moultrie, who later laid out Fort Moultrie during the War of 1812.

In 1848, the Horton family came to Iowa, settling at Muscatine. For two years the Hortons remained in town, but in 1850 moved to a farm two miles distant. Young Horton had started his schooling in New York State, and continued it at Muscatine and in a district school near his father's home in the country. In 1857 he returned to New York State and entered the Delaware Collegiate Institute at Franklin, from which he graduated in 1859.

When the first warnings of civil strife came in 1861, Horton, then a young man of 22, talked of enlisting, and at Muscatine, in July of that year enlisted as a private in Company A, Second Iowa Cavalry. He was commissioned second lieutenant on Aug. 1 and promoted to first lieutenant on Nov. 2. On June 4, 1862, he was made captain, and on Sept. 20, 1863, major of his regiment. From that he rose to lieutenant colonel, on Sept. 27, 1864 and was mustered out Sept. 19, 1865, at Selma, Ala....

During his four years' service Colonel Horton participated in thirty-one engagements. His first fight was the battle of Monterey, where William Paxton, of Indiantown, Tama County, was the first man of the regiment to be killed. Horton was in the fighting at New Madrid, Island No. 10, the two battles at Booneville, in the second of which Phil Sheridan won his first star; Farmington, Iuka and Corinth, Tupelo, Jackson and Nashville. In the famous charge at Farmington, made by the Second Iowa on May 7, 1862, Horton had his horse shot from under him. He was wounded in the battle of Coldwater in September, 1863 and carried a musket ball in his hip to his death.

Directly after the war Colonel Horton went to Alabama where, in company with Captain Brunton, of the Second Iowa, he engaged in a coal mining enterprise near Toledagoula. The business

*did not prove profitable, however, and in 1866 Horton returned to
Iowa and went to farming. He specialized in the raising of small
fruits and fine stock, largely horses. Later, for several years, he was
in the abstract business in Muscatine in company with John Kemble,
under the firm name of Horton & Kemble.*

A year after his return from Alabama, Colonel Horton married
Isabella Ogilvie of Muscatine on October 31, 1867. She was the
daughter of Adam Ogilvie and Isabella Milne of Muscatine. Colonel
Horton and Isabella settled down on the farm and did not have their
first child until James Lisle arrived on April 24, 1874. In the next nine
years they had three more children: Skipper and his two younger
sisters, Mary Milne and Bertha.

While Colonel Horton farmed after the war, and as he raised
his children, he was active in the community, a trait which his son
Skipper would inherit. He served in various capacities including
supervisor of his township, vice president and president of the
Muscatine County Agricultural Society, and trustee and treasurer of
the Soldier's Orphans Home in Davenport, Iowa. He also served two
terms in the Iowa legislature and represented his county in the 15th
and 16th General Assemblies. Colonel Horton was a candidate for the
Republican Party for Congress and narrowly missed election at the
party convention on the 125th ballot. In 1880 he was appointed as a
special land agent of the government and also was appointed as a
special agent for the Pension Bureau and supposedly he lived in
Athens, Tennessee for several years. In 1897 Colonel Horton was
appointed as commandant of the Iowa Soldiers' Home in
Marshalltown, Iowa. He served in this position until he resigned just
before his death in 1916.

Skipper's Birth

Skipper's birth date is uncertain. The conventional wisdom is that he was born on October 18, 1882, in Muscatine, Iowa. This date is used in the Horton Family History posted on the Brockway Family website. The same birth date was used in Frank Horton's Congressional Biography and other miscellaneous pieces written about Skipper over the years.

Yet, evidence exists that places the 1882 date in dispute. For instance, the 1880 Federal Census lists Skipper as two years old at the time of the census yet, supposedly, he was not even born yet. There are other anomalies. Skipper's youngest sister, Bertha, was born in July 1883. This would have been only a scant nine months after Skipper's birth.

Further, Skipper's nephew, John Brockway, discovered that Frank enlisted for the Spanish American War on April 26th, 1898 at the stated age of nineteen, but no birth date was entered. If Skipper was nineteen at the time, then his birth year would have been in 1878 or 1879. But, the year 1879 has to be ruled out. Skipper's other sister, Mary Milne, the mother of John Brockway, was born in November 1879 and John Brockway knows that his mother and his aunt, Bertha, were younger than Skipper. Skipper could not have been born in 1882.

Other documentation about Skipper's age is equally confusing. For instance, he is buried in Willow Grove Cemetery in Buffalo, Wyoming. The date of birth carved on the headstone is October 18, 1880, when, according to the census he was already two years old. The funeral home records state that Skipper was sixty-eight years old when he died, but there is no birth date listed on the funeral home record, which, according to the staff, is very unusual. There are no probate records in the Johnson County Courthouse (he was buried in Johnson County) or in the Sheridan County Courthouse (he died in Sheridan County).

Census data is equally confusing and highlights the inaccuracy of these types of data. For instance, the 1910 Federal Census listed Frank as thirty years old, which meant that, if true, he would have been born about 1880 which is not probable. The 1920 census lists his age as thirty-eight which is strange because ten years passed between censuses yet Frank only seems to have aged eight years. Similarly, the 1930 census lists his age as forty-six. Again, he only aged eight years in ten?

Two other circumstances convinced me that Skipper could not have been born in 1882. In 1937, his youngest sister, Bertha, sent Skipper an application for his entry into the Illinois Society, Sons of the American Revolution. Bertha urged him to join since she was a Daughter of the American Revolution. To encourage him she filled out the application for him so that he had only to sign, which he never did. Bertha listed Skipper's birth date as 1877.

A last fly in the ointment is the information entered on Skipper's transcripts at the University of Chicago. The transcript states that Skipper was born on October 21st (not the 18th as recorded elsewhere) in 1877 in Marshalltown, Iowa (not Muscatine, Iowa).

So, why discuss these genealogical aberrations? Does it further the story of Skipper? Well, no, not really, but it does add slightly to the mystery of the man. And, in my mind, Skipper was a bit mysterious. We will have to content ourselves with the reasonable certainty that he was born on October 18th or 21st, in either Marshalltown or Muscatine Iowa, in either 1877 or 1878.

Chapter 2

Frank O. "Skipper" Horton

Early Days

Skipper was a typical Iowa farm boy. He grew up on the family farm about two miles out of Muscatine with his older brother and two younger sisters. Their household was probably fairly regimented because of his father's military background and because of the work it takes on the part of all family members to make a farm work. No doubt his father instilled in young Skipper, and his siblings, a sense of hard work and social responsibility—traits which Skipper would display throughout his life.

Skipper went to public schools in Muscatine and graduated from Muscatine High School in 1897. For reasons unknown he was dispatched to the Morgan Park Academy in Chicago, Illinois. There is no history of any family connection with the school. He was probably sent there simply because his father believed Frank needed some additional schooling before he attended a university.

Morgan Park Academy was first called the Mt. Vernon Military and Classical Academy and was founded, according to the Morgan Park Academy website:

...on a ridge above "Horse Thief Hollow" during Ulysses S. Grant's second term as president, just in time for the "Panic of 1879". It survived that economic dislocation—and a few others in its venerable history—and has endured and flourished as an

independent school for more than a century and a quarter.

...It became Morgan Park Academy in 1874, with the civil war still a vivid memory and while U. S. military operations were concerned primarily with the resistance of Geronimo and other Native American leaders in the West.

...When William Rainey Harper became the founding president of the University of Chicago in 1892, MPA became the co-ed (quite unusual for that time, although the experiment did not last the decade) preparatory school for the university.

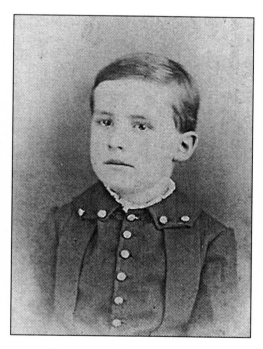

Frank O. Horton as a youth.
Age unknown.
(Courtesy of the HF Bar Ranch)

According to the Academy history, teachers at the Academy held university rank. One of them, Amos Alonzo Stagg, who was to become a legend, coached football at both institutions. When Mr. Harper died in 1907, the University of Chicago ceased its relationship with the Academy and the school once again became a military boarding school.

So, when Skipper went to the Academy it was a co-ed preparatory school for the University of Chicago. Not much is known about his academic career there. It is very likely that he played on Alonzo's football team because it will be seen later that Skipper played a major role on Stagg's University of Chicago football team.

The most significant thing about Skipper's career at Morgan Park Academy was that it was interrupted by the Spanish American War; not to the extent, however, that it kept him from graduating in 1899.

Skipper entered Morgan Park Academy in the fall of 1897 and on April 26th the next year enlisted in the Iowa National Guard. He became a member of Company C, Fiftieth Iowa Volunteers. His brother, James Lisle (usually called Lisle), who was four or five years older than Skipper, was a member of the same regiment and served with the rank of Sergeant, so it is assumed Lisle had been in the regiment some time before Skipper joined. Skipper was a private.

No sooner had Skipper enlisted than the regiment was dispatched, in May, to Jacksonville, Florida and nearby Camp Cubra Libre. They did not see combat action because in late July Spain sued for peace and in the fall of 1898 the men of the Fiftieth returned home to Iowa. Apparently many men of the regiment died of disease during the Florida rainy season but Frank and his brother returned unscathed.

Skipper's service in the military did not really interfere with his education at Morgan Park Academy. He went to war, literally, on his summer break.

Skipper graduated in the spring of 1899 and went on to matriculate at the University of Chicago in the fall of the same year.

His college career was noted in 1933 by Francis Birkhead Beard in an article entitled *Wyoming From Territorial Days to the Present* for the American Historical Society:

> *...From 1899 until 1903 he was a student at the University of Chicago, being graduated in the latter year with the degree of Bachelor of Science. Mr. Horton had a brilliant college career, being an excellent student, a member of the Alpha Delta Phi Greek letter fraternity and a member of the football team under Coach A. A. Stagg during all the four years of his university attendance...*

Frank O. Horton in 1899,
the year he served in the
Spanish American War.
(Courtesy of the HF Bar Ranch)

There is a problem with Mr. Beard's statement. I queried the University of Chicago Registrar about Skipper's attendance at the university and received the following reply:

I've checked our records (microfilm transcript, matriculation card which agrees with the transcript) that his birth date is Oct. 21, 1877 in Marshalltown, Iowa and the absence of a graduation card, so it seems safe to say that he doesn't have a degree from the University of Chicago...Mr. Horton attended the University of Chicago from Autumn 1899 to Spring 1902...

Another source stated that Skipper attended Rush Medical School which at that time was affiliated with the University of Chicago. However, a query to officials at the University of Chicago about that possibility also resulted in the firm declaration that there is absolutely no record that Skipper graduated from the University of Chicago or the Rush Medical School.

I assume that the records of the University of Chicago are correct. This casts a shadow on Skipper's representation that he was a graduate of the University of Chicago. However, Skipper's self promotions, including highly visible campaign literature, firmly declared that he was a graduate. So, could the University of Chicago records be mistaken? Or, did Skipper stretch the truth? The subject remains a mystery.

Whether he was a graduate or not, Skipper was a real presence on the University of Chicago football team while he was enrolled. An article from an unidentified newspaper describes the situation, believed to be in the fall 1900, before a forthcoming game between the University of Chicago and Northwestern.

The pending game was between two intense rivals and apparently Skipper had been out of action to the consternation of fans and the coaches. But relief was in sight. The article proclaimed:

Horton Back in Line-Up

When Horton appeared in his football togs yesterday he was greeted by cheers from his teammates. His injury of Saturday was not so serious as it was at first thought to be. He has recovered rapidly. While he is still lame, he was able to do light work yesterday, and is confident that he will be in condition by Saturday. Stagg is counting on him to play.

Frank O. Horton as a star football player
for the famed coach Alonzo Stagg
at the University of Chicago. Circa 1900.
(Courtesy of the HF Bar Ranch)

There were several other players on the injury list but Skipper provided hope to Stagg, for as the newspaper article reported:

If Horton is able to play but one substitute will be necessary...Horton is the best general utility man on the team...

A subsequent article reported that:

...The strong defensive game which the University of Chicago played against Northwestern has given Coach Stagg and his pupils new hope for the contest on the gridiron with Michigan next Saturday...with Horton back on the team next Saturday the offensive play ought to stand out to much greater advantage...

I had always assumed that Skipper met Gertrude Scovel Butler, of Indianapolis, Indiana, who was to eventually become his wife, while they were both students at the University of Chicago. Gertrude was born in Indianapolis on September 30, 1881 and had also attended Butler University in Indianapolis. Butler University was founded by Gertrude's grandfather, Ovid Butler in 1855.

Again, the registrar at the University of Chicago cast doubts on the assumption that Skipper met Gertrude while they were fellow students because Gertrude:

...attended classes from the autumn of 1902 to the autumn of 1904 and got a "two year diploma" similar to an associate's degree and something we have not awarded in many decades...

So, if Skipper left the university in the spring of 1902 and Gertrude entered in the autumn of the same year, how then did they meet? The issue is further confused by the fact that many years later Skipper would receive a letter from an old classmate who would refer to the time that he, Skipper and Gertrude were up at the University

of Chicago. It is possible, I suppose, that Skipper could have still been in Chicago in a non-student status and met Gertrude when she was enrolled as a student. We do not know exactly how and when they met, but we do know they did because they eventually married.

Their marriage would make possible, in later years, a family partnership with Gertrude's sister, Demia, and Demia's husband, Warren Gorrell. Warren was born in 1874 in Taylorville, Illinois and was raised there and in Chicago. Demia and Warren were both graduates of the University of Chicago and were married in Chicago in 1900. We will observe later how Warren and Demia Gorrell would go west to visit their Horton in-laws and become partners in a historic venture.

Skipper also had strong university connections through his fraternity Alpha Delta Phi. In 1900 Skipper and Warren Gorrell were fraternity brothers. Fraternity brothers would be called on frequently in later years to help him finance the HF Bar Ranch operations.

Skipper's activities between 1902 and when he arrived in Wyoming in 1905 are not known, except for the fact that Francis Birkhead Beard, mentioned previously, stated that Skipper took a position with Barnhart Brothers & Spindler, but I do not know for how long. Regardless, Skipper was definitely in Wyoming by 1905.

Chapter 3

Skipper Goes West

Why did Skipper go west? A popular legend is that he had aspirations to be a surgeon. As the story goes his ambition was frustrated by his color blindness and so he followed a medical recommendation to go west on the chance that life in the West would improve his condition. This theory has been embellished by several writers. One even went so far as to state that Skipper had to give up a successful medical practice because of his eyesight. As has been discussed, there is some doubt as whether or not Skipper obtained a bachelor's degree, much less attended medical school.

This issue is confused further by a door knocker. On the front door of the Horton house at HF Bar there is a brass door knocker inscribed "Dr. Horton." Was this the result of wishful thinking on Skipper's part? Or, is it possible the door knocker belonged to his grandfather Dr. Samuel Horton and Skipper put it on his own door because of wishful thinking, a lark, or to honor his grandfather? We will never know the answer.

So, Skipper may have harbored an ambition to be a doctor, even to the point of inscribing his door knocker, and he may have had a medical condition which thwarted his ambition. Whether or not his situation caused him to go west is conjecture. So, why, then, did he go?

He may have been influenced by his brother Lisle. Lisle was four years older than Skipper and they had served together for a short time in the Spanish American War. Skipper's nephew, John Brockway, wrote in a letter to Margi Schroth, the current owner of HF Bar, in 2002:

...I believe Frank's older brother Lisle was already in Wyo.—Clearmont area...Anyway, when Frank finished school, he, sister Bertha and Aunt Sarah (his father's sister) went to Clearmont area and each homesteaded a quarter section. Where the four corners of the sections met they made living quarters on the point and stayed there a year. After that I don't know what they did with the land, but Frank moved to where Saddlestring is now...

Lisle may have preceded Skipper to Wyoming. John Brockway's statement, however, that Skipper's sister and aunt accompanied him to Wyoming in 1905 is, I am afraid, family lore that cannot be substantiated. It is true that the Hortons took up homesteads in Wyoming—but not in 1905.

In fact, none of the Iowa Hortons with which this story is concerned owned any land in Wyoming before 1911 when Lisle purchased 158 acres from a Henry Klein who was the original homesteader. Lisle paid $750 for the property and then the next year, when he paid off the mortgage, he transferred ownership to his wife Grace for some unknown reason.

In 1918 Lisle leased a large parcel of land from the Leiter Estate to add to his livestock production capacity. The first homestead was not filed until 1919 when Lisle and his wife Grace filed on 320 acres and 160 acres respectively. It was not until 1926 that sister Bertha and Aunt Sarah filed their homesteads. Bertha filed on 320 acres and Sarah filed on 640 acres. What is curious is that when Bertha filed she was approximately forty-three years old, but there is no evidence she ever lived in Wyoming. Even more curious is that when Aunt Sarah filed she was eighty-two years old and would die the next year, 1927. One can only assume that Bertha and Sarah filed on homesteads so they could be used by Lisle in his ranching operation.

The Big Red

Even though the exact reason for Skipper's journey west is uncertain, where he went is not. Skipper first went to the Buffalo, Wyoming area where he got his first job herding sheep for Bud Cass in the Big Horn Mountains above Buffalo. There he learned enough of the sheep raising business to strike out on his own, which he did with the Big Red.

The history of the Big Red is best described in a brochure issued by the Ucross Foundation which currently owns and operates what was once part of the Big Red:

The property on which the Ucross Foundation stands was once the Wyoming headquarters for the Pratt & Ferris Cattle Company, a ranching operation founded in 1878 and made up of four ranches that stretched from present-day Ucross, Wyoming to the Platte River near the Nebraska line. All of the four ranches were situated on former Indian hunting grounds where large herds of buffalo had once migrated with the seasons. The ranches in the Powder River basin were on Clear Creek and included Big Corrals and Big Red. The village of Ucross that settled around Big Red went through several name changes before settling on Ucross—a word derived from the configuration of the original PF (Pratt & Ferris) brand. (Note: "Big Red" is derived from the fact that the main ranch house was painted red.)

The Pratt & Ferris Cattle Company was incorporated in Wyoming Territory towards the end of the Indian Wars by four partners—James H. Pratt, a former colonel in the Civil War, two of his brothers-in-law including Cornelius Ferris, and Marshall Field (of the famed Chicago department store)...Big Red became the headquarters for all four ranches in the mid-1880s...

In the 1890s, Marshall Field sold his shares to his

former Chicago partner, Levi Leiter. A sharp-minded and astute businessman, Leiter eventually became the dominant partner in the cattle company, holding more than 2,900 shares of the 4,000 shares that composed the company's assets. Leiter and Pratt bought out the smaller shareholders and by 1900 they became its sole owners. That year, 3500 cattle were run on the two Platte River ranches and 13,000 cattle were run on the Powder River basin ranches...

Levi Leiter died in the summer of 1904 and his widow, daughters, and only son Joseph inherited his shares of the Powder River holdings...The Leiter family would continue to be involved in the operations of the ranch for many years, as the senior Leiter's will had stipulated that no part of the ranch be sold until all his children had died...

History relates that the Pratt & Ferris cattle company would dissolve over time due to changes in ownership and a myriad of other factors, until today when the ranch comprises about twenty-two thousand acres and is called the Ucross Land and Cattle Company. It is small when compared to the original ranch that stretched from Wyoming to Nebraska.

Horton Bros.—Woolgrowers—Bankers

The early part of the century was a benchmark period at the Big Red. Levi Leiter died in 1904 and his son Joseph became the manager of the estate along with a board of trustees. Additionally, the cattle business in Wyoming, and most of the West, had become a losing proposition in the late 1800s and early 1900s and beef prices were at rock bottom. Many big ranches had already gotten out of the cattle business, but the Big Red hung on longer than most. However, the handwriting was on the wall and finally, in 1905, the Big Red virtually abandoned the cattle business and engaged heavily in sheep production.

The Big Red searched for people with sheep experience (they had twenty-three people in the sheep division). The first evidence of the Horton brothers' involvement in the Big Red sheep operation is found in family letters that Helen Platt wrote to her children.

Helen Platt was the wife of Henry Platt, a young lawyer for the Leiter interests in Chicago. He took an assignment with the Big Red in Wyoming so that he could go west for his health and gain first hand familiarity with the "livestock business and irrigation operations of the company." He was a member of the law firm of Mayer, Meyer, Austrian and Platt and would later coordinate Joe Leiter's team in a lawsuit when his sister sued him for mismanagement of the estate in 1926.

Helen's first letter was written back to her family on September 9, 1905 from Clearmont, Wyoming. The series of letters she sent back to her family provide a remarkable glimpse of life in Wyoming and on the Big Red. Her first mention of Skipper was on October 6th when she wrote:

...Yesterday Mr. Leith, the sheep manager, & two other men came to dinner. One of the two was a Mr. Horton from Chicago. He

is a graduate of the University & is right attractive. He has been up in the mountains all summer, & now is learning the sheep business...

On October 17th Helen described the experience she and her husband, Henry, had while they were out on a trip to look over the sheep. Skipper was in the party and Helen wrote about him again:

Mr. Horton is a very handsome attractive young man of twenty five or so. He is a graduate of the University of Chicago, & knew Chicago pretty well. He is out here learning the sheep business & next spring will go into it for himself together with his older brother. A long training on chafing dish suppers has made him an elegant cook, & his willow grouse were nice enough for an indoor meal...

Henry and Helen Platt would return to their home by Thanksgiving time, but it was not the end of the Platt acquaintanceship with Skipper. After HF Bar was established they went there as guests. Their son, Sherwood K. "Que" Platt wrote to his son, Austin P. "Bob" Platt in 1977:

...I was 12 when the family first took me to (the) HF Bar. (Note: 1915). *Part of the reason was to get me better acquainted with my cousins, Francis Chase and Isabelle Platt (now Mrs. McClumpha) whom they also took along. Another reason was to get me away from Malcolm Kerr and the Kerr boys, of whom my parents were not particularly fond, my Evanston pals. At the Ranch, I made many boyhood friends: Ned Tilt, Bill Robinson, Gregg Vecker (?), Ginger Gorrell, Benton Foley, Josephine and Ralph Wallace, etc...* (Note: Sherwood took the opportunity to carve his initials in the base of a prominent sandstone geological feature, Castle Rock, which overlooks the ranch. He carved his initials just below where a C. J. Hepp carved his name in 1877.)

Sherwood Platt visited HF Bar again in 1927 with his wife Dorothy Pickard "Dottie" Platt and her parents Henry Austin Pickard and Minnie Verna Pickard of Evanston, Illinois. The Platt family would continue to have a relationship with HF Bar which still exists.

Helen and Henry Platt's grandson is Austin P. "Bob" Platt. Bob visited the ranch in 1962 as a guest of his parents with his wife Pam and baby son Steve. Since 1968, Bob and Pam and members of their family have been guests at HF Bar every summer. One of Bob and Pam's children, Richard, has been to HF Bar literally every summer as a guest and employee since he was born. He has been a permanent ranch employee for the last ten years.

Bob and Pam's grandchildren from their eldest son, Steve, have also been guests at the ranch. So far, the HF Bar Ranch has hosted five generations of the Platt family and become a major part of their lives.

Helen Platt commented about Skipper's plans to get in the sheep business with his brother, James Lisle. Those plans were implemented when on December 19, 1905, W. A. Leith, the sheep manager of the Big Red, wrote a letter to the Leiter estate headquarters in Chicago:

...Herewith I enclose Bond of F. O. Horton—James L. Horton in sum of $5,000—as per yours of 12th inst...

So, the Horton brothers were in the sheep business. The bond was required because the brothers would run sheep on shares for the Leiter Estate. In fact, Robert A. Murray documents the Horton Sheep Contract in his 1981 treatise entitled *The Pratt and Ferris Cattle Company's Ucross Ranch on Clear Fork*:

...In 1906, Horton signed a contract with the Leiter Estate to take care of 3000 head of sheep for the company, using water points they controlled on Powder River and grazing the sheep out east of

that stream. The company furnished the sheep and the wagons. Horton and the company split the wool clip and the increase in the flocks and it turned out to be a profitable arrangement for both. By 1911, Horton amassed enough capital to start a major dude ranch at the foot of the Big Horns that is still in operation today... (Note: It will be seen later that Skipper didn't amass quite enough capital. He had major financial backing from his relatives Warren and Demia Gorrell.)

Skipper provided a more candid version of this state of the situation when he wrote an article about his Wyoming beginnings in the HF Bar Ranch newspaper *Bridle Bits* in 1928:

...I came out here from school, herded sheep for a while, and finally got a band of sheep on shares, made a little money and lost a little money, made some more and went broke; then made a little more and got married and had to settle down more or less and give up the good old times and the good old, free bachelor days of the wild and wooly west when she was in her prime...

Skipper's brother Lisle did not figure into any of the accounts about the early days of the sheep business with the Leiter Estate. For sure, Lisle was around. Beginning in 1908-9 the Horton brothers were listed in the Sheridan County Directory in the Woolgrowers Section. They were a repeat listing in the 1910-1911 edition.

The Horton brothers also got into the banking business as officers of the Clearmont State Bank. In about 1909 or 1910 Frank Horton was listed as Vice President and J. L. Horton as cashier. Little is known about this banking operation or how the Horton brothers became involved.

At about this time Skipper and Lisle began to take divergent career paths. In the 1910 Federal Census, Frank Horton is listed as "Woolgrower and Employer" in Clearmont and James L. Horton is listed as bank cashier, Clearmont. The census also documented that Lisle had a wife and daughter.

Lisle was already married when he went to Wyoming as he had married Grace Cora Jobe in Rock Island, Illinois in January, 1899, the year young Skipper began his studies at the University of Chicago. Lisle and Grace would have two daughters born in Sheridan, Wyoming: Harriet Lisle was born in 1909 and Maribel the following year. Both would live into their eighties and die in Cheyenne, Wyoming.

In 1911 Lisle began to ranch in the Clearmont area on the land he acquired through purchase and homesteading as was mentioned previously. Eventually, Lisle and Grace divorced and he married Marjorie Stowell Akers in Golden, Colorado on July 7, 1934. Grace died on June 18, 1941 at sixty-seven years of age. Lisle would eventually move to Nebraska and then Hot Springs, South Dakota , where he died at the age if seventy-three on October 22, 1947.

The relationship between Skipper and Lisle does not seem to have always been particularly close. No known correspondence between the two exists. There was contact, however. After they went their separate ways Skipper often sent livestock to winter on the "homestead" which was Lisle's place near Clearmont.

Some insight into their relationship can be gleaned from a letter Skipper wrote to his attorney, Burt Griggs, in Buffalo, Wyoming about 1946. The Horton siblings had been left some property in Kansas by their uncle and it was sold. The paperwork for the transaction was sent to Skipper and his brother and sisters for signature. Apparently, when Lisle received it he marked it all up and it had to be reaccomplished. This prompted a telling reaction from Skipper:

...I suppose all of these papers must be made over and sent on to my sister Bertha C. Horton...She will send them on to my sister Mrs. James Brockway, widow, and to the idiotic brother J.Lisle

Horton. I see he spells his name Lise, which is probably correct (Note: How could he not know how his brother should spell his name?) *but you better make it Lisle. I sometimes wonder whether people are born fools or whether they acquire the habit by practice...*

Skipper must have had some brotherly feelings for his big brother Lisle because he had been known to help him out during difficult times in later years. Skipper's sister, Bertha, reflected on one such instance in a personal letter to Skipper on May 14, 1937. She also expressed her feelings about their brother:

...I think it is pretty fine of you to send Lisle $25.00 a month toward a car and to keep it up for 8 mos. after the way he has done. (Note: There is no evidence to show what Lisle had done.) *I don't know that it's right to help him anymore. Of course it does help him to get established in what should be his line of work I suppose, but here is hoping he sticks to it and makes good...*

Marriage—The Gorrell In-Laws—Visitors

The 1910 Wyoming census did not state that Skipper had a wife, but that is probably because she was not in Clearmont. She was in Chicago having their first son, William Scovel Horton. Skipper and Gertrude had been married in Lakeside Minnesota on August 25, 1908. No correspondence or family stories about their courtship have survived. They were married three years after Skipper went west. Whether or not there was talk of marriage before he left is not known, nor do we know if Skipper paid periodic visits to Chicago to court Gertrude. At any rate, Skipper did go back to marry Gertrude and then took her to Wyoming.

They lived in a sheep camp somewhere on the Leiter Estate and in 1909 Gertrude's relatives came to visit. Her relatives would join with Skipper to co-found the HF Bar Ranch and would be closely associated with them for the next twenty years.

As stated previously, Gertrude's sister, Demia, married Warren Gorrell in 1900 in Chicago. They were both graduates of the University of Chicago and had four children: Anna (Nan) born in 1901; Warren, Jr. (Ginger) born in 1904; Demia (De) born in 1906 and Sarah (Sally) born in 1909. One child, a son named Scovel, died in infancy. Warren Gorrell was an investment banker in Chicago from approximately 1908 to 1929 and became a multi-millionaire. He was president of Warren Gorrell & Company in Chicago.

Warren and Demia Gorrell
(date unknown)
They partnered with Skipper
to establish and develop the
HF Bar Ranch.
(Courtesy of Henry S. Stewart)

Demia and Sarah Gorrell,
daughters of Warren and Demia Gorrell.
Date unknown.
(Courtesy of Henry S. Stewart)

Sarah Scovel Gorrell (Stewart) daughter of Warren and Demia Gorrell.
Date unknown.
Her son, Henry S. Stewart, would champion the recognition
of his grandparents' role in the establishment and
development of the HF Bar Ranch.
(Courtesy of Henry S. Stewart)

Warren Gorrell relaxing with his horse at the HF Bar Ranch
away from the hustle and bustle of Chicago. Date unknown.
(Courtesy of Henry S. Stewart)

In 1930, Warren Gorrell would recall his first visit to the
Hortons in an article he wrote for the *Chicago Commerce*:

*...My first visit to Wyoming was in November, 1909—not the
most propitious time in the Big Horn Mountains. I landed in what
was then my brother-in-law's sheep camp, and my first impression
was of the bleakness, the inconveniences and the loneliness. In those
days neighbors were far apart and one could see for miles over the
hills and never see a person or fence. It was not long before I had
forgotten all this and was learning to dress as fast as a fireman, in an
unheated room, at the call of "roll out" at 6 a.m., and be out on
horseback wrangling horses and cattle before daybreak. I arrived*

worn out physically and nervously, but at the end of six weeks when I reluctantly returned to Chicago, I was hardened as never before, and found I had stored up physical and nervous energy which carried me through the winter and spring with a zeal for my work and no loss of time through illness—a new experience...

The Gorrells were not the only people to visit the Hortons. Apparently there were a lot. Skipper described the situation in *Bridle Bits* and explained how he got started in the dude business:

...It was all on account of happenstance that we ever got started on this dude ranching business...the wife had a lot of eastern friends who kind of found it convenient to come west to eat on us. They got to be pretty numerous by the time another hard winter came along and I almost went broke again, and with the long list of free boarders in sight for the following summer, had to do something to keep my head above water. I therefore decided to put it on a commercial basis, and early that spring (1910) built Trail Lodge where we had 10 or 12 friend guests, receiving from them about $35 per week and giving them in return about $10 a week in value...

What Skipper does not explain in the article is that he had discovered the site of Trail Lodge when he herded sheep in the mountains above Buffalo which was about forty miles northwest of Clearmont. The mountain sheep camp was probably where he built Trail Lodge.

In the early 1920s it sometimes took two kinds of horsepower to get to Trail Lodge in the Big Horn Mountains. Rider in business suit is Skipper Horton. Second rider is unknown.   *(Courtesy of Cynthia Twing)*

So, with Trail Lodge, Skipper was in the dude business, whether he liked it or not, before the site for the HF Bar Ranch was ever discovered. Trail Lodge would remain the mountain camp and be used extensively during the summer months for many years. Trail Lodge was described in the first HF Bar and Trail Lodge booklet published in 1911 as follows:

Trail Lodge, the Mountain Camp...is located in Clear Creek Canyon (Big Horn Forest Reserve) at an elevation of 9,134 feet.
The surroundings are beautiful; the Canyon is about seven miles long and at the Lodge half a mile wide. At the west it

gradually narrows to a creek bed between towering peaks and abruptly ends in the rock wall of the great divide of the Big Horns at an altitude of 11,500 feet.

The equipment consists of a kitchen, mess hall and bath house on the cleared south bank of Clear Creek, and cabins and tent houses set back three hundred feet in the pine forest.

There is good fishing up and down Clear Creek. Seven lakes, known as the Seven Brothers, are within ten minutes climb of the lodge, and the Piney Lake Fishing Preserve within an hour and a half's ride...

Trail Lodge was a great place to go and get away from it all, and it is where Warren Gorrell went in August of 1910. Gertrude was not there at the time, because, as was mentioned before, she was in Chicago, presumably with her sister Demia, to give birth to their first son Bill.

The corral at Trail Lodge in the late 1920s.   *(Courtesy of Cynthia Twing)*

Discovery of HF Bar

This is when Skipper and Warren discovered the place that was to become HF Bar. He described the event in *Bridle Bits*:

...After the guests had left that fall, my brother-in-law, Warren Gorrell, and I happened to roll off the mountains one day, coming down the trail that we are now using to go to Paradise. My first sight of the present HF Bar Ranch, therefore, was from the top of Stone Mountain. We drifted down to the ranch house where we were heartily received by Bill Robbins, then owner of the ranch.

That night, Mr. Gorrell and I slept out in a little tent about where the Glass Door now stands. (Note: The Glass Door was the name of a bungalow which for some reason had a glass door, a unique feature in those days. The bungalow no longer exists). *The tent in which we slept was rather a clever contraption consisting of four stakes driven into the ground, with poles connecting the four stakes. On the poles, ends and sides, was nailed a large canvas and through the center of the canvas underneath was run another pole in order to keep the two of us from rolling together. I say "slept"—I am not quite sure this is the true word. Anyhow, the next morning we went over the ranch and found it even more beautiful than we had thought from the top of the mountain...*

Apparently Skipper and Warren expressed an interest in their new discovery and intimated to Bill Robbins and his wife, Cora, that if they every wanted to sell the place, he and Warren would be very interested. In fact, Skipper must have asked a lot of questions because sometime shortly after his visit he recorded his thoughts about the place on a piece of Clearmont State Bank stationery, on which he was listed as vice president:

Billie Robbins Ranch

520 acres deeded land—120 acres of this under cultivation and under the ditch. The water right is O.K. Always have plenty of water. There are 1220 acres of lease land, 1120 of which are state lands, 100 acres forest reserve land. The leases on state land amount to $56 a year on the forest reserve land $6 per year. Twenty acres of the state lease land are now under cultivation under the ditch, at least 30 acres more can be put under the ditch. Between 40 and 50 acres of the deeded land can still be put under the ditch making a total of more than 200 acres which can be cultivated. State land can be bought any time at $10 an acre until such time there is any trouble in renewing your lease. There are no taxes on state land, the deeded land pays a tax of about $60 a year. There is a $5,000 mortgage on the ranch paying 7% interest which runs for 3 or 5 years. Mrs. Robins didn't remember which. This mortgage can be paid any month by giving 30 days notice at any other time by paying an additional 3 mos. interest. The soil is rich and will yield a great crop if properly farmed. A lot of the alfalfa is of poor stand and should be reseeded. There would have to be 6 good work horses and a couple of saddle horses for the ranch alone which would cost close to $900. Plenty of machinery save plows go with the ranch.

When Skipper and Warren left the Robbins place they had no inkling of the forthcoming turn of events. In Skipper's property description, he neglected to mention, although he was aware of it, that there was a sawmill on the Robbins place. Just a few months into the winter it would take Bill Robbins' life. No one was around to observe the accident but when Bill Robbins was found he was almost cut in half by the saw blade.

This tragedy was recalled years later, in January 1983, by Clara Thompson of Kaycee, Wyoming, when Clara gave an oral history interview to Patty Myers. Clara was the granddaughter of Thomas and Clara Haynes, who owned a place on Rock Creek that would eventually be acquired by HF Bar.

Clara's interview was about Cora Robbins and she recalled that the Robbins:

...had lived up on what is the Horton place now. And he was running a sawmill and he fell, and it cut him right in two...they had a boardwalk over the saw part, and he was walking out, and it was kind of slippery that morning. I can remember the morning well enough, it kind of sleeted, half snow and half rain. I went to school that morning, we were going to school out on Rock Creek, my brother and I. He slipped on that board and fell right into the saw. I will never forget that, it made a horrible impression on me...

The Robbins hadn't lived on the place that long and Cora Robbins was left with three children ages eight and five and one less than one year old. Cora had to sell the ranch to settle the estate and so she turned to Skipper and Warren Gorrell because of their expressed interest in the property on their earlier visit only a few months before. They obliged and took over the place.

The transaction was completed on April 17, 1911 when an Administrative deed was prepared. The deed was issued with Warren and Demia Gorrell as the purchasers. The price was twelve thousand dollars and was paid for with a seven-thousand dollar down payment and the assumption of an existing five thousand dollar mortage. Later it would be refinanced and Warren and Demia Gorrell and Skipper and Gertrude would be named as mortgagees.

There it was. In just a few months time, a tragic turn of events provided the opportunity for Skipper to leave behind his sheep herding days and with Warren and Demia Gorrell create a historic ranch near Buffalo.

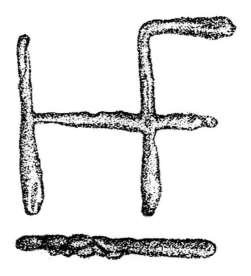

Part II

A Joint Venture

The Hortons and Gorrells

1911-1930

Chapter 4

HF Bar Beginning

Skipper was anxious to get started and took early possession of the ranch in March, 1911, a month before the deal was officially closed in April. He also had to get his family, Gertrude and young Bill, to the ranch, so, as Skipper wrote in *Bridle Bits* in 1928:

> *...Mrs. Horton was spending the month in Greeley and did not come to Wyoming until March. I met her at Clearmont with the buckboard with a couple of broncs hitched to it, and drove straight through to the ranch.* (Note: Gertrude went to Greeley, Colorado after she gave birth to Bill in Chicago. I do not know who she stayed with in Greeley and I assume Skipper had never seen his firstborn, Bill.) *Bill at that time was a husky kid of about six months. The only thing in the way of improvements on the ranch when we arrived was a log house about 20 by 40, covered over with boards...Then, too, there was the log building which we are now using as a garage, and another*

which stood near the present power plant...

> *...Since we had a number of people lined up for July and August, it didn't take us long to get Old Tom and Ollie Clark on the job.* (Note: Old Tom and Ollie must have worked for Skipper in Clearmont). *Before the first of July we had completed the Gorton, Hole-in-the-Wall, Boulders and LaRobida which at that time was called the Monkey House...* (Note: The cabins Gorton and LaRobida have disappeared in time, but Hole-in-the-Wall and Boulders are still in use today, albeit greatly updated.)

The local press took note of the happenings on Rock Creek. *The Sheridan Post* printed the following article in July 1911:

Johnson County Summer Resort

> *Another summer resort is being built in the Sheridan country. The latest man to bid for eastern tourist trade is Frank O. Horton of Johnson County who is building accommodations on his Rock Creek ranch and on an adjoining tract of the forest reserve for a large number of guests. Already with his cabins half completed and without having done any advertising he is said to have had requests for accommodations for far more guests than he could care for.*
>
> *Mr. Horton's plans include the building of two groups of cottages, one on his ranch and one on the north fork of Clear Creek on the reserve. Thus the guest may enjoy a fine outing in the lower country, in the foothills, or if he is so inclined may go up through the mountains to the highest accessible altitude.*
>
> *The location is an ideal one and the equipment being installed is to be the best. Mr. Horton is said to be backed in his enterprise by eastern capital...*

In the *Bridle Bits* article Skipper describes further the living conditions offered to the guests:

> ...*Of course, none of these cottages had a private bath. Remember that the west was not only still wild and wooly, but also the Great Unwashed...It was not until 1917 that we installed bathrooms. This was quite some innovation in the dude ranch business because up to this time there was no dude ranch in the country that could boast of a private bath. We tacked a frame building on the end of the log house, which served as a dining room. Later, when we remodeled the entire ranch house, this frame dining room was moved away and now is the present store and office.* (Note: It would later be replaced with a new structure which is the present store and post office.)

Skipper also reminded the reader of other conditions that existed when they started HF Bar. For instance, there was no electricity and it wouldn't come to the ranch until 1925, and:

> ...*in those good old days, there were no good roads, not even good bridges, leading into the ranch. The automobile was unknown in these parts, and all our transporting of guests, baggage and provisions had to be done in buckboard. That meant 40 miles of mud or snow or sleet, or whatever happened to lie on the road between the ranch and Sheridan, and it certainly was some job transporting people to and fro! Many a time we found it necessary to send guests clear to Sheridan on horseback, with their luggage on pack horses, because the roads were well nigh impassable...*

Some operations had to be fine tuned with experience. Skipper relates in *Bridle Bits* how:

> ...*In the early days the saddle barn and corral occupied the*

spot where the garage (Note: original old log barn) *and baseball diamond now are. Harry Huson had worked for me for a number of years before I took over HF Bar but did not come with me here. We tried to operate the corral without much success during the first two years of HF Bar. Then Harry came and it has been smooth sailing ever since...*

Harry Huson, longtime HF Bar corral boss from about 1913 to 1935.
(Courtesy of the HF Bar Ranch)

Harry Huson was a mainstay of HF Bar for many years. He was born near Tabor, Iowa, in 1879. His family went west and was the first to homestead on Crazy Woman Creek. Harry and his brother Fred also homesteaded on Lone Tree Draw, in what is now the Clearmont area, to add to the family holdings. Harry was raised in the Clearmont area and for about ten years was a cowboy with the Big Red.

Harry wasn't very big. His sons, Harry and Russell, believe he was probably no more than five foot six inches tall. But, he was all tough. His sons know for a fact that during his lifetime he broke his legs seven times riding broncs. Apparently, some of the breaks he set himself without the assistance of a medical doctor. Surprisingly, Harry never developed a limp!

At some point in time Harry linked up with Skipper. Whether or not they worked together or Harry worked for Skipper is not clear. There is reason to believe that Harry was involved with the Trail Lodge operation as his son, Harry, has vivid memories of his father talking about helping to build a cabin at Trail Lodge for Warren Gorrell.

When Harry went to work for Skipper in 1913 he was about thirty four years old, approximately the same age as Skipper. Harry had been married twice before but, tragically, both of his wives had died without having children.

He married in 1927 while he was still working at HF Bar. His wife, Mae, was a New Yorker who was a guest at the IXL ranch near Dayton. Harry, who had a sideline as a square dance caller, and performed at many ranches in the Sheridan area, met Mae, who was twenty-four years younger than Harry, and they were married.

Harry and Mae had three children, Harry, Edward and Russell. Harry was born in 1928 at HF Bar on the old Haynes place. When Russell was born, Harry was fifty-seven years old. Harry and Mae were at HF Bar until 1935.

A rare photo of Gertrude Horton who by all accounts
was a gracious hostess to the guests
of the HF Bar Ranch.
Date unknown.   *(Courtesy of the HF Bar Ranch.)*

Saddlestring

While Skipper wrote about the early days of HF in the 1928 issue of *Bridle Bits*, Gertrude also recorded her memories on the twentieth anniversary of HF Bar Ranch in the 1931 issue. The charming article is quoted here in its entirety first, because it is so descriptive of the very early days, and it repeats some of what Skipper said, and second, because so little is known or has been written about Gertrude. She wrote:

...The Skipper reminded me the other day that this was the twentieth year of our HF Bar, and suggested that I write something about it for Bridle Bits. *I got out our old Kodak book and lived again in the days when we seemed most remote from the rest of the world.*

At that time arriving at the ranch was a glorious adventure. Our guests arrived from Sheridan in a more or less reliable automobile stage, as far as Lake DeSmet. There they were met by the Skipper or some of the boys from the ranch in a buckboard, well-named by the way. Their suitcases and duffels, the only luggage encouraged, were roped on behind or wired on with barbed wire if the rope ran short. The passengers were crowded into the seats and the real adventure started. The rest of the way to the ranch led through grain fields, over irrigation ditches and up rocky lanes. All the way people wondered how on earth the Horton's ever happened to locate in such an out-of-the-way spot. They expected to find the ranch at the end of each long lane—then there would be a turning to the right or left and another long, steep land stretched ahead. It was a few years later that it became a frequent thing for people to arrive on foot, later when motor vehicles came into use in our hills, but could not always make the grade.

Courageous were those early guests, accepting the comforts and the discomforts with high spirit, with humor even. They did not exaggerate the hardships or dangers for there were dangers on the rough trails and in the rapid waters of the fords that called for steady nerves. Perhaps the sunshine, the varying skies, the moon, the howl of the wolf and the calling of the coyotes from hilltop to hilltop meant more in those days. There were few distractions. That was twenty years ago.

We had four cottages that first year,—the Gorton, the Hole-in-the-Wall, Boulders and LaRobida. The ground all about was untrodden, soft and fragrant with sage and wild flowers, but when it rained—and it did rain often then—the mud was—well, why bother about the mud. The cabins had no baths; at all hours we passed on the paths to and from the bathhouses guests with towels, sponges, and soap. At night candles glowed in drinking glasses like fireflies, as people groped their way about.

The dining room was a lean-to addition to the then small white ranch house. It held about thirty people, the capacity at that time. The small room was lighted by kerosene lamps hung from the low ceiling. These would smoke and smell but they gave out a soft, mellow light. There are still some old-timers who ask us to dig out the old oil lamps and get them in order because they love the yellow light.

This little dining room was our one place on the ranch to dance, and dance we must. So at least once a week the tables were piled high and chairs stacked on top, cornmeal sifted on the floor and with a mouth harp, fiddle and drum for an orchestra we danced till we were dead—and it was never very late at that. There was an old dance hall over the store in Story, to which we used to ride on horseback, dance till midnight and ride home afterwards, arriving back about sunrise. The girls used to carry their party dresses tied on back of their saddle and change from their long, khaki divided skirts (so feminine) on a dingy little back porch, a distracting performance for the store pump was on this porch and all the cowboys must needs have a drink just at this time.

People camped out in the mountains or went on long pack trips more frequently then. They went up on top for two weeks, or took a five week trip making the circle of Willow Park, Elk Lake,

# Saddlestring

Lake Geneva, Trail Lodge and back to the ranch. They took eight or ten pack horses, a cook and several guides, slept on the ground in sleeping bags and often stayed less than three days in any one camp. On these trips, which took them above the timber line, they used to see the mountain sheep, even photographed them, and sometimes the bears would eat up their bacon.

I often wonder why our long mountain trails have been so little traveled these last few years. I think the congenial life here at the ranch holds people. They hate to leave even for a week, lest they miss something of interest or some excitement here on the HF Bar.

Speaking of long, divided skirts, well I remember with what alarm we first witnessed the arrival of breeches worn without the skirt—alarm only exceeded by that caused by the smoking of cigarettes by women and girls.

Has it justified itself, all this labor and building during these twenty years, establishing a little bit of civilization in a valley under the Big Horns? Yes—the work has kept us contented and happy. The wonderful people who have loved our mountains and the life here have been our best friends—our greatest blessing—and they have made the HF Bar what it is today.—Gertrude B. Horton

HF Bar Brand

Skipper used the HF Bar brand in his other endeavors before HF Bar Ranch was established. It must have been agreed by the corporation that it be used for the joint venture as it was registered on November 17, 1915. HF Bar stands for Frank Horton backwards. As he explained:

...It...is a reversal of my initials, as FH would not have made a good-sounding brand...

Even before the brand was registered, the name "HF Bar" was mentioned in the first Articles of Incorporation.

Incorporation

HF Bar had been in operation for two years when it became apparent that more capital would be needed to make necessary improvements and so an HF Bar Certificate of Incorporation was issued on June 21, 1913. It stated:

KNOW ALL MEN BY THESE PRESENT: That we, Warren Gorrell, Demia B. Gorrell and Frank O. Horton have associated ourselves together as a company under the name and style of the HF Bar Ranch...

The principal object and purpose of said company is and shall be to engage in the general business of conducting pleasure resorts...

The stated purpose, conducting pleasure resorts, was certainly a remarkable departure from the original intent for HF Bar that was expressed in the first HF Bar and Trail Lodge booklet published in 1911 that proclaimed the enterprise was to be a ranch—not a resort!

Two year's worth of operating experience must have caused the onset of reality. Skipper and the Gorrells seem to have changed their minds about the purpose of HF Bar Ranch. On the other hand, it is possible that the resort end of the business was emphasized because it would be more attractive to potential investors. At any rate, the livestock end of the business was certainly not abandoned; in fact, at the time, they were looking for ways to increase it.

The company issued capital stock for one hundred thousand dollars divided into one thousand shares of the par value of one hundred dollars each.

The Certificate of Incorporation also stated that the affairs of the company were to be controlled by a board of three directors which were Warren Gorrell, Demia B. Gorrell and Frank Horton.

The first balance sheet of the incorporated company was

issued in January of 1914. It stated that $48,000 worth of capital stock, a major portion of which was owned by Warren and Demia, had been sold (of the $100,000 authorized) and issued in payment to the Ranch. The status of the ranch upon incorporation was:

ASSETS:

Ranch and Improvements	$34,000
Live Stock	10,500
Equipment, machinery, etc.	8,300
Trail Lodge (Bldg.)	1,000
Store Supplies	200
Commissary	250
Hay and Grain	550
	$54,800

LIABILITIES:

Capital Stock	$48,000
Mortgage on Ranch	6,000
Sundry Creditors	800
	$54,800

The Corporate Team

From the outset, it is important to examine the Horton-Gorrell relationship. The working arrangement was basically that for most of the time Warren Gorrell was president of the corporation and Demia was, at times, an officer. Skipper was a minority stockholder and officer as well as the designated manager.

Skipper lived at HF Bar and managed it all year. Warren was in Chicago except for summer vacations and occasional visits at other times of the year. Skipper managed the operation, but consulted regularly with Warren through a voluminous correspondence consisting of letters, telegrams and telephone calls. Skipper often traveled to Chicago for meetings with Warren to conduct ranch business. Skipper also made comprehensive annual reports to stockholders.

We do not know exactly how all decisions were made about ranch matters. When significant expenditures for property acquisitions and construction were required, Skipper consulted with Warren. That is not to say, however, that I believe Skipper consulted with Warren on every single detail of the operation. Warren could not have possibly micromanaged every detail from Chicago. I doubt he would have had time for that as he was busy managing his financial empire. Neither do I believe Skipper would have tolerated extensive micromanagement of everyday operations. However, Skipper had a corporate responsibility to keep Warren apprised of what he was doing and as we shall see, he did.

One curiosity about the arrangement is that only the Horton name was used to promote the HF Bar Ranch. The first ranch brochures, printed in Chicago in 1911 and 1912, only mention Frank O. Horton. Surely the Gorrells had an input to the brochures and if the truth were known Warren probably arranged the printing. Did they agree to the singular use of the Horton name in ranch promotions? Did Warren and Demia wish to be only silent partners? We simply do not know.

In later years, in local newspapers and other published articles about HF Bar the Gorrell name is not to be found. Locally, the ranch was referred to as either "Hortons" or "Frank O. Horton's HF Bar Ranch." This is understandable, I suppose, because Skipper and his family were an ingrained part of state and local society and the Gorrells were not.

The lack of recognition of the Gorrell family involvement with HF Bar is of some concern to some Gorrell descendents. Whether or not the absence of recognition bothered Warren and Demia at the time, we'll never know.

Growth and Development

From the very beginning Skipper and Warren seemed hell bent to grow and expand. On the ground, Skipper did all the work and looked for opportunities. Warren Gorrell, back in Chicago, found ways to finance them.

The Gorrell's did more than just arrange financing. They also made extensive purchases for the ranch, particularly with regard to building and furnishing the cabins. Henry Stewart, Warren and Demia Gorrell's grandson stated that:

> ...I particularly recall check registers showing thousands of dollars in purchases by my grandmother at Marshall Fields on an ongoing basis for the benefit of providing furnishings for the ranch...

All the transactions were accomplished under a corporate umbrella but they controlled the corporation as majority stockholders. At early stockholder meetings it would be Skipper and Warren and Demia, the major stockholders, each with a fistful of proxy votes, mostly from their friends whom they had convinced to buy stock in HF Bar. Skipper's early reports to the stockholders and other documentation from the ranch files tell the story.

The report for 1915 reported that the gross income for the year was $43,519.39 as against $29,290.79 for 1914 and the gross expense increased from $23,720.20 to $32,098.42 in 1915. Skipper explained that the gross income increased about one-half while the expenses increased by only about one-third. The report continued:

> ...It is interesting to note that the store profit for 1915 is about $1,000 as against a loss for 1914. The greater increase in income is from guests' board. This figure for 1915 is $33,583.25 as against $20,038.35 for 1914. This increase is due first to higher prices

charged for board and second to a larger number of guests. In order to take care of a larger number of guests it was necessary to purchase additional horses, hence a larger hay and grain cost during 1915 than during 1914.

Then Skipper lays some groundwork to dampen any stockholder expectations for a dividend:

...It will be impossible, short of three years, to show much if any profit from ranch or livestock activities. Practically all that the dairy herd produces goes to the resort at cost, therefore this department will never show a real profit...

Then he puts forth ideas for expansion:

...As a matter of fact the HF Bar should take over another ranch in order to produce sufficient hay, grain and other ranch products required for its needs. The management proposes to recommend such purchase to the directors. The only drawback is that the purchase of another ranch will necessarily defer a dividend to the stockholders as additional purchases should come from earnings rather than additional issuance of capital stock...

Skipper then provides more reasons why there will be no dividends:

...As you will note from the balance sheet, the greater part of the 1915 profit went into additional equipment, building, land, a tractor and a Ford and horses. Very little equipment will be required during 1916 but it will be necessary to complete the barns, build addition to store so as to accommodate a tea room, build a suitable commissary, construct tennis courts and systematically beautify the ranch. With these additions being made from 1916 profits it is quite

likely that there will not be a dividend declared for at least another year...

Lastly, Skipper gave a pep talk to the stockholders:

...closing this report the manager wishes to urge upon each stockholder the importance of talking ranch when ever the opportunity arises. You can do more than any one else to send guests here and make the HF Bar a dividend paying proposition...

The guest population was definitely on the rise. By 1915 the number of guests had increased from about thirty per year in 1911 to 223. The number of first time guests which included maids and children was 189 and there were thirty-four guests that stayed for the second or third time.

Skipper sent his second report to the stockholders on March 1, 1916, when the ranch had been in operation for almost five years. The draft of that report is quoted in full because it gives remarkable insight into the life and challenges of the times:

I herewith submit the financial statement for the year ending December 31, 1916 together with the following explanations.

The total amount of capital expended was $23,120.75 divided as follows:

For Bungalows, land and ranch house $11,540.04. For Equipment $6,622.71, For Horses $2,958.00, For Cattle $2,000.06. The amounts expended for Bungalows, Ranch House and Equipment exceeded estimate greatly on account of the very bad weather and the condition of the roads encountered while freighting all building materials and equipment from the railroad to the ranch. This distance is about forty miles and when every mile is mud it greatly increases the cost of transportation. The weather also delayed construction on the buildings so that it was necessary to put on a *great deal larger force than was deemed necessary in the estimate. Not only did the condition of the roads enhance the cost of transportation but it pulled down our horses to such an extent that they were in no condition to do farm work when the time came. The consequence was that very little farming was done and consequently a short crop harvested. This necessitated the purchase of large quantities of hay and grain during the fall and winter months.*

This year with very little freighting to do I estimate that we will derive a profit from the ranching operations three times greater than last year. This will to a great extent eliminate the necessity of buying hay and grain for next fall and winter.

When this ranch was taken over four years ago the farming lands were in very bad condition. Little improvement has been made in this respect for the reason that all of our time has been given to develop the resort end of the business. I believe it will take three years yet to make the ranch produce to its maximum. At the end of that time the ranch should be able to produce sufficient grain and forage crops to care for three hundred of livestock. Since only this limited number of livestock can be cared for, I strongly recommend that we get into purebred stock as soon as possible. It costs no more to feed the best stock than it does the poorest and the profits are much greater.

Four years ago at this time there were no accommodations on this ranch for guests. By the first of July Bungalows had been built as well as dining room and kitchen, so that we were able to make comfortable thirty guests. Since that time the ranch has steadily grown in popularity as well as in accommodations until last July we were able to care for eighty guests at one time. It has never been the policy of this ranch to receive as guests more than sixty but the above mentioned eighty was but for a few days and was a special occasion. During the past season we received as guests 150 different people, 122 of whom were guests at the ranch for the first time. The building of the ranch house last spring made it possible for us to accommodate comfortably guests for the winter months. During December we had eight guests at the ranch. In order to make this ranch a paying proposition every month of the year it is necessary to develop the winter end of the business. The stockholders can greatly help in this respect. Our winter climate is ideal and wonderful and you need feel no hesitancy in sending your friends here at that time of year, especially those that need a rest and change. There is no question but what this place will do more for people who have broken down from over work or nervousness than any other place you could send.

This ranch has about passed its period of constructive work. From now on we will devote our time to improving in every respect what we already have. The grounds, the roads, the bridges, the Bungalows, the service will receive more attention and will be made as ideal as possible. No great outlay for improvements will be necessary and the departments will be better organized and waste and needless expense eliminated so that the ranch will show good earnings.

I believe that every department will show an earning this year. It is our desire to produce on the ranch practically every thing that we consume during the year. It is with this idea in mind that we are collecting one of the finest dairy herds in the west and preparing to house them in model dairy barns. The ranch gardens, the chickens, the hogs and sheep are all receiving their share of attention and I feel sure by another year will be furnishing us well in the way of their products. Our new cold storage box installed last year makes it possible to kill all of our own beef—something we have been unable to do before.

Some of the first cabins at the HF Bar Ranch.
Note the temporary tent cabins. Circa 1911.
(Courtesy of Henry S. Stewart)

Buildings

In the years from 1911 to 1915, the increased number of guest reservations created the need for an aggressive building program. In 1911 and 1912, for instance, twenty-eight guest bungalows were built and in 1913 the ranch house was constructed which provided a larger dining hall and many rooms to accommodate the increasing number of guests that found their way to HF Bar.

The numbers associated with the construction are interesting. For instance, the cost for the new ranch house was $10,000 and its estimated life was fifteen years. The new barn cost $1,486.58 and its estimated life was fifteen years. Both buildings stand today, albeit the ranch house has been remodeled many times, but the barn remains the same.

After the initial surge of construction to 1915, the ranch continued to expand. In the 1920 Directors meeting it was reported that, in the past year, the ranch had spent $17,000 on buildings which included Meadow Lark Bungalow, La Rabida, Manhattan, Paradise, Monkel, Sun Bungalow and the Horton House which cost $7,000. Today the Horton House and Meadow Lark Bungalow are still in use.

Skipper presented a report to the stockholders every year, but the one prepared for the year ending December 31, 1919, amply illustrates the vicissitudes of the ranch business and sets the stage for the 1920s.

...The weather conditions which made this the very best year we have ever had for the resort business played havoc with our farming and livestock interests. Our grain crop was an almost complete failure, our hay crops and ensilage crops a half failure and our range grasses almost a complete failure. These conditions have made it necessary to purchase quantities of high priced feeds in order to put our stock through the present winter. Not only that, but it has

*been necessary to ship 130 head of cattle and 120 head of horses to
Nebraska for feed. All of this stock will be brought back to Wyoming
in the spring. The almost failure of the grass crop made it necessary
to employ additional men to move the stock from place to place to
find feed so that our payroll has been very high. This same condition
of the range also reflected on the condition of the cattle so that we
did not receive the full market value for the stock sold.*

*Range Cattle. Present inventory 377 head valued very
conservatively on our books at $26,620. Some 60 head were sold
during the past season. 76 calves were born.*

*Dairy Cattle. Present inventory $4,720. Also very low value
placed on them. Count 43 head. We had the misfortune to lose 8 of
our best cows from alfalfa bloat during the past season.*

*Horses. Horses of all kinds have been greatly depreciated in
value because of the poor horse market in this country. A book value
of only $7,635 is carried.*

*Sheep. Present inventory count 600 head, valued on books at
only $7,500. In October of 1918 we bought 500 head at $8562.50. In
June we sold wool for $2723.08 and in October we sold 276 head for
$2,113.18 and still have 100 head more sheep than when we started.
I strongly recommend that we buy 2000 head of breeding ewes at
once.* (Note: No record exists as to whether this recommendation was
adopted or not.)

*Hogs. All hogs have been sold. We have gone out of the
hog business.*

*School. The new school department has done extremely well
and will break even the first year. We set as a limit 15 boys for the
first year and had no difficulty in getting that number. Another year
we plan to take 30 boys and should be able to show a nice profit. In
conjunction with the school we will this coming summer operate a
boy's camp. From the interest already being shown in this matter we
do not anticipate any difficulty in securing the 20 boys wanted.*

Saddlestring

The HF Bar Ranch before 1921.   *(Courtesy of the HF Bar Ranch)*

The HF Bar Ranch in 1921.   *(Courtesy of the HF Bar Ranch)*

Skipper would reflect later in *Bridle Bits*:

...Not many people know that during the winter of 1919 the ranch operated a boy's school. Fifteen boys completed the year's work most successfully. But we found that we were faced with the big expenditure for suitable ranch buildings and master's houses, etc. Since everything financial was on rather wobbly pins in 1919, we gave up the idea rather than make the additional capital expenditures...

Prospects for 1920: Already practically all of our larger and better accommodations are spoken for so we are sure to have the best resort year in our history. There is more snow in the mountains than there has been in years, which means we will have plenty of water for irrigation, hence a splendid farm crop. From all indications 1920 should show the best profit we have ever earned.

So, in the first nine years of operation, the HF Bar Ranch dude and livestock business grew by leaps and bounds in spite of occasional weather and financial challenges. On other fronts, production was also notable. For instance, in a 1919 inventory book there appeared this fact:

Meals

The total number of meals served during the year 1919 was 37,511 to guests and 18,489 to help making a total of 56,000.

Saddlestring

Land

Skipper seized every opportunity to expand the ranch. The first opportunity occurred when he filed a personal patent for 40.39 acres in 1915. He then deeded it to HF Bar in 1917.

Another opportunity presented itself in 1916 when the next place down the creek became available because the owner, T. J. Haynes died and his widow, Clara, wanted to sell the place on which they had lived for thirty-two years. A *Sheridan Post* 1905 newspaper article about area ranches had described the place as:

> ... *right at the junction of north and south forks of Rock Creek with a good house, nice large fenced lawn and a rock basement barn.*

In the corporate minutes the HF Bar Board of Directors authorized Skipper to negotiate with Clara Haynes for the 760 acre holding and also purchase of all hay, grain and livestock at prevailing market prices. The deal was done for $20,000. Clara Haynes accepted a $4,000 down payment and took a note for $2,000 a year at six per cent interest. Forever after, the Haynes place would become known as the middle place at HF Bar.

Three years later HF Bar would be able to purchase the lower place, but before that some minor land acquisitions were made. In 1916, Gertrude was able to file a patent on 160 acres of adjoining land and she deeded this to HF Bar in 1917. Then in 1917, as well, HF Bar Ranch received a warranty deed for 80 acres from Marcus D. Richards and Helen Gillette for the sum of $1.00. The reason of this transfer of ownership is not known.

The largest purchase in the history of HF Bar Ranch was made two years later in May, 1919 when Warren Gorrell purchased the adjoining UM Ranch from Abraham C. and Cora Warburton for $84,000. The ranch had 2400 acres plus leased federal and state land for which figures are not available.

Other writers have stated that the HF Bar Ranch purchased the UM Ranch in the 1930s from Edward Moore. This is incorrect. In fact, Edward Moore purchased the UM Ranch in the 1930s when he helped bail Skipper out because of financial difficulties encountered by Warren Gorrell.

It is clearly recorded in the Johnson County Courthouse, Buffalo, Wyoming, that Mr. and Mrs. Warburton sold the UM Ranch to Warren and Demia Gorrell. Years later, in 1928, Skipper wrote a passage in *Bridle Bits* in which he demonstrated his propensity for using "I" instead of "we" to include the Gorrell interest. He wrote:

...As for the UM brand, it was the brand used by Mr. Warburton, and I continued to use it after I bought the place...

Skipper neglected to acknowledge that Warren Gorrell's name was on the mortgage paperwork or that the UM brand was registered with the State of Wyoming to Warren Gorrell and Frank. O. Horton.

The purchase of the UM Ranch sheds some light on the roles that Skipper and Warren Gorrell played in the HF Bar Ranch corporation.   The only way they could finance their expanding operation was to issue bonds. In 1916, Warren Gorrell had organized a ten year one hundred thousand dollar gold bond issue with the Chicago Savings and Trust Company. Later, in 1923, this issue would be increased by an additional one hundred thousand dollars. This bond issue became a problem for HF Bar Ranch—in particular for Skipper—a few years later.

The exact financial arrangements for the largest purchase to date are not exactly clear, but it is known that Chicago Savings and Trust held the mortgage in conjunction with the bond issue. This transaction was typical of most HF Bar transactions—little money down with large mortgages or contracts.

Shortly after the purchase of the UM Ranch another opportunity

arose. HF Bar, which was at the head of Rock Creek, had never had good access. Other places on the creek below HF Bar restricted access and caused travelers to take a circuitous route over the hills. A big part of this problem was solved when the Haynes place was purchased. The final piece was the Tathwell Ranch which was a 440 acre place that extended down to the yellow school house, which still stands today.

When the Tathwell place was put up for sale, Skipper, on behalf of the corporation, was quick to seize the opportunity to buy it. The place had 440 acres and was purchased for $25,000. The purchase price included a lot of other assets including 127 head of cattle, five head of work horses, one hog, fifty chickens, one-third interest in two shocks of wheat, all necessary farming machinery, harness and wagons, one-hundred twenty five tons of hay, one large straw stack and one and a half shares of Rock Creek and Piney Ditch stock. In other words, the place was bought lock, stock and barrel—but not the brand.

Mr. Tathwell's brand was TAT. He retained the brand and sold it separately. It changed hands several times and today is registered to Ralph I. Goodwin, Jr., of the TAT ranch in Banner, Wyoming. The Goodwin family is, today, close friends with the current HF Bar owner, Margi Schroth.

To help sell the bonds, Warren Gorrell wrote the following letter to potential investors in the spring of 1920:

Frank Horton, of HF Bar Ranch, has asked me if I would not write you regarding some HF Bar First Mortgage 6% Bonds, due May 1, 1927, which he is having this office arrange to take down for him in connection with the purchase of the Tathwell Ranch. This purchase extends the land holdings down to the yellow schoolhouse, which will enable him to run a road right up the creek and avoid the climb over the hills; his purpose in asking me to write you was that I might present the merit of the security clearly to you, and say that it

*was his desire that these be held by friends and patrons of the Ranch
rather than anyone else. The denominations are $500 and $1,000.*

*The total amount outstanding when this financing is
completed will be $65,000, secured by a first mortgage on land and
improvements valued at about $200,000, with additional security in
the form of quick assets, including live stock and equipment worth
about $100,000. The earnings each year are several times the
interest. The net earnings have increased steadily and have been
reinvested in the property and will be for the next three years. After
that Mr. Horton proposes to apply net earnings to calling in these
First Mortgage Bonds.*

*I know Frank would be tickled pink if you saw your way clear
to taking any of these securities. It is also apparent that you would
be getting a good security. The price is par and interest.* (Note: I find
it curious here that Warren would refer to "Frank Horton of HF Bar
Ranch" instead of a more collective term that would include himself
as a major stockholder. It adds fuel to the discussion about how much
recognition the Gorrells really wanted in conjunction with HF Bar
Ranch.)

Acquisition of the Tathwell Ranch, which was to be known as
the lower place, allowed better access. Now the ranch could build a
road all the way up the creek to the main ranch. The purchase also
increased the capability of the ranch to be self sufficient and provided
a place for a dairy and a chicken production operation.

HF Bar Ranch acquisition of land was not over in 1919. More
would be purchased in the 1920s but not to the extent of the
1911-1919 period. The size of HF Bar Ranch at the end of 1919 was
approximately 4400 deeded acres—not a bad increase from the
original 520 acres purchased from the Bill Robbins estate to start the
ranch. There was also a sizeable amount of federal and state leased
land that ran with the purchases but the amount is unknown. In eight
and half years, Skipper and Warren Gorrell had put together a
significant holding.

The Gorrell Chicago Connection

The Chicago connection was not only financial; there was a huge social element which caused many Chicagoans to flock to HF Bar Ranch "out in Wyoming." Skipper and Gertrude had some connections in Chicago from their University of Chicago days, but the real impetus for HF Bar support from the Chicago area was due to the efforts of the Gorrell family. The word about HF Bar Ranch in Buffalo, Wyoming, got around fast. In fact, as early as 1915, there was an article in the local Evanston (just north of Chicago) newspaper:

SOCIAL ACTIVITIES
and PERSONAL MENTION
By Dorothy Palmer

Fifteen miles from Buffalo, Wyoming, made famous by Owen Wister in the "Virginian" there is a place known as the HF Bar Ranch, which has a particular fascination for a number of Evanstonians this year. The ranch, consisting of more than two thousand acres is in an irrigated valley at an altitude of 5,300 feet, and is thirty-six miles to the nearest railroad station, which is at Sheridan. The approach to the ranch is by a winding road through the foothills and along the heavily wooded banks of Rock Creek, ending at the ranch house; from this point the ranch slopes upwards to the first range of the Big Horn Mountains, which forms the eastern boundary of the forest reserve...

The equipment at the ranch—for it must not be called a summer resort—consists of the old original ranch house, to which have been added a large dining room and a large clubhouse, comfortably furnished bungalows, a ranch store, a cold storage and a saddle house with one hundred riding horses for on the HF Bar Ranch riding is the order of the days. There is, besides, fishing, hunting and camping on the trail, varied by occasional spectacular exhibitions of broncho (sic) busting and by visits to the round-up camps to see the roping and branding of cattle. And it is this—the "call of the wild"— that has drawn a number from our city...

In an article in the Chicago *National Hotel Reporter* there was an article about dude ranching in the west. It declared:

...The particular ranch which seems to have met with especial favor among Chicagoans is the HF Bar Ranch...owned and managed by Frank O. Horton. This season as many as 95 residents of Chicago and vicinity have spent a portion or most of their summer there, and the fact of this large number from one locality makes it seem like a great big family, rather than a crowd of strangers, for everybody knows each other and absolute informality and good fellowship is the rule.

Going west to dude ranches was absolutely the thing to do for much of Chicago society. While some Chicagoans went to other dude ranches in the area, articles in Chicago newspapers often declared that *...The HF Bar Ranch is especially popular this season with Chicagoans...*

In another article:

...HF Bar Ranch is one of the most popular of the so-called "dude ranches" of the far west, and Chicago society folk flock there every summer...

In the summer months the Chicago newspapers were filled with society notes like:

...Mrs. Warren Gorrell...with her children has left for the HF Bar Ranch, Buffalo, Wyoming

Mr. and Mrs. C. C. Chickering and family...have left for an extended stay at HF Bar Ranch...

...Warren Gorrell has left for the HF Bar Ranch in Buffalo, Wyoming, to join his daughter who has been there for some weeks...

An article in the *Chicago Herald* in 1917 even described how the Chicago connection was helping the war effort:

...Letters from HF Bar Ranch...tell of many gay camping parties in the mountains, of dances and other festivities and of much work accomplished by summer guests for the Red Cross. Every Monday and Thursday the women at the ranch meet in the tearoom for the purpose of making surgical dressings for the Red Cross. Mrs. Charles Nagel of St. Louis instructs them, Miss Anna Gorrell is shampooing their hair and Mrs. Edward Concklin of New York is telling fortunes for the benefit of the Red Cross. September will be University of Chicago month at the ranch when a number of members of the U. of C. faculty and their families will arrive...

In the wintertime, Skipper and Gertrude would travel to Chicago to promote the ranch at occasions organized by HF Bar dudes and aficionados:

...A unique event of the week will be the "get together" dinner-dance which will be given on Saturday evening by Mr. and Mrs. Tracy Drake at the Blackstone Hotel for Mr. and Mrs. Frank Horton of the HF Bar Ranch in Buffalo, Wyo. The guests will include many of those who have spent their summers at the ranch, and there will be shown some moving pictures taken there last summer...

Skipper was a tireless promoter of the ranch and carried on a voluminous barrage of correspondence with past guests and potential future guests. He would often mail them a postcard which allowed them to make an appointment to visit with him when he was in Chicago to promote HF Bar. He also took advantage of his college fraternity connections from the University of Chicago. One year, sometime in the "teens" he sent a brochure to all of his Alpha Delta fraternity brothers. The foreword read as follows:

When HF Bar was equipped for guests, I sent an announcement to a number of my Alpha Delt friends who manifested a keen interest and asked why I did not include all the Brothers. The suggestion appealed to me, as I could imagine nothing more pleasant than to have the ranch become an Alpha Delt Playground. To that end, I extend to you and your friends a cordial invitation to spend your vacations here. Having once experienced western ranch life, you will not need a second invitation.
                    Yours fraternally...

(Author's Note: When I discovered this brochure I was startled to find that it was dated Chicago, 1902! This was an obvious misprint as in 1902 Skipper was still a student at the University of Chicago and HF Bar was not even a dream. I have seen the date 1902 used before in articles describing HF Bar. Possibly this misprint is the reason why, although the brochure could only have been seen by a limited number of people.)

The influence of the Chicago connection would extend well into the 1920s and 1930s. It would continue to provide a steady stream of dudes to the HF Bar Ranch.

Other Ventures

Skipper was ambitious and took advantage of every opportunity. When HF Bar was acquired, there was an active sawmill which unfortunately led to the demise of the former owner. There are no ranch records available that indicate how the sawmill was used. But, Robert A. Murray stated in *175 Years of History at the Foot of the Big Horns*, which he wrote for the Buffalo Chamber of Commerce in July, 1981, in reference to Skipper:

> *...he engaged in lumbering ventures, which in 1916 and 1917 produced 105,946 board feet from his Pheasant Creek unit in the Big Horns. He nearly repeated that in 1924 producing over 100,000 board feet from the same unit...*

This information must be true. It is hard to imagine that Skipper would fail to take advantage of a ready-made capability for lumber production, especially since the ranch was engaged in a heavy building program at the time; lumber was definitely in demand. But it is curious that lumber production was never mentioned in year end reports to the stockholders.

Activities

Skipper was an active person and he saw to it that his guests had every opportunity to be active in western pursuits. This is how Skipper summed up the possibilities in an early HF Bar Ranch and Trail Lodge brochure:

Life on the Ranch

Each guest has his own horse and cowboy equipment, and parties go out daily over the trails which lead in every direction to nearby points of interest. Longer trips to remote parts of the mountains can be arranged at nominal expense. Guides, pack-horses and necessary equipment are furnished. This country has always been open range for cattle and sheep, and there are opportunities to see the life on the range, round-ups, frontier-day celebrations, bronco busting, stage coach travel and Indian battle grounds and reservations. (Note: Skipper would take guests on horseback rides to the Crow Fair on the Crow Indian Reservation. That's a fair piece— fifty or sixty miles as the crow flies.) *In the early fall there is excellent hunting for game birds, such as grouse and ducks; in late fall and early winter for deer and elk; and in the winter big game hunting, trapping and snow-shoeing. After a few days of horseback riding and tramping in this wonderful Wyoming air, eating becomes imperative and insomnia is unknown.*

As early as 1912 Skipper took a small hunting party through the Jackson Hole Country and did so for several years. Skipper was always looking for fun things to do at the ranch. In 1915 he had the first guest ranch rodeo called "September Roundup," which brought people from all around and featured such events as a grand costume

parade, children's flat race, bareback race, a potato race and many others. Usually, some of the local cowboys would come and ride bucking horses to the wonder of the dudes.

The *Sheridan Post* newspaper provided a colorful account of one of the early HF Bar celebrations in an undated article but it was in the period before 1920. Some excerpts from the account follow:

CELEBRATION DAY AT THE HF RANCH ON ROCK CREEK

Many automobiles from Sheridan, Buffalo and other sections headed for the HF Bar Ranch of Frank O. Horton last Sunday, among which was The Post car, top take in the Frontier day celebration...The dude ranch was a lodestone that attracted somewhere near 150 autos and their parties. Many took their lunches and picnic dinners were in order at almost every point nearby where there was shade.

This resort is one of the great attractions for easterners and it is booked to the limit this year and could have taken care of many more. Many of these people come from the top social life of the east, and the pleasure they get out of the mountain life was evident to all. The freshly sunburned faces and arms gave evidence of their lack of familiarity with the regular western wind and sun, and then the costumes of some were an attraction, especially those worn by some of the ladies, which were of the dignified eastern variety. The ladies in pantaloons and semi-male attire distributed through the throngs and gatherings by themselves, impressed on many westerners the comforts which they attain in the mountains and bent on out-door exercises, and to which styles of dress many of our western women have not yet taken to. Various styles of costumes were in evidence, and they all seemed to fit in very nicely with the occasion. However, there were some there who still held to the ordinary feminine attire.

The HF Bar Ranch is situated at an altitude of 5,300 feet, and the climb from the valleys told on many of the autos. The ranch comprises about 4,000 acres...and located as described "just at the boundary line between civilization and untouched nature"...

The event of last Sunday is one that is looked forward to each year by the patrons and there are eastern out-door sports to mix with western features, so there is new sport for each class. One of the regrettable features was the absence of manager Frank Horton, who went into the mountains with many others to fight the forest fires which are raging back of the ranch.

The author then talks about some of the events:

...Dave King, an Australian, was in charge of the events of the day, and one of his exhibitions was the throwing of a steer from a horse by a tail twist. Bill Eaton (Note: Bill Eaton of Eaton's Dude Ranch, located west of Sheridan and the oldest Dude Ranch in the country, established at Wolf Wyoming in 1904) *gave a very interesting exhibition of roping, and put the rope on the horse of each rider who passed in front of him, riding in groups of two, three and four, and for his accomplishments was greeted with much applause. It would be hard to tell of the many interesting events, aside from the prize-winning events given below:*

100 yard pony race for kids—first prize, Judy Tilt,
                    second prize Martha Love.
200 yard ladies' race—first Katherine Gossler, second Katherine Tilt.
Men's potato race—first, M.C. Huntoon, second Ralph Goodwin.
Ladies' potato race—first Katherine Gossler, second Lavinia Gadson.
200 yard race for men—first Scranton Platt, second H. B. Huntoon.
Ladies' cigar race—first Roger Sergent, second M.C. Huntoon.

Saddlestring

FREE-FOR-ALL EVENTS
(Note: Contestants in these events were not dudes, but mostly locals.)

Steer roping—first prize Ruben Barkey, time 57 seconds;
second prize Bill Eaton, time 1 min. 16 sec.
300 yard cow pony dash—first Roy Barkey, second Dave King.
Cavvy race—first Ruben Barkey
Stake race—won by Reuben Barkey
Bucking—first Fay Harper, second, Archie Braemer.
Horton's "Croppy" took the first prize for the best outlaw horse.
Reuben Barkey's "Jerry" took the second prize as the best
outlaw horse...

Annual celebrations would be held well into the 1930s and then occasionally thereafter. The events were always well attended.

The core of all daily activity at a dude ranch is horseback riding. Skipper related the story about one of the very early female dudes in the 1928 edition of *Bridle Bits:*

Mrs. J. Gordon Wilson of Chicago was the first woman to appear in knickers in Wyoming so far as I know. She so shocked the natives that she found it necessary to wear a little ruffled skirt about 10 inches wide, which she called a "modesty," and which she wore around her waist. August Hettinger, a German, was forest ranger in the mountains at that time. He used to tell me that it embarrassed him so much that he couldn't talk when he happened to run across Mrs. Wilson in her knickers. His embarrassment was greatly alleviated when she wore the little "modesty." All the girls in those days wore the heavy divided riding skirts reaching almost to their ankles, and it took at least eight or ten years to oust the riding skirt and substitute the knickers and, later, the overalls.

There was other entertainment for the dudes as well, some of it kind of scary. Skipper described that:

...Lots of bear and wolves and coyotes roamed the hills in those days. Nearly every night of the winter we were awakened by the howling pack, and the next morning found a deer or cow or calf that had been pulled down by the wolves. That winter, too, we killed 21 wolves right here on the ranch property. Many a guest, with face gone white, would point out of a cottage window to the main yard where a big black bear was playing with one of the dogs.

So it was at HF Bar Ranch in the early days.

Family

    While Skipper was busy helping the HF Bar Corporation to expand the ranch in this period, he and Gertrude expanded their family. Jack Ogilvie was born on October 18, 1911, just a year after his brother Bill. A third son, Ovid Butler (Bobby) was born on April 19, 1916.

Chapter 5

The Twenties

The HF Bar Ranch was at its peak in the 1920s. Land holdings were increased even further, though not to the extent of the decade before. The ranch was engaged in the cattle, sheep and horse business in a very significant way and the dude business was on the increase. As if these major efforts were not enough, Skipper's social conscience came to the fore and he became an active politician. It was a busy decade, and Skipper was a busy man.

Skipper Horton in cowboy gear in front of the Horton house, circa 1920.
(Courtesy of the HF Bar Ranch)

Skipper Horton, a man for all seasons—
sheepherder, rancher, community leader,
Wyoming state legislator, and United States congressman.
(Courtesy of the HF Bar Ranch)

Skipper would pitch in wherever there was work to be done.
He is pictured here with unknown helper at the corral.   Date unknown.
(Courtesy of the HF Bar Ranch)

Land

No sooner had the HF Bar Ranch acquired the UM Ranch than another opportunity presented itself. An additional 320 acres was added to the ranch with a purchase from an Edgar Scott and his wife in 1920. This was followed by a purchase of 200 acres in June 1926 from James Woodling and his wife for $300.

Then, in June, 1920 Skipper acquired another personal patent of 120 acres. This addition was the last one until 1926 when the HF Bar purchased another ranch, not for acreage to increase agricultural production, but for accommodation to increase dude production. The ranch was Paradise Ranch.

The origin of Paradise harkens back to Mr. Norman Meldrum who in the late 1890s drove a herd of cattle from Colorado up to Buffalo, Wyoming, where he had acquired some land. The Paradise Guest Ranch takes up the narrative of the history on its website:

...The cattle were wintered near the present Soldier's Home and summered in the upper meadow range of the Big Horns, which was to become Paradise Ranch. Mr. Meldrum liked the mountain meadow so well that he proved up on the land and acquired title. In his youth, Mr. Meldrum had served with a New York cavalry regiment, coming to Colorado to seek his fortune. In Colorado, he became engaged in politics and served a term as the Lieutenant Governor. Once he had acquired title to his mountain meadow, he built the original log cabin which still stands and has been restored by Apache Oil Company. (Note: A later owner.)

Paradise Ranch is located sixteen miles west of Buffalo at an elevation of 7,500 feet above sea level and developed gradually as Norman Meldrum's friends came up to the meadow for camping trips. His son, Dr. Gordon Meldrum, returned from the war in the Philippines and decided to settle in Buffalo and establish a practice.

Gordon Meldrum was enchanted with the cabin in the mountains and encouraged friends to visit him there. It was these visitors who eventually called the meadow "paradise." The name stuck and eventually became the name of the dude ranch. Shortly after Dr. Meldrum married Mabel Lee in 1903, they began to invite guests up to the meadow cabin. They soon added a few other cabins to accommodate their needs. This developed into paying guests and the infant dude ranch was on its way. The official date for the beginning seems to be 1905. (Note: HF Bar has always laid claim to being the second oldest ranch in the state, second only to Eaton's which was established in Wyoming in 1904. If the Paradise 1905 date is even near correct then the HF Bar claim is a bit ambitious. Remember, 1905 was when Skipper arrived in Wyoming to herd sheep. HF Bar may have to settle for being one of the oldest dude ranches.)

...After Dr. Meldrum's death in 1911 (Note: The year HF Bar was established), *Mabel elected to continue Paradise Ranch and it was operated from June through September and used as a hunting camp during big game season. Log cabins were erected and a main lodge built with a community bath house to serve the guest's needs. Riding, fishing and pack trips were the featured activities. In 1909, Jack Meldrum had arrived on the scene just two years before his father Gordon's death. He grew up with the summer dudes at Paradise. Mabel was an expert manager, good with horses and a pretty fair hunter. She was indeed, a liberated woman for her time...As young Jack grew up, he helped his mother with the operation during the summer. Paradise was only seven or eight miles on horseback from Frank Horton's HF Bar Ranch and dudes from Horton's often rode up for the day. Horton's was growing and in 1927, Mabel Meldrum sold Paradise Ranch to Frank O. Horton...* (Note: This is a prime example of the lack of recognition, or lack of awareness of the Gorrell involvement in HF Bar.)

Skipper verified the chain of events when he wrote in *Bridle Bits*:

...In 1926, feeling the pressure for accommodations at HF Bar, we took over Paradise Ranch and accommodated there that summer about 30 guests, without making any improvements whatsoever, with the exception of the installation of a bathhouse. (Note: It must have been a replacement or an additional one since the Meldrums built a bathhouse at one point in time.) *In the spring of 1927 we built the new clubhouse and the dining room, and remodeled the kitchen; in 1928 we added the four new log bungalows.* *Now we can accommodate 60 guests comfortably at Paradise and with the 160 guests whom we can take at the height of our season at HF Bar we have a total guest list of some 220 guests.*

HF Bar Ranch paid $15,000 for Paradise Ranch and Mabel Meldrum took five $3,000 notes in payment. The notes had to be extended in 1935 and 1940.

Paradise Ranch became an integral part of the HF Bar operation for many years. It was operated separately, but under HF Bar supervision. One of the earlier managers was a Mr. Sherwood Smedley and at various times the Horton boys were sent up to try their hand at managing the place.

Sanfords "Sandy" Jacques was the manager for many years. Sandy Jacques married Eleanor "Jimmy" Watt who was a dude at HF Bar in the early 1930s. Sandy and Jimmy Jacques left Paradise in approximately 1932 and established their own dude ranch, Pass Creek Ranch, outside of Parkman, Wyoming, just north of Sheridan.

Pass Creek Ranch was a 2500 acre spread which the Jacques owned and operated until the late 1940s. It was not operated as a dude ranch during the war. In about 1948, they sold the ranch and moved into Dayton, Wyoming for a few years and then moved to La Jolla, California.

Sandy and Jimmy had two sons, Sandy and Dave, who worked

HF Bar and Paradise Ranches

E.W. "Bill" Gollings worked for the HF Bar Ranch in the 1930s. He created many drawings for the HF Bar Ranch brochures. When Paradise Ranch was acquired in 1926, Bill Gollings created a brochure for the combined dude ranch operation. *(Courtesy of the HF Bar Ranch)*

at HF Bar during the summers for several years in the 1950s and for many years after her husband's death in 1955 Jimmy would work in the HF Bar store.

The acquisition of Paradise Ranch was not the last land purchase. In November, 1926, at a sheriff's sale, HF Bar paid $350 for 80 acres that belonged to Joseph Sayles. No other land would be acquired until 1933 when Skipper was granted another patent for 80 acres. That was the end of HF Bar expansion.

HF Bar Ranch was at its maximum size during the late 1920s but it is unclear how many acres were leased from the state and federal governments. I suppose we have to take Skipper at his word when he stated in *Bridle Bits* in 1928 that:

...The original ranch consisted of about 500 acres. Since then we have taken over eight other ranches and have increased our holdings until we now have about 28,000 acres in feed and nearly that much more land under leases from state and federal governments...

The HF Bar Ranch also had leases in Montana. In 1924, Skipper signed a lease with Virginia B. Spear who leased forty sections of land on the Crow Indian Reservation. Virginia was the wife of Willis Spear, a notable rancher and politician. The Sheridan County Heritage Book published in 1983 describes Willis Spear's involvement in the land and cattle business:

...In 1896, Spear Brothers Cattle Company was formed...From 1899 until 1914, Willis went to Old Mexico, Texas and New Mexico buying cattle and shipping them to Wyoming to feed and ship to market when four or five years old.

The Spear Brothers owned land on Dutch Creek and five ranches on Powder River, north of Arvada, in Montana. They leased the Leiter ranches (Note: The old Big Red mentioned previously where Skipper first worked in Wyoming.) *which extended 17 miles along Clear Creek. In 1908 they leased over a million acres on the Crow Indian Reservation. They ran 36,000 head of their own cattle and pastured 22,000 head for other people. This continued until 1915 when Spear Brothers sold out.*

Willis Spear continued to be interested with others in the livestock business until his death October 11, 1936...

Willis and his wife retained leases on the Crow Reservation even after the dissolution of the Spear Brothers Cattle Company that enabled them to sub-lease the land to other livestock growers like Skipper. Skipper and a person named O. E. Wartensleben obtained the right to graze cattle and horses on 8,840 acres of the Spear lease. These leases would run well into the 1930s. The lease conditions were that Skipper could run one animal for each thirty acres per year or one animal for each fifteen acres per six months.

Even with the Montana leases it is difficult to corroborate Skipper's claim that he had control of 56,000 acres deeded and leased land. Public records do not account for more than approximately 6,000 acres of deeded land. Neither can I account for "eight other ranches" unless I count homestead acreages (patents). It is probable that Skipper's claim that he had over 50,000 acres of land under his control was exaggerated, or, if he rounded out the numbers, he rounded them way up.

HF Bar West

In his land estimate, Skipper may have included 10,000 acres in California, for that was where Skipper and the Gorrells planned to establish the California HF Bar Ranch. In 1928, in the *Bridle Bits* newspaper, the headline read:

Frank O. Horton Buys Ranch in California

On the coast, eighty miles south of Monterey, in Monterey county, half way between San Francisco and Los Angeles, directly west of King City, is the future home of the California the HF Bar Ranch. At this point, the coast turns east so that the property is protected from the north and northwest winds; the coastline is very broken and rough. So rough, in fact, that our entire ten miles of coast has only two bathing beaches, both of them at the mouths of streams as big and beautiful as our own Rock Creek...

The property itself contains about 10,000 acres, is bounded on the west and south by the sea, and on the north and east by the Santa Barbara forest reserve...

Skipper continued to describe the wildness and beauty of the country and discussed the plan:

...The present plan is to set aside the most beautiful part of the property for a dude ranch and to utilize the adjoining forest reserve in much the same way as we do our own Big Horns. Lodges will be established a day's ride apart in the forest reserve so that guests can take comfortable trips back to the mountains. At first, the main ranch will be equipped with a comfortable log lodge and, later on, individual log cabins will be added—all built of redwoods. In a word, we are going to try to do in California what we have done

in Wyoming.

During the coming winter we will be ready for only a few pioneer friends, but it will be another year before any but the tough ones will enjoy it.

Unfortunately, Skipper was premature with his announcement because the California HF Bar never materialized. Warren and Demia Gorrell did in fact purchase at least twelve miles of California coast line. Much of 1928 was taken up with negotiations between Warren Gorrell in Chicago, lawyers in California, the various land owners involved, and a Marion Hollins who lived in California and was a potential investor in the project and at times acted as the local contact with property owners.

Skipper was heavily involved. He made several trips to California with Gertrude to view the property and advise Warren Gorrell on how the property could best be developed into a dude ranch. Warren Gorrell relied heavily on Skipper as a front man but occasionally they seemed to get at cross-purposes and Warren Gorrell would complain. After Skipper had taken the initiative on a certain matter in the negotiations Warren Gorrell wrote the following to Skipper in May, 1928:

...I must insist on running my own business. This is a big deal and I am putting up the money. You seem to get so heated up over a proposition and putting it through you go off kind of half-cocked. Take for example that Gamboa option—why not investigate the situation first and let me know the basis so that I can decide whether I want to enter into it or not! That must be the rule on anything in the future, and I cannot quite understand why you have not seen it before...

This would not be the only time that Skipper and Warren Gorrell would have their differences. Warren Gorrell's position was that he made all financial arrangements, including the investment of his own money and so he should be able to call some of the shots. Skipper's position was that although he didn't make significant monetary investments, he put in the majority of the sweat equity and made things work and so was an equal partner. It is also pretty evident that Skipper didn't appreciate being second-guessed from Chicago. There would be later disputes of the same nature between Skipper and Warren Gorrell.

In fact, only a month later, in June, 1928, Skipper and Warren Gorrell had a similar clash about Wyoming HF Bar matters. Skipper happened to be in Kansas City, Missouri, when he got the following letter from Warren Gorrell:

...I am not pleased with your long-hand letter of the 7th, about the larger expenditures not contemplated nor authorized, nor am I with the new cottages. Did you stop to figure what all this runs into in the way of money; and just what is the use of going on on the same basis year in and year out, always promising that it is the last year that such a thing will happen?

What difference does it make if the income is larger if it all goes out in expenditures? I agree with you about the highest price requiring a correspondingly well-equipped place, but it doesn't make it any more attractive to have it bigger—I think it will detract.

I have expressed myself so many times in so many different years in exactly this way, that I wonder why I never made any impression. Is it because you think I am a soft and easy mark? The thought comes to me whether for the next 15 or 20 years I will be going through the same proposition with you in California. If so, I would rather not make the start.

Well, they never did make the start. Aside from the acquisition of the property by Warren Gorrell, the project never really got past the idea stage and was overtaken by events—notably the worsening relationship between Skipper and Warren Gorrell, the nearing financial depression and Warren Gorrell's financial collapse.

Agricultural Pursuits

Agricultural production at the HF Bar Ranch was the most prolific during the twenties. Skipper recorded all the agricultural transactions that occurred in the cattle, horse, sheep and crop business of HF Bar in a series of daybooks. The content of the daybooks is much too comprehensive to record verbatim here, but I have extracted excerpts from the day books to give the reader a flavor of the agricultural dynamics.

The daybooks began in 1923 when Skipper noted that on May 12 they branded five steers and four heifers with the UM brand and on May 20 branded eighty seven steer calves and sixty heifer calves with the HF Bar brand. Skipper then notes that some calves were to be branded HF Bar because the UM is "selling all calves to HF Bar to square up accounts." The background of this transaction is unknown but it is known that separate accounts were kept for the UM Ranch, which was technically owned by Warren Gorrell, and HF Bar. There are other references to separate accounts in other daybook entries.

Skipper also had a lease arrangement with his brother Lisle in Clearmont because he notes that on July 2nd

...98 head 2 yr old cows bot (Note: Skipper often uses "bot" for brought and bought) *up from Lisle's by Perry...*

and then on July 6th:

...Perry takes down (Note: To Lisle's place) *137 head of steers and heifer yearlings. There should be about 100 head of two yr old steers at Lisle's or a total of about 237 head all told...*

On the same date Skipper noted that 325 cattle including eleven bulls were put in summer pasture in the mountains and a separate lot of 115 cattle (mostly two year old heifers) including five bulls were also put on summer pasture in the mountains.

Another entry:

...total number of calves branded HF Bar during 1923=274. Half of these, 137, were really UM...HF buys these 137 head at $20.00=$2,740 ...

On September 5, Skipper noted that they sent one hundred thirty three horses to Lisle's for winter pasture. The inventory included one hundred fifteen geldings, thirteen mares and five colts. Skipper notes that:

...13 mares branded O on jaw all bred to the government horse.

The government horse was a United States Army Remount stud that was part of the Army's program to upgrade the quality of horseflesh in the United States. Skipper joined the remount program. The arrangement was that he maintained the stud and bred it to ranch mares. The crop of foals was then shared with the U. S. Army, but the exact nature of the sharing arrangement is unknown. Later in the month, Skipper would send more horses to Lisle's homestead so that 273 horses would spend the winter at Lisle's.

The daybooks also show that HF Bar was in the sheep business in a pretty significant way. In October 1923, he recorded the purchase of over a thousand sheep (1171) from John Esponda for $5,427.00 and another lot of over thirty-five hundred sheep from various sellers for over $18,000. The transactions were not limited to cattle and sheep, for near the end of 1923 Skipper recorded that they had hogs as well which amounted to:

...121 winter pigs in feed lot...7 old sows in feed lot...103 weaners in feed lot...about 52 brood sows outside...

In 1924 the daybooks record several bunches of cattle that were sent to the Spear lease on the reservation. The herd included 500 head from HF Bar and the UM. That winter a total of 640 head were wintered on the reservation and that fall HF Bar would ship cows from the reservation, Arvada (Note: near Clearmont) and Buffalo.

Horses were also wintered on the reservation as well as Lisle's homestead near Clearmont for Skipper noted on September 15, 1924 that:

> ...*Tud Smith took the following to the Reservation...Grey Fox, Horse Creek Brownie, Spotty, Cheyenne, Have, Ranger, Bay Colt, Whoa, Arvada, Indian, Ray...*

By the end of 1924, HF Bar had 860 head of cattle, mostly yearling heifers, at the reservation. In years subsequent to 1930 there were entries like this:

...Dec 31, 1925 Inventory

Bulls from Res	*16*
Grown stuff from Res	*451*
Grown stuff always on HF	*12*
Calves branded during 1925	*251*
	730 Total...

The January 1, 1927 inventory listed 873 cattle of all sorts and a total value of $37,540, of which half the value accrued to HF Bar and the UM Ranch each. The sheep inventory for the same time was 3,016 head of all sorts valued at $35,557 and, again, the value was split between the UM Ranch and HF Bar.

For some reason, in the spring of 1927 the ranch got out of the sheep business, temporarily, for as Skipper recorded in the daybook:

...sold all sheep to Hinton April 1927...bucks sold to Antoine Silva and Ed Twing

HF Bar did get back into the sheep business again later in the year but on a more modest scale. The inventory on January 1, 1928 was only 110 ewes and wethers. This number would increase somewhat later on in the 1930s but was much less than the previous inventories.

The 1920s, then, ended with a very modest sheep inventory, but throughout this time the cattle inventory remained fairly stable. At the beginning of January 1930 Skipper listed 852 head of cattle of all types.

Skipper also kept detailed records on farming operations from 1926 to 1942. He planted and harvested crops of all kinds-hay, barley, oats and wheat at various locations depending on his crop rotation scheme. In 1926, Skipper recorded his method of keeping accounts:

...All farming operations considered an expense account against livestock, therefore, all hay and grain and ensilage to be figured at cost which price holds for all H and G (Note: Horton and Gorrell) *inventories...all cattle, sheep and hogs are joint livestock...all farming operations are joint farming...all farm machinery is joint farm eqpt (sic) acct. starting 1927.*

A joint H & G inventory is to be taken of the crops produced by the two corporations (Note: HF Bar Corporation and Mowry Basin Development Corporaton, which will be explained later.) *The corporation producing the smallest amt of H or G is to buy from the other corp and amount of each shortage so that each will put up # for # and ton for ton. The price of same to be the production price per # or ton of the H & G produced by the purchaser...*

An example of how the above worked is that in the 1927 farm report the UM Ranch put up 908 tons of hay and HF Bar put up 451 tons. So, HF Bar bought 228 tons of hay from the UM so that each place ended up with 680 tons of hay.

So it was in the agricultural business at HF Bar in the 1920s. The livestock operation was spread out between HF Bar and the Crow Reservation and the Clearmont area, both of which were many miles away, mountain grazing leases and the adjoining UM Ranch made for a far-flung complicated, labor-intensive operation. The intensive farming operation, when added to this, resulted in the portrait of a busy and ambitious man—Skipper Horton.

Skipper summarized the agricultural position of HF Bar when in 1928 he declared in *Bridle Bits* that:

> ...*We always have run cattle, horses and sheep on the ranches. At the present time we are practically out of the sheep business, but are running about 2,300 head of cattle and 600 head of horses, with about 2,000 tons of hay, and harvest about 6,000 bushels of grain...*

Skipper's figures may be absolutely true, but I was unable to verify them from the comprehensive set of daybooks he left behind which portray more modest holdings.

Mowry Basin

Warren Gorrell had established the Mowry Basin Stock and Development Company sometime before 1923 and probably in Illinois. In 1923, a letter was sent to all subscribers and notified them that they must pay the final installment on their subscriptions because after May 1st the company would be incorporated as a Wyoming corporation and certificates of stock would be distributed.

Mowry Basin had an authorized capital of $200,000 divided into 2,000 shares with a par value of $100. Warren Gorrell sold mostly to his friends and no more than about $100,000 worth of stock was ever sold. In 1928 the corporation reported a value of $328,527.80 and listed the nature of investments as Livestock and Feed, Investments & Notes Receivable, Real Estate, Buildings and Improvements, Machinery and Equipment, and Irrigation Ditch Shares. In addition to ranching interests the corporation began purchase, in 1926, of Ohio Oil Company common stock. By 1930, the corporation owned 4,706 shares of the stock at a value over $98,000.

The UM Ranch mortgage, and several other minor land purchases, and various lots of livestock were purchased and placed under the Mowry umbrella. Skipper had some financial interest in Mowry Basin but how much is unknown. His is the only name listed on the company stationery. At one point he was listed as president of the corporation, and at other times he was the vice president and treasurer. Of course, another director was Warren Gorrell who at one time was listed as president. Demia Gorrell, Warren's wife, was also listed as a director in one annual report. One of Warren Gorrell's employees in Chicago, F. J. Sohm, was also a director and was instrumental in the operation of the corporation.

Early in the next decade, when Warren Gorrell fell on hard financial times, the dissolution of the Mowry Basin Stock and

Development Company presented a real challenge to Skipper. The future of the HF Bar Ranch would be placed in jeopardy and Skipper would have to arrange a bail out plan.

Politics

Skipper inherited the family interest in public office and service and so in 1922 he threw his hat in the political arena when he opted to   run for state representative in the Wyoming State Legislature. On October 28, 1922, the *Buffalo Bulletin* published the following article about Skipper:

*...Mr. Horton became a candidate at the solicitation of his many friends who are of the opinion that he is the very man who should represent the county at the next session and who believe that if there is any legislation that will be of advantage to the county it can best be obtained by one who is in harmony with the state administration. Mr. Horton came to this county a good many years ago and after his arrival here herded sheep for B. C. Cass, later buying a band of his own. He later purchased a ranch on Rock Creek adding to it gradually until he now has one of the largest and best improved ranches in the county and a part of which is fitted up as a resort for those who enjoy the out of doors. (*Note: Again, no reference to the Gorrells.) *He is interested in cattle, sheep and horses, and understands the wants and needs of those engaged in these lines. He is also interested in the schools of the county and stands squarely on the Republican platform which was adopted at Sheridan, which declares that the Republican party favors salaries for teachers commensurate with their services and the country pupil should be able to receive the same advantage as those of the city pupil. Mr. Horton is a veteran of the Spanish American War, is a large taxpayer in the county and is one of the public spirited residents of Johnson County. He is just the man for the position and the voters will make no mistake if they decide that they want him to represent them at Cheyenne.*

Well, the people decided that they wanted Skipper to represent them as he was elected to the 1923 legislature. He received 1,063 votes which gave him a majority of 374 votes over his opponent who was a man named Hawkes.

Skipper's first term in the Wyoming Legislature was successful and obviously pleased his constituents for he ran for the state senate in the next term and was elected. In a prelude to the election, the *Buffalo Bulletin* again characterized Skipper:

The first name appearing upon the county ticket is that of Frank O. Horton for state senator. Mr. Horton is present state representative from this county to which position he was elected two years ago. He has therefore had experience in the legislative body. Mr. Horton served well the people of this county as well as the state in the legislature. He is very largely interested in livestock and ranch lands. His ranch, known as the HF Bar, enjoys a patronage of prominent people from every section of the country. It comprises several thousand acres of land and is undoubtedly the best improved ranch in Johnson County and one of the best in the state of Wyoming. Mr. Horton is well informed and deeply interested in all phases of agricultural work. He is the present president of the Johnson County Farm Bureau and in that capacity he has served well the farmers of Johnson County. He is also deeply interested in the game and fish laws and the public schools. Mr. Horton's experience in the legislature and the acquaintance he has gained there together with his knowledge of all phases of Wyoming industry makes him an invaluable asset in a state legislature both from the standpoint of the state of Wyoming and of the county which he serves and we expect that Mr. Horton will be elected by an overwhelming vote on November 7th.

The *Buffalo Bulletin,* reported that Skipper was elected by a "...most substantial and satisfying..." majority to the sixteenth legislature

.

Skipper served two four-year terms as a state senator which covered the seventeenth through twentieth legislatures. In the last legislature, from 1929-1931, Skipper served as President of the State Senate.

A respected state legislator, Skipper was also a recognized spokesman and advocate for the livestock industry and served honorably as a member of the Wyoming Stock Growers Association. His achievements in the association were documented in a history of the association called *Guardian of the Grasslands,* written by John Rolfe Burroughs in 1971. He described the role that Skipper played in an important moment in the early 1920s:

Frank O. Horton, who was destined to play a crucial role in preventing the fragmentation of the Association and its possible demise, first figured prominently in its affairs at the annual convention held in Cheyenne on June 5, 1923. Some months previously, W. J. Thom, pioneer Buffalo, Wyoming banker, had written an article in which he referred to "Tommy Haynes, whose home on Rock Creek (in northwestern Johnson County) has, since his death, been converted into a dude ranch...(by)the Honorable Frank O. Horton, our State Representative." President Jordan introduced Horton to the convention and the latter in a brief response, remarked that "I have to explain my position because I think nearly everybody here thinks I have a dude ranch. As a matter of fact, I have about 1,500 head of cattle up there (in Johnson County) besides a lot of horses."

(Note: The reader will recall that the Haynes place was actually the second place down the creek, i.e., the middle place. It is also amusing to observe how Skipper sometimes slanted his point of view depending on his audience. He definitely wanted to make sure that this audience believed he was a stockman first, and dude rancher second; in other instances, he preferred to be known as a dude rancher who also had a lot of livestock.)

Later, according to the Rolfe article, there was another crisis looming in the Stock Growers Association in 1929. What the crisis was is not particularly important to this story, but the role that Skipper played provides an insight into the man and the high regard in which he was held by his stock growing peers. John Rolfe wrote:

...In accordance with a custom established during the regime of John B. Kendrick, President Jordan had arranged a program of guest speakers for the 1929 meeting, one of whom was State Representative Frank O. Horton of Johnson County. It is doubtful that Representative Horton thought of himself as a figure of destiny as he approached the podium in Sheridan, Wyoming on that fateful day in 1929, but such he proved to be. Not only because of the subject matter, but because of its timing and because of the decisive action it evoked, Representative Horton's speech was the most important ever delivered to a Wyoming Stock Growers Association convention.

Skipper's influence as a member of the Wyoming Stock Growers Association during the 1920s would cause him to be elected by the membership as a trustee in 1928. He held this position until 1942.

Skipper's influence expanded beyond the borders of Wyoming. His views on the livestock industry were sought after, and he was not above combining those views with his political views. The following article was published in the *Denver Post* in January, 1928, and illustrates the typical kind of coverage that Skipper received from the press:

PEAK PROFITS ARE SEEN AHEAD FOR CATTLEMEN
Wyoming Senator Visions an Era of Record Prosperity

Colorado and Wyoming cattlemen will acquire fortunes in the next five years and sheepmen of the two states will make millions.

And Colorado and Wyoming will go Republican in the presidential campaign, with either Hoover or Lowden the west's candidate.

Frank Horton, Wyoming state senator, cattle baron and proprietor of the largest dude ranch in Wyoming, made those predictions in Denver Thursday when he arrived to meet a number of big cattlemen now assembling in Denver for Stock Show week.

Predicts Record Prosperity

"Colorado and Wyoming stockmen face the most prosperous period of their lives in the next five years", declared Horton, "for cattle markets are stabilized with good prices prevailing. The small fellow has been eliminated from the cattle business by the years of low prices we have experienced since the war, and those who are now in the cattle game do not have to rush unfinished stuff to the markets, do not have to do so much begging at the banks for finances, and do not have to compete on the market with men who must sell to lift mortgages.

"Colorado and Wyoming cattlemen had a big year in 1927. But 1928 is going to put the past year in the shade. And 1929 will be even better. Denver's stockyards records, which have been smashed in many instances in the past year, will fade compared to the records to be made in the coming five years."

Forecast G. O. P. Victory in Wyoming

Horton, who has served eight years in the Wyoming Senate, believes that the cattle and sheep markets will be helped if a Republican candidate is elected to succeed Calvin Coolidge as president...

Horton is the owner and proprietor of the HF Bar dude ranch in the Wyoming Big Horns. There he has over 15,000 acres devoted to stock raising and giving eastern millionaires the times of their lives during the summer season.

(Note: It is interesting that the article claims that the HF Bar Ranch consisted of 15,000 acres. The source of the number is unknown, but it is a far cry from Skipper's claim in the same year that he controlled approximately 50,000 acres. Also, his optimistic predictions about the livestock industry would become victim of the Depression.)

For reasons unknown, Skipper did not run for the state legislature when his last term expired. There is no discussion of the matter in the local newspaper. Others have offered the conjecture that he ran for governor in this period, but the local newspaper does not bear this out as Skipper is not mentioned as a primary candidate either in 1931 or 1934, the two gubernatorial primary years. Skipper disappeared from the political radar until 1938 when he was again elected to public office.

It is entirely reasonable to assume that Skipper was too preoccupied with more important matters than running for public office. In 1930 we will see that Skipper had to mount a rescue effort to save HF Bar from financial disaster.

Family Matters

There is no surviving correspondence or other records that help paint a picture of what the Horton family life was like in the 1920s. Surely, because of Skipper's upbringing and his pretty intense work ethic, the children were put to work in some capacity as soon as they were old enough. And that was probably at a pretty young age. No doubt, Gertrude tended to the children and did whatever she had to do to help Skipper.

It has been written that when the children became of school age they attended the Rock Creek District School, the yellow school house on the old Tathwell property that was now the HF Bar lower place. In 1923, however, the boys appear in the Sheridan County School census. Bill was twelve years old, Jack eleven and Bobby was seven.

The fact is that the boys attended Sheridan schools, with a brief exception, until 1929 when Bill and Jack graduated from high school. Sometime in the early 1920s Gertrude and Skipper discovered California. Gertrude spent parts of several winters there and must have taken the children with her. In fact, the Sheridan High School yearbook states that Bill and Jack started high school in La Jolla, California, but they returned to Wyoming sometime during that year and finished their high school career in Sheridan.

In the wintertime, Gertrude and the boys lived in Sheridan at various addresses. It was not a viable proposition to commute to school in Sheridan from the ranch every day. This was not unusual. Ranching families even today often rent or buy a house in town so the children can go to high school. In fact, Skipper's brother, James Lisle, rented a house a block down the street from Skipper so his daughters, Maribel and Harriet, could attend school in Sheridan instead of Clearmont. (Note: The Skipper and his brother both had Sheridan addresses during the period 1925-1929. Skipper was listed in the

Sheridan City Directory as a rancher and James Lisle was listed as a car salesman for Riley Motors, the local Buick dealer, but he still had the homestead near Clearmont.)

These days are documented in *Backward Glance*, published by the Clearmont Historical Group in Clearmont, Wyoming. In the book, Carl Bauer, wrote about his sister Evelyn, that:

> *...Clearmont didn't have a four year high school. Dad made friends with the Sheridan Buick man, Lyle (Note: Lisle) and the Horton's became close friends of ours. Harriet was a close friend of Evelyn's, so when she had to go to Sheridan for two more years of high school she stayed with the Horton's...*

This arrangement also afforded Gertrude the opportunity to participate in the social life of Sheridan in such organizations as the Sheridan Women's Club in which she was an active member. Gertrude was also active in the Red Cross. In 1928, the Sheridan Journal wrote the following article about her:

In Charge of Sheridan County Red Cross Roll Call

> *Mrs. F. O. Horton, head of the Sheridan County roll call for the Red Cross, has brought to her aid in this campaign a number of ladies who are equally interested with her in raising the budget which has been placed at $3,000. Workers are busy about the city and county, and when Thanksgiving day comes and the campaign ends, those who know Mrs. Horton know she will have done her best in a wind-up of the work.*
>
> *In talking with a representative of* The Journal *this morning Mrs. Horton expressed her great appreciation of the fine spirit of co-operation which had been given her in this campaign. "The people have responded beautifully, and while the full quota has not been subscribed we hope it will be reached within the next week*

or 10 days...

One of those interesting ladies, always willing to help in any public or civic enterprise, Mrs. Horton is the wife of Senator Frank O. Horton, and is associated with him during the dude season in looking after their large number of guests at the dude ranch in Johnson County, southwest of Sheridan...

Even though there was a year difference in their ages, Bill and Jack graduated from Sheridan High School, Sheridan, Wyoming in the same year—1929—when Bill was nineteen and Jack was eighteen.

Bill was an active student. The yearbook listed his activities: In his freshman year (when he was in La Jolla) he was class treasurer and he held the same office in his sophomore year at Sheridan High School. He was a member of the Future Farmers of America (FFA) in his sophomore through senior years, and was president of the organization in his junior and senior years. He was also a member of the stock judging team which represented Sheridan High School at Laramie, Wyoming, in the state judging competition. The team won third place out of eighteen competing schools and gave the team the right to represent Wyoming at the Kansas City Royal Stock Show. In his senior year, Bill was also on the high school yearbook staff. In the school history, the quote that Bill selected as his motto was:

...I had rather be a kitten and cry "mew" than one of those some metre ballad-mongers...

Yearbook photo of Jack Horton, Sr.
on graduation from Sheridan High School in 1929.
(Courtesy of the HF Bar Ranch)

Yearbook photo of Bill Horton
on graduation from Sheridan High School in 1929.
(Courtesy of the HF Bar Ranch)

There has always been a certain amount of horseplay
at the HF Bar Corral.
Here a young Bill Horton and two unidentified partners in crime
baptize an unidentified girl at the water fountain.
(Courtesy of the HF Bar Ranch.)

A young Bobby Horton. Date unknown.
(Courtesy of the HF Bar Ranch)

Clearly, Bill's major interests were agricultural. Jack, however, had a different bent. He was on the debate team in his junior year and a member of a young men's Christian association in his junior year as well. He was also the business manager for the school yearbook. Jack had a literary flair, and in his senior year wrote a short story for his school annual which was titled *Concerning The Monster of Lake DeSmet* and revealed a pretty vivid imagination and an ability to express it. He also wrote a poem for the annual titled *The Faculty Play*. The quote which Jack selected for the school history was:

...He hath a wisdom that doth guide his valor to act in safety...

When Bill and Jack graduated from high school, Bobby was thirteen years old and about to begin his freshman year. Nothing is known about his secondary education. I assume he went to high school in California because there is no record of his attendance at Sheridan High School. The year when he would most likely have graduated at age 17 or 18 would have been 1933 or 1934 when he was living in California.

During the summers throughout the 1920s the entire family would be at the ranch. These were formative years for the children. Life at the ranch would give them all opportunities to be cowboys. Jack was the more studious type, and while he could ride and probably do all the things that needed doing on the ranch, he could take it or leave it. Bobby was still young, but there is no indication he had any inclination in the cowboy direction whatsoever.

Bill, on the other hand, became, in the vernacular of the West, a real "hand." He became an excellent roper, a skilled rider, a good judge of horseflesh and was involved as a contestant, and later as the primary organizer of the HF Bar rodeos that were held for many years. By all accounts, Bill Horton was a fast living, fun loving, and hard drinking kind of guy whom one old timer described to me as "funny as hell, especially when he was drinking."

In the summers of the 1920s the Horton children would have spent a lot of time playing with their cousins, the Gorrells. Warren and Demia had four children: Anna (Nan), Warren, Jr. (Ginger), Demia (De) and Sarah (Sally). The Gorrells came every summer, though not always at the same time.

Often, news correspondents visited dude ranches to give first hand reports of ranch activities. A reporter from the *Chicago News* filed a dispatch on August 5, 1927, and mentioned the Horton and Gorrell families:

...State Senator and Mrs. Frank O. Horton are the inspiration of HF Bar, and a joy to every dude family there. Their three boys, Bill, the roper; Bob, who is looking after Paradise (Note: Bobby was only eleven years old. I doubt he was looking after Paradise) *and Jack, who has had a pack train down to Cheyenne to the round-up with Ritchie Grant and Bob King this week are the capable aids.*

"Ginger Gorrell," son of the Warren Gorrells of Chicago has been here all summer and the rest of the family arrived yesterday, with the exception of Nan, who is abroad. This is the Gorrell's fourth season at H. F. Bar (Note: The reporter got that wrong. The Gorrells had vacationed at HF Bar since 1911.) *and they have all become proficient steer ropers and range riders. "Ginger" is in a class with "Tud" Smith and Johnny Scott when it comes to cattle wrangling, and all are popular as cowboy escorts for the dude girls...*

The Gorrells built a substantial house at the ranch and lived in it during their vacations. It was located on the hill just west of the Horton house. Nothing remains of it today except a few remnants of the foundation.

The Gorrell children are not mentioned much in surviving correspondence except for Warren Gorrell Jr. who everyone called

The house that Warren and Demia Gorrell built
for their family to live in during their annual visits to the HF Bar Ranch.
The house no longer exists.
(Courtesy of Henry S. Stewart)

"Ginger." Ginger did not quite fit the mold of his father. Ginger was educated at Northwestern University and Amherst College but he did not have much use for the establishment. Instead he was somewhat of an free spirit who loved the West—in particular HF Bar Ranch and its environs. He worked there in the summers and spent as much time as he could in the mountains. In the mid-1920s he built a cabin in the mountains above HF Bar and the cabin still stands today.

Skipper, at times, acted as a link between Ginger and his father, Warren. The earliest record of this situation is a letter from Warren to Skipper when Skipper was vacationing in New Mexico in the fall of 1927. For some reason, Ginger was with him. This was at a time when Warren was trying to guide Ginger toward some kind of a career. Warren had arranged an introduction to a Mr. Levi Smith, who was involved in the oil business, to show Skipper and Ginger around. Warren wrote Skipper:

*...I am hoping Levi is there, because he is one of the most interesting men I think I ever met. If there I would like to have him give Son (*Note: Warren always referred to Ginger as "Son."*) a talk on the oil business, and I think you know how to bring that about...Son seems to be in seventh heaven turning over the soil in New Mexico for what he can find. Yet I judge from one of his letters that there isn't anybody on top of the ground that could hire him to do it on a salary...I am enclosing draft for $50 to Son's order, which he can have as a reserve...Make sure that he has enough warm suitable clothes, and at the proper time see that he gets rid of the motorcycle...*

A year later Warren would write another letter to Skipper:

You will recall my telling you about Son's desire to go into ranching for his own account. I want you to discuss with him the experience and training he must have to be eminently successful, and I am not interested in it any other way. It occurred to me that the McDonald place might be one for him to start on and cut his eye teeth. If he failed, Mowry could take it over...

Warren's suggestion was never implemented. Ginger never became a rancher. But he did have other ambitions.

One was, apparently to set up some kind of operation at Trail Lodge which Skipper opposed. This resulted in the following letter in October 1928 from Skipper to Warren, and illustrates the complex relationship between the three men.

I was right in the midst of one of the Count Luckner stories when your telephone call came through. Son had been up with me most of the evening, so that he was also on hand, as you know, when your call came.

It never entered my head when I wrote you a few days ago about my opposition to the Trail Lodge plan that you did not already know about it. Son had been getting ready for three or four weeks; everybody here knew it, and I supposed that you back there knew it also. I think Son was inclined to be a bit sore at me because he thought I had been tattling, but I made him see that there wasn't anything else for me to think except that he had taken the matter up with you, and that in writing I was simply voicing my opposition to the plan. I told Son after my talk with you that I rather thought it was up to you to suggest something that would be of interest to him, but worthwhile as well, and I think that you should do this. One thing is for sure—the kid is not going to get anything out of his Trail Lodge experience. I tried to point out that fact to him, that is, that there is not enough up there that he doesn't already know, and that the only experience he could possibly have would be to see the same old thing with a coating of snow. If he were going into a country which he didn't know, there would, of course, be added a thrill, and the kid would not only get a big kick out of it, but such an experience might help him find himself.

I didn't have much of a chance to talk to Son last night; in fact, I didn't want to because I felt that he should sleep over the things you said to him. He has been off all day and I haven't seen him at all except at breakfast for a moment this morning. I will try to have a little talk with him tonight—it will have to be tonight because tomorrow I have to go out on a speaking tour again and will not return until the end of the week...

Another exchange of letters between Skipper and Warren in May, 1929, shed even more light on the situation. This letter is from Warren to Skipper:

I have your letter of the 27th regarding Son, and as long as you are frank with me, I ought to be with you. He loves it out there, and would like to be identified in some way with an enterprise in which I was interested, but that (Note: I do not know what "that" was.) *seems to be the only one that draws him as it is out of doors.*

There has been some previous experience in working under you that has cut pretty deep into his soul, and I have regretted it, but never understood clearly enough to attempt any correction. I should like to see the best feeling between you two. I do not believe I can say anything more about his working there this summer—or ever working there—until there is some clear understanding between you which sets everything right forever.

This is not an easy letter to write, and as I am writing it I have the feeling that I am more or less of a dumb-bell in sending it, yet there has been the basis of an unhappy feeling and I have had the wish that matters might be cleared up. Right at the moment I have the uncomfortable feeling that if you went to him saying that I had written this letter, that the results would be futile. I guess it's a case for diplomacy, or nothing.

As far as I know, Ginger did not go back to work at HF Bar, and in the next year the relationship between the Hortons and Gorrells would change dramatically. However, Ginger would reappear in later years in the area; in fact he would die there, and would have a special relationship with Skipper's granddaughter, Trudy.

Social

Dude ranches in the 1920s were at their full hue and cry. Eastern newspapers and other publications were full of articles that described the western way of life complete with photos. The Burlington Northern railroad even ran special trains, called "dude ranch specials," to bring hundreds of easterners to the Sheridan railroad depot where they were met by representatives of the many dude ranches in the Sheridan area.

HF Bar and Paradise always figured prominently in the publications and were the sole subject of many. Typical of the coverage was an article published in the *Chicago Daily News* on Aug 4, 1927. Excerpts from the article describe the allure of dude ranch life in the West:

WANTS TO STAY IN WEST AS COWBOY
Albert Goodrich Jr. Likes Life on Dude Ranch in Big Horn Range
By Jessie Ozias Donahue

H F Bar Ranch, Buffalo, Wyo. Albert Goodrich Jr. has found Paradise, so he says. It is Paradise Ranch, Wyoming, and he is so keen about it he threatens to stay on indefinitely and become an honest-to-goodness cowpuncher.

Paradise is one of Senator Frank O. Horton's dude ranches and it is away up in the Big Horn mountains, a bit of the old West, according to Mr. Goodrich.

Joe Cassard of Chicago agrees with him and passes most of his time there. With no electric lights, just candles and kerosene lamps, with no private baths—just a big general bath house; with all the necessities but no enfeebling luxuries, one gets a taste of early frontier life and primitive experience at Paradise that gives color and atmosphere not existing at the modern dude ranch.

Mr. Goodrich drove a cavvy of horses up to Paradise today— a real responsibility even for a regular cowboy. I doubt if any society girl in Chicago who ever dinner-danced with Al Goodrich at home would have recognized him in his western togs as he started off this morning.

The whole camp, including the Chicago contingent—the Frederick T. Hoyts, the Clifford Chickerings and the Robert Grafs— were seated on the rails of the corral fence, to cheer him on his way. Seated on his bronc bearing the HF Bar brand, with his slicker—without which no true cowboy sets forth—and his blanket rolled neatly behind his saddle, he rode forth with his "outfit"...

A trip over the 55,000-acre tract is an interesting experience. There are 2,000 head of cattle and one of the best dairies in the land. There are 5,000 head of sheep and 2,000 horses besides a big poultry farm. (Note: These figures are highly exaggerated). It is no small undertaking to run a dude ranch, but it is gratifying to see the pale girls and boys from the cities blossom out into rosy-cheeked, sparkling-eyed, healthy human beings after a few weeks of the right kind of recreation—riding and swimming, eating and sleeping in the fresh, invigorating mountain air.

Families Get Acquainted

Ranch life affords a good time to families—they get acquainted with each other somehow when they are all together in a tiny cottage.

At home father has his business and his clubs; mother has her social life, her domestic cares and her charities. Sons and daughters have their studies and their individual interests. Here the family is united—they have the same interests. The very remoteness of the ranches is a health asset. There are no distractions and the simplest pleasures are enjoyed with zest. The family applauds as father,

fishing from the cabin porch, pulls in a mountain trout from the brook that rushes past the door.

There is good bathing in the stream but the water is very cold, yet many of the young folk take a daily plunge in the pool fed from the mountain spring. No one thinks of taking a drink at Horton's—there simply is no liquor on the place. (Note: Remember that prohibition was in effect and Skipper was a state senator and had a reputation to uphold.)

H F Bar and Paradise were also popular spots to honeymoon and were often mentioned in eastern wedding announcements. One, which concerned the Gorrell family, was in the *Chicago Tribune* on August 2, 1928.

And speaking of romance, the quiet marriage of Miss Anna Scovel Gorrell, daughter of Mr. and Mrs. Warren Gorrell...to Bradford Hinckley Burnham, son of Mrs. William Newton Hartshorn of Cambridge, Mass., and the late Frederick Lyndon Burnham, which took place on Tuesday, July 24, was replete with that quality. Miss Gorrell was studying art abroad, and met her husband when she was on a winter holiday in Egypt last Christmastime. Mr. Burnham is a graduate of Harvard in the class of 1924, and the Union Theological seminary, from which he received his degree in 1927. During the last year he has been a student at Jesus College at Cambridge, England. The wedding was attended only by a small group of relatives and intimate friends, and Mr. and Mrs. Burnham have departed for two months at the HF Bar Ranch at Buffalo, Wyo. Mr. Burnham is to have an Episcopal church in New England, where they will go to live this fall.

While HF Bar was a social focal point for a very large Eastern clientele, it also figured prominently in the local social scene. Skipper also used the ranch to entertain local civic organizations. A good example of the Horton hospitality was noted in the *Sheridan Journal* on June 26, 1929. The headline on the front page read:

HF BAR RANCH IS HOST
TO SHERIDAN AND BUFFALO ROTARIANS FRIDAY

Splendid Courtesies Extended by Senator and Mrs. Frank O. Horton—Ask Rotarians to Make This An Annual Occasion—Visitors Given Splendid Idea of This Splendid Dude Ranch, Which Ranks With the Largest and Best in Wyoming

Mr. Horton gave a splendid talk to the visitors following the dinner hour, stating that the HF Bar Ranch began its operation in July 1911, with 20 guests the first year and which has since been increasing each year with the exception of the war period. He also gave his impressions of the Republican National Convention which he attended. In concluding, he made a motion proclaiming that hereafter this should be an annual custom and the Rotary clubs would visit that ranch each year on the second Friday in June.

The overall program was a great success. The only problem was the weather. Rain fell during most of the program and the roads became very muddy. Everyone had to put chains on their cars in order to make the trip home by way of Buffalo which was a long trip in those days and under those circumstances.

Building Program

During the Rotarian visit to HF Bar, Skipper also discussed the building program in progress at that time. The newspaper article told about the pleasure the visitors had:

...of following the winding trails thru the cottage grounds across the creek and back through another avenue of cottages, each one of which is given a name, the "Tower," the "West Tower," "Meadowlark," and other such designations rather than by numbers

WIFE DESIGNS COTTAGES

Senator Horton credits Mrs. Horton with being the architect and designer of the various cottages, and remarked that if they "were comfortable for guests it was not his fault." They are beautiful and cozy, with many having porches extending out over the Rock Creek, with trees and shrubbery surrounding...

MANY NEW COTTAGES

A number of new cottages are being erected this year and several workmen were busy getting ready for the big rush to come at the end of this month which Senator Horton stated would be the largest in the history of the ranch...

There is no definitive record of the evolution of cabin construction at HF Bar. There is lore about how some guests, after they fell in love with the ranch, would pay to have a personal cabin built for their use and at their cost. Often, it has been purported, the designs for some cabins were drawn out on the back of a cocktail napkin. It has also been said that in later years the "Washington, D. C. crowd" had some influence on cabin design and alteration. However, there is no documentation to substantiate cabin construction stories; the real facts are lost in time as are the reasons why the cabins are named as they are.

Private ownership of cabins on the ranch could become a complicated business. Witness the cabin named "Cubist's Flare" that was built by Warren Gorrell's daughter Nan and her husband Brad. Warren wrote Skipper and told him that Nan and Brad were staying in the east that summer of 1929 and that their cabin would be available. Warren asked Skipper what rent the cottage would bring in for two months and how the proceeds should be divided. Skipper wrote the following to Warren on April 19, 1929:

I have just been up to take a look at Cubist's Flare. (Note: Even today there is speculation about the name of the cabin, which disappeared from the scene many years ago. Some people believe the cabin was actually called Cupid's Flare since it was originally built as kind of a newlywed abode. But Skipper called it Cubist's Flare and I believe he, of all people, should know.) *It seems to me that the cottage as it isn't anything—one little bedroom and looks like a barn. Why not put in $500 and make a real cottage out of it. This could be done by adding another bedroom and by stuccoing it on the outside similar to our other cottages.*

We already have it lathed ready for plaster on the outside. This was done last fall. With the two bedrooms you could put four people in, and certainly we would have no difficulty in finding three people to occupy it for both July and August. The cottage would bring $255 a week for three people and $320 a week for four people. I figure that the board is of course on HF Bar and represents about one half the income. We should get about one fourth of the other half in order to take care of the linen, laundry, housekeep, etc.. In other words, HF Bar would take five eights of the gross and Nancy and

Brad three eights. I suggest that you get the information from Nan by wire and wire me because daily we are turning people away for August, and as stated in a former letter, are almost entirely filled for July also...

How complicated was that? Such exchanges between Skipper and Warren Gorrell were common in that Skipper was definitely a detail man on even some of the most seemingly mundane matters. He was thorough to a fault—not a bad trait for a businessman.

There were several major improvements in the 1920s. The present day clubhouse was constructed in 1924 and the next year brought electricity to HF Bar. This feature, added to the installation of plumbing and bathrooms in 1927, brought HF Bar out of the era of kerosene lamps and hand pumps. It was now modern and up to date.

Another big improvement was the relocation of the horse corrals and the construction of a saddle barn. Until sometime in the early 1920s the corral and saddle barn had been just across the creek from the main ranch house but by 1925, at least, a new set of corrals and a two story saddle barn were built across the creek on the hill south of the main ranch house. (Note: I had originally thought the corrals and saddle barn were not moved to their present location until about 1928, but John Gordon, who first went to HF Bar in 1925, distinctly remembers the corrals and saddle barn were in their present location the first time he visited the HF Bar).

Above is the original corral. Below shows the present location of the corral and saddle barn viewed from the location of the original corral. *(Courtesy of the author)*

Activities

The annual HF Bar rodeo continued to be a major summer activity in the twenties, especially in 1926 and 1927. The following advertisement appeared in the *Sheridan Press* in 1926:

TODAY SEE THE HF BAR RODEO
Starts Promptly at 1:00
So You'll Get Home In Time To Milk
At Horton's New Ranch Arena
Same Stock Used In Sheridan-Wyo-Rodeo Will Be Used Here

There was a follow- up article on the next day, which described the new arena that was located in a natural amphitheater. (Note: This is the same arena in use today). The article further described how the HF Bar rodeo was one of the outstanding day shows in the Big Horn region and that Bill Horton had complete charge of the arena. The rodeo drew quality contestants; for example, Jake McClure, world champion calf roper and Pete Knight, world champion bronc rider competed at HF Bar.

The rodeo drew even more attention the next year when Prairie Lilly Allen came to the ranch. *The Sheridan Post Enterprise* reported the event:

Noted Cowgirl Will Ride At Horton Rodeo

The article reported that Prairie Lilly Allen, who was one of the world's greatest riders, was in the region for a short time on her way to a Chicago rodeo and was to put on a bucking exhibition at the HF Bar Ranch, which she did, to the amazement of the dudes.

Actually, it was her second visit to the region, for she and

Alice Roosevelt, the daughter of Theodore Roosevelt, were at Eaton's ranch in 1917. Prairie Lilly Allen won the championship at some of the biggest rodeos and at that time had won more bucking contests than any other woman. On the same visit she also rode at the Sheridan County Fair.

Aside from activities that were geared to be entertainment especially for dudes, there were some spontaneous activities that took place behind the scenes that sometimes involved the hijinks of the employees.

Marian Devine was a graduate of St. Luke's Hospital in New York City and in 1927 she came to Wyoming. She left a charming account of one night at HF Bar in an unpublished manuscript that she prepared for her friends.

"HEY NURSE"

I was spending the summer on a dude ranch in Wyoming and earning my board and keep, as a nurse. I gave first aid wherever necessary and otherwise had the most wonderful time of my life.

The staff consisted of a number of good looking, unattached cowboys, and since I had only recently graduated from nurse's training, they enjoyed teasing me and testing out my first aid knowledge, on every possible occasion.

One evening, as I was about ready to go to bed, someone knocked at the door. There was Johnny with his gorgeous green eyes, as concerned as could be. "Marian," he said, "Shakespeare has been hurt and we are bringing him down to your cabin." (Shakespeare was a real old timer, and got his nickname because he was such a talker.)

I hurriedly cleared off my bed and got out my hypo-syringe and first aid equipment. That ranch was thirty miles from town and the roads in that day were not as good as now, so I was prepared for any emergency. And soon they came, bearing Shakespeare very tenderly—Johnny, Tud, Jack, Bob, and Harry. (Note: Johnny Scott,

Tud Smith, Jack Dalhart, Bob Cutler and Harry Huson.) *They put him on the cot and then stood in the doorway, hovering anxiously.*

Shakespeare was seemingly unconscious. Someone had wrapped a towel around his head and there was a good deal of blood all over it—or was it blood?

I felt his pulse. If it were a serious head injury, the pulse would probably be irregular. But it was steady and strong.

I unwrapped the towel and examined his head for the wound, but found no wound of any size, only a slight scratch over one temple. I was a little puzzled—but who was I to question? That's what I was here for, wasn't it? I hesitated to go much further with my examination, before such an audience. "Do you want me to go for some water?" asked Johnny. "Do you need some help?" asked Tud. Pondering, I turned, and caught the gleam of several rows of white teeth in suntanned faces beneath the large hats. Without a word to any of them, I backed up and sat down heavily, in the middle of Shakespeare, who came back to consciousness in a hurry. The boys roared with laughter and pounded each other in glee. The game was up.

Finally they told me that a guest, who was a doctor, had put them up to the trick, when one of them had thrown a chair that hit Shakespeare's head. They thought they'd find out if that nurse really did know anything. I don't know what they decided, but from then on, regardless of where we met, I was hailed with, "Hey, Nurse!"

(Note: That summer Marian met her future husband, Fred Buckingham at HF Bar and they lived a long life together. They worked on various ranches, and at one time had their own place. Eventually, many years later, they operated the Lariat Motel in Sheridan until 1969 when they retired and moved to Cody, Wyoming. Tragically, they both died in an automobile accident near El Paso, Texas, in January 1976.)

Sometimes activities at the ranch could take a turn for the worse. In 1925 a ranch employee, William Gamble, had an awful experience in the mountains. *The Sheridan Post Enterprise* headline read:

Horton Guide Brought to Hospital
After Terrible Trip from Solitude.
William Gamble Is Paralyzed
by 175 Foot Fall Friday Afternoon
Rescuers Get Him To Hospital Monday Night
(By Vera Kackley)

Unnerved by seventy-eight hours of incessant pain and exhausted by a tortuous trip down the mountain side from Lake Solitude, William Gamble, 28 years of age, assistant guide at the Horton HF Bar Ranch near Buffalo lies at the Sheridan County Memorial Hospital, shaken by the horrors of an experience few men are called upon to face.

The three column newspaper article described the rescue effort in great detail and how a series of people were able to eventually get to him and get him down off the mountain and to the hospital. Many people helped with the long, involved rescue operation, and two of the major players were Skipper and a man named Lanfall. One of the men involved, a man named Crosby, stated to the newspaper that:

"...Of course, the whole thing was hard on everyone but none of the rest of us could have done what those two men did," he said. "Lanfall walked every step of the twenty-two miles, and Horton walked almost the entire distance. The only time he rode was when he was on the back of Gamble's saddle.

"If it had not been for their heroism, sure-footedness and downright grit Gamble would have been killed on the rocks, or he

would still be lying out there on that cliff. Both of them are real men and they saved a life."

Fortunately, William Gamble's paralysis was temporary and he fully recovered from his harrowing experience.

People

Many interesting people, both employees and guests, passed through HF Bar in the 1920s. Sometimes the employees and guests formed close relationships. One such relationship was between Ben Cook, a wrangler, and his wife, and the family of President James Garfield, who was assassinated in 1881. Those family members included Garfield's widow and his son, Abram, and his wife.

The Garfields spent many summers at the ranch. Their main activity was to head to the mountains where they stayed at Trail Lodge and used it as their base camp while they explored the area. Ben Cook was their guide and wrangler and they became good friends. The Garfields and Cooks exchanged Christmas cards every year and for several years the Garfields sent small sums of money for presents.

Ben Cook's father, Herbert Cook, had also worked at the HF Bar, and died there in 1940 while fighting a fire. The incident was described in Herbert Cook's obituary published in the *Buffalo Bulletin* on August 15, 1940:

Death came to Herbert J. Cook, 57, at the scene of the Rock Creek fire about 4 p.m. Tuesday. Mr. Cook, who was superintendent of the Wyoming Land Company and manager of the Cross H Ranch had taken a truckload of men to the HF Bar Ranch and then rode with them horseback to the scene of the fire.

The fire leaders had not yet arrived so he plunged into the combat. The heart attack which took his life came almost at once.

Mr. Cook was born in Elk Mountain, Colorado, April 14, 1883 and came to this part of the country with his parents that same year. For fifteen years he was foreman at the HF Bar Ranch and has for the past several years been associated with the Wyoming Land Company.

He was married October 29, 1906, to Bird Wolfe and is

survived by his widow, two sons, M. H. Cook of Hansard, British Columbia and Ben C. Cook of Buffalo and a daughter Annabelle of Buffalo...

A corral crew circa 1928.
Left to right: Harry Huson, "Peelingen" Nels Larson,
Tud Smith and Perry Bryant.

A descendent of Ben Cook is his granddaughter, Cynthia Twing, the director of the Johnson County Library in Buffalo, Wyoming.   Cynthia has a scrapbook which contains cherished mementos from the days her grandparents worked at HF Bar.

One of the mementos is a Christmas card the Cooks received from E. W. "Bill" Gollings in 1924. Bill Gollings was employed at HF Bar in the 1920s and left an artistic legacy. He was a noted Western artist in his time and became even more notable and more appreciated after his death in 1931. While at HF Bar, Bill Gollings created many western images for exclusive use by HF Bar in brochures and catalogs. Some of his original works still adorn the walls of Farthest West, the residence of Margi Schroth, the current owner.

The Platt family relationship with the Hortons and HF Bar took a curious turn in 1926. Henry Platt, whose wife first mentioned Skipper in 1905 when they were all at the Leiter Estate, had remained as an attorney for the Leiter Estate. (Note: Many years later the Leiter Estate was dissolved. Sherwood K. "Que" Platt, Henry Platt's son, was the principle attorney involved in the dissolution of the estate holdings in Wyoming and Montana. Sherwood was reputed to be the top real estate attorney in Chicago at the time.)

Henry, Skipper and his brother, James Lisle, would all come together again in an amusing incident which shed some light on the nature of the Horton brothers.   The following article from the *Sheridan Press* explains it all:

J. L. Horton, Wyoming's cow-punching rancher and an eastern automobile company's go-getting salesman of the wide open crossroads, cashed in on the double talent yesterday in Judge Denis Sullivan's court when he talked up right smart to Attorney Henry Russell Platt, counsel for Joseph Leiter.

Called to the stand by attorney Frank Scott, representing Lady Marguerite Hyde, Countess of Suffolk and Berks, in her charges that her brother, Joe, has mismanaged the estate of their father,

Levi Z. Leiter, Mr. Horton testified to Joe's mercurial business ability.

Then, on cross- examination by Mr. Platt, he was asked to loiter on the western plains long enough to admit, reluctantly, that sometimes, mayhap, it was the sugar beet, the rainfall, or the hay that had a temperamental up and down curve, and not Mr. Leiter's farming judgment.

Funny for Every One but Them

The impact, and it was a vigorous one, between the two men was amusing to everyone save those two men. Mr. Platt, the lawyer, was quiet, easy, and exasperating, very. Mr. Horton, the rancher, was brisk, resilient and provoking, quite.

For instance, Mr. Platt was trying to minimize Mr. Horton's statement that he "knew every acre of the Leiter ranches" and rode over them frequently in his journey from his ranch to Clearmont.

"What time did you get to the Leiter ranches on these rides?" the attorney asks.

"That depends on when I left," the rancher clicks out.

A moment later, attorney Platt queries:

"How many acres of grain did you grow in 1908?"

"Oh," replies J. L. Horton, "about the same as in 1907."

"And how many did you grow in 1907?"

"I don't recall."

There were other outbursts of repartee between J. L. Horton and Mr. Platt and then the subject turned to the testimony of Skipper.

...Earlier in the day attorney Cranston Spray of counsel for the Countess read into the record a long deposition from J. L. Horton's brother, Frank, operator of the fashionable HF Bar dude

ranch. Legally, the deposition dovetailed with the other Mr. Horton's testimony.

An Aside on Dude Ranching

Extra legally, it gave easterners something to think about, since it reports Mr. Horton as saying:

"We make more money off the dudes than we do off the other livestock."

"A dude," Mr. Platt took no small pleasure in explaining to Judge Sullivan, is "anyone whom Mr. Horton puts on an old horse and makes believe he is a red blooded American."

Some employees would rise to national prominence. One such person was a young man from Minnesota who worked at HF Bar in 1925. Many years later, in 1994, he wrote the following letter to the current HF Bar owner, Margi Schroth:

My cousin, Patricia Coen, of Mount Pleasant, Michigan, has written me describing her visit to the Ranch this last summer. She was most enthusiastic in her description and sent me a brochure.

I write because her letter brought back for me many happy memories of being at the Ranch in 1925. (What a long time ago!) Frank Horton was then running it. I had the ranch store with morning and early afternoon hours and then I was free to join the dudes. Always present in those days were members of the Garfield family from Ohio. It was a happy interlude, and meant a lot to me at the time. In fact, it changed my life, but that is a long story I need not impose on you.

I hope the ranch is doing well...

Margi promptly wrote back and asked him to please, impose on her. He replied:

...You intimated that I should comment on a few things that I recall from the summer of 1925. There was a New York actress whose name was Fay. I am embarrassed that I cannot recall her last name. She was playing in the big time, however, and, of course, as a youngster just out of high school, I was most impressed. (Note: This would have been Fay Wray who starred in the movie *King Kong)*

I mentioned the Garfields and the kindness of the president's widow in strenuously encouraging me to go to Harvard when a tuition scholarship came through. Without her presence, I probably would not have gone, and in that respect my life was utterly changed by my presence at the HF Bar.

One of the persons at the Bar was a delightful middle-aged cowhand who had no knowledge whatsoever of his ancestry. Rumor at the time was that he was the lost Charlie Ross, a white baby that had been found or kidnapped by the Indians. In any event, he was brought up in a tribal community, spoke their language fluently, and lent an air of mystery. I liked him.

I was proud, of course, when, as summer moved on, Mr. Horton had enough confidence in me (or took an awful chance) to have me lead a party of dudes into the mountains near Cloud Peak. Wasn't there a lovely waterfall not too far away that I recall? Perhaps it was up beyond the saddle....

The man who fondly remembered his early days at HF Bar was Harry A. Blackmun. He graduated from Harvard with a degree in mathematics and then completed his law degree as well. Upon graduation, he clerked for a federal appeals court judge in Minneapolis and was then appointed to the United States Court of Appeals for the Eighth Circuit. He was appointed to the Supreme Court of the United

States by President Richard Nixon and sworn in on June 9, 1970. He served until August 3, 1994 when he retired. Justice Blackmun died on March 4, 1999.

End of a Decade

If there were halcyon days in this era, they were probably the 1920s. The Hortons and Gorrells, together, worked hard to build one of the premier combined resort and working ranch operations in the area. In addition, Skipper established himself as an important civic figure and successful politician whose opinions carried weight in local and state government.

In the late 1920s the future seemed bright. The next decade would have some bright spots; but there were to be some very dark spots as well. Many challenges lay ahead.

Part III

Truly the Horton Place
1930-1948

Chapter 6

The Thirties

Financial Difficulties & Family Strife

The routine exchanges of letters between Skipper and Warren Gorrell early in 1930 gave no hint of the problems to come. The first letter on January 13th was simply to provide Warren the status of the family accounts at the ranch so they could be paid.

There were several letters between Frank, who by the end of January was in Carmel, California, at the property they proposed making into HF Bar west, and Warren, in Chicago. At this time, the California deal was still on the front burner. There were still occasional disagreements between the two men.

Skipper must have indicated in a letter that he thought they should buy "the McDonald" place and a property owned by a Mr. Walter. Whatever Skipper said, it did not sit well with Warren Gorrell, who replied:

...I do not get it in regard to McDonald's place. You have told me before it was not essential. Our plan has been to stop expansion, and yet the Walter situation comes up unexpectedly as something essential to do, and now McDonald. Walter's deal necessitates more livestock. I think it about time to ask where the line should be finally drawn, and then adhered to....

In one letter, Skipper also discussed whether to buy more sheep and cattle. In a telegram Warren advised that he had completed a loan for over thirty-four thousand dollars for operations but to go easy on purchases.

In April, Skipper wrote a letter to Warren advising him that things looked promising at the ranch and the prospects for the year were good:

...We are absolutely booked full for August, and July is coming along very nicely. Believe we're going to have just as good a year as we had in 1929.

The ranch is lovely—green grass and flowers starting every place. I have never seen it look more lovely at this time of year. Herb has done corking good work in getting in the crops. Practically all the fields are seeded down and everything will be absolutely done in the way of spring planting by the middle of next week if the weather holds good. I am mighty glad of this because from all indications it looks like a darn dry year. You have probably noted the upturn in wheat on account of drought. I think that the advance is justified. If we happen to get a dry year the wheat problem may be solved for a few years at least. All the cattle are looking fine and we already have better than two hundred spring calves.

Gertrude and Bobs are due home some time next week...
(Note: From California)

The first indication in correspondence that something was wrong in Warren's financial world was in November when Skipper wrote Warren and asked him to forward all the HF Bar papers, and Skipper's personal papers, to the ranch. Five days later Skipper asked Warren to send all the HF Stock Certificate books to the ranch as well.

I imagine there were many telephone conversations about the looming financial problem with Gorrell and Co., but the first piece of correspondence is a hurried note written in pencil by Warren on a piece of scratch paper and dated November 21, 1930:

Dear Frank:

The bad and dangerous position for the two ranches (Note: HF Bar and the UM) *is that Sohm* (Note: Sohm worked for Warren Gorrell and was secretary of Mowry Basin.) *had 428 4/7 shares Ohio of HF Bar and 1676 6/7 shares Ohio of Mowry tied up in Gorrell Co's. affairs and I don't know the outcome. It looks bad at the moment & I'll do the best I can. It breaks my heart to tell you this.*

We do not know the exact circumstances of the situation. However, Henry Stewart, Warren's grandson, noted in his review of the manuscript for this book that he understood that Mr. Sohm committed suicide and:

"...that certain of the circumstances that added to the catastrophe caused by the Crash itself resulted from improper actions that Sohm had taken without the awareness of, and contrary to, the interests of Warren Gorrell. Despite of or in consideration of such lack of awareness, Warren Gorrell handled his difficulties by accepting considerable responsibility for such circumstances...

At this alarming news, Skipper wrote Warren a long, hand written four page letter. It expressed his feelings about his business associate and brother-in-law:

> *...No matter what happens old fellow I want you to know that my thoughts for you are as always. I know you have been absolutely square and that your plight is caused by conditions beyond your control. I am for you and everything I have or ever have is yours and you know it—that's that.*

The letter also put forth a detailed action plan and said that if it were adopted he, Skipper, would:

> *...do my darndest to find someone or someones to take over the balance of the property on some such basis or better and of course I'll do that anyway...*

It didn't take Skipper long to find someone to bail them out. He found Edward "Eddie" Moore. Eddie Moore was a New York millionaire who had come west and bought a lot of property. He purchased the 2,800 acre Meade Creek Ranch from Malcolm Moncrieffe and Formed Meade Creek Ranch, Inc. (Note: In most correspondence Mead is spelled with an "e." However, at other times it is spelled without an "e." Today it is spelled Meade.) He also eventually owned, among other things, the Willis Spear Ranch in Big Horn, Wyoming, and the local newspaper the *Sheridan Press*.

How Skipper became acquainted with Eddie Moore is unclear, but he definitely found a willing investor. In December, Skipper wrote the following, which was a dissolution proposal for the Mowry Basin Stock Development Co:

...Because of desperate need, I propose to accept the $100,000 ......offer of Meade Creek Inc. for all the real and personal property of this corporation excepting 4705 shares of Ohio Oil Stock—free of all encumbrances.

This corporation owes the following which must be paid at once and has not the funds to pay same unless the proposal of Meade Creek Inc. is accepted.

Gorrell and Co.	$53,000.00
HF Bar Ranch Inc.	40,000.00
Warburton Mortgage	32,800.00
(Note: UM Ranch)	
State Mortgage	18,901.85
State and Fed Tax	663.93
	$145,365.78

The Meade Creek Inc. $100,000 plus the sale of 2699 shares of Ohio Oil Company stocks will provide sufficient funds to pay all the above and leave 2,006 shares of Ohio Oil stock for the benefit of the stockholders of this corporation. I propose to give two shares of Ohio Oil stock in exchange for each of the 1,003 outstanding shares of this corporation...

As it turned out, Eddie Moore also bought the Ohio Oil stock to provide the extra cash to be added to the $100,000 he had already put up. He wrote to Skipper, who was in California, on December 19 1930:

...I wired you at Sheridan this morning that I would be glad to take over the Ohio Oil stock in the mortgage transaction at the market price day of closing, namely $51,700.

Eddie Moore also took the time to lecture Skipper on his handwriting:

...I think I will have to do for you as I have done for my Mother, buy you a typewriter so that I can read your writing. I have had a hell of a time trying to make out what you are trying to say but I think I have been able to make it out....

Skipper's bail out plan was adopted. On December 12, 1930, the Gorrell family returned all their HF Bar stock to be reassigned to the new stockholder, Eddie Moore.

On January 10, 1931, the HF Bar Board of Directors met. The meeting place is unknown but the purpose of the meeting was to elect officers and consider salary questions for the various officers. Warren Gorrell was still involved, at least in name. The officers elected were:

Frank Horton	President
Warren Gorrell	Vice President
Frank Horton	Treasurer
J. D. Hart	Secretary
Frank Horton	Manager

The discussion about the salary question read as follows in the minutes:

...The question of the salaries of the various officers was next discussed. It was pointed out that the newly electedpresident of the corporation was really the only official who ever had and was giving his entire time and energy to the affairs of the corporation and that the success of the corporation was due entirely to him. Therefore, he, not as president, but as manager, should be allowed the combined salaries of the heretofore president, vice-president and manager; namely, $7,600 per annum. This opinion prevailed...

The next action occurred on January 19th when Skipper wrote a letter to Jimmie Hart, the corporation secretary and said:

...Eddie Moore comes in and Gorrell steps out of HF Bar...

Enclosed were the stock certificates from the Gorrells with instructions to reissue one stock certificate for 345 shares to Eddie Moore.

Even though Warren was no longer a stockholder he remained on the books as vice president and he and Skipper corresponded. (Note: It would not be until June 1, 1931, that the board held a special meeting to officially recognize that Warren and Demia Gorrell were no longer stockholders and no longer connected with HF Bar Ranch. At that meeting Edward S. Moore and James D. Hart were elected to the board.)

In fact, in February, 1931, Warren Gorrell wrote a note to Skipper informing him that he wanted to set up a syndicate in which he was looking for subscribers to acquire assets from Gorrell & Company. He asked for Skipper's opinion and Skipper gave a long one, but unfortunately the reply is not legible. At any rate, the proposal was never adopted. In the same letter Warren Gorrell wrote:

...It is 5 months today since I entered the portals of hell. Have hung on this long & I'm hoping we can continue to. Sorry to have to use you so much, but it is great to have a friend who is willing...

Warren must have been a tortured man.

In the meantime, Skipper received letters from concerned Mowry Basin investors. In his reply to one of the letters, in April, Skipper lamented his frustration:

...I have lost everything I put into Mowry to say nothing of

ten years of hard work for which I have never received one cent. Conditions have been and are impossible for the farmer—it was impossible to continue longer.

Last year was a bad one for HF Bar and the coming year doesn't look good. We are reducing our rates but even that doesn't seem to interest many because everybody is naturally hard up...

In the midst of all his difficulties, Warren Gorrell was concerned about his son, Ginger. In April, he wrote to Skipper and asked for his help:

...Son has been waked up by my misfortunes and is a different lad. He has tried hard to get a job but you know the conditions. He came to me recently, expressed his love for the Ranch & said he knew more about it as a business than anything else. I wondered if you would take him on & let him develop as an understudy. He is a caged animal working in the city...Son is miserable because he can't help me himself. If he could be happy out there with you it would take a great load off an already tortured mind...

Skipper wrote back that he would like to do all that he could but that:

...Son was not cut out for this kind of work and might as well train to be a banker...

Warren replied:

...I have your letter regarding Son, and perhaps you are right. However, he was so much in earnest & proposing to go out to see you, that I took the liberty of writing you. By reading

between the lines I gather that I did not put it up to you in the right way. If so, I am sorry...

The first six months of 1931 must have been very difficult for the Horton and Gorrell families. They had been close for many years, and now this huge financial problem was driving a wedge between them. Of course, the sisters, Gertrude and Demia would be forced to side with their husbands. A glimpse of the stress that developed between the two families is illustrated in a letter which Skipper wrote to Warren on June 29, 1931:

Dear Warren:

Have been back in the mountains several days. There is nothing personal. The only thing is De's (Note: Demia Gorrell) attitude which makes it impossible for us all to be happy here together. Just remember De's rotten remarks to me in Chicago which have never been retracted. Also know that G (Note: Gertrude) has written De seven letters and no answers. I don't want you this summer because I am still too sore—perhaps time will heal the wound...

That is the last known correspondence between Skipper and Warren Gorrell but not the last contact between the families.

Henry Stewart imparted the following information about the situation:

...Warren Gorrell, having lost his fortune in and after the Stock Market Crash of 1929, was able to build a smaller fortune later in the 1930s; that he greatly wished to at least buy back into the

ranch that he loved very much and had been significantly involved in creating; that he went to the ranch to explore the possibility with Frank Horton; and that Frank Horton chased him off at gunpoint, stating, "This place is mine now; you're not part of it any longer...

Henry Stewart also revealed that Warren died in Hinsdale, Illinois in December 1943. His wife, Demia, died in Troy, New York, in January 1956. They were survived by their children, Anna Scovel Gorrell Burnham, of Troy, New York, and Duxbury, Massachusetts, who died in 1989; Warren Gorrell, Jr., of Buffalo, Wyoming, who died in 1963; Demia Butler Gorrell Lewis, of Palatka, Florida, who died in 1976; and Sarah Scovel Gorrell Stewart, Henry Stewart's mother, who died in 2003.

Warren would continue to loom in one aspect or another for a few more years. At a special directors meeting of the HF Bar Ranch, Inc. in September 1932, the board took up the matter that Warren had kept some interest on certain stocks and that he should be instructed to pay it over to the company. There was also the matter of some outstanding accounts he still had remaining at the ranch. The minutes also mentioned Warren Gorrell's status:

...Then followed a discussion of a rumored question as to whether or not Mr. Gorrell, or any member of his family, may now have in HF Bar Ranch Inc., or in any property of that ranch, an interest of any kind or character. After a full discussion of the situation, it appearing that the Gorrell interest in the property of the corporation has never been other than as represented by the corporate stock formerly held by him and members of his family, either in an individual capacity or as trustee; and it appearing that all of said stock was long heretofore transferred to Edward S. Moore, of Nassau County, state of New York, and that the transfer of the stock to Mr. Moore carried with it all of the Gorrell interests...it was

the unanimous decision of the board that the corporation is in no way indebted to the said Gorrell...and neither Warren Gorrell, nor any member of his family...has any right, equity or interest in the property or any of the property of the corporation since the transfer of the said stock to the said Edward S. Moore...

That was final!

In the same meeting it was announced that Edward S. Moore had resigned as director and disposed of his stock to Mr. John Hutton of Sheridan and that John Hutton was now a director of the corporation. This statement is contrary to the actual fact that the stock records show that Eddie Moore's stock (405 1/2 shares) was transferred direct to Skipper. Perhaps the plan changed and John Hutton really only loaned money to Skipper to purchase the stock.

Why Eddie Moore resigned is not known. Perhaps it was agreed in the beginning that he would only be on the board long enough to help Skipper with his rescue operation. When Eddie Moore resigned and sold his stock to Skipper, HF Bar remained intact, but the UM Ranch was placed under the corporate umbrella of Meade Creek Ranch, Inc. and so belonged to Eddie Moore since, after all, he did pay off the mortgage.

In 1933, the bankruptcy hearing for Gorrell and Co. was held and Skipper was sent copies of the transcript of Warren's testimony to verify certain matters. Skipper provided the information required and was finally out of the matter.

By March of 1934, Skipper had managed to acquire 759 shares of HF Bar stock. He made his three sons major shareholders by issuing each of them 253 shares.

The other big financial challenge to be dealt with in the 1930s was the HF Bar six percent bond issue which was to fall due May 1, 1937. This was the issue organized by Warren ten years before which added $100,000 to the original $100,000 issue. Skipper had to find some way to retire the obligation, but it wasn't that easy.

Basically, Skipper needed cash to retire the bond issue and he had to find someplace to get it or get the bond issue extended. But, there was a problem. Apparently, Warren Gorrell still owned one bond and was making noises to some of the bond holders that Skipper did not know what he was doing: that an extension was not necessary and that the issue would be paid in full when due. To which Skipper retorted:

...Unfortunately, Mr. Gorrell and I do not get on...As a matter of fact, Mr. Gorrell has no knowledge what-so-ever of the financial situation of HF Bar, so that any information he may be giving, is not information based on fact. My only fear is that misinformation may be followed to such an extent as to create a most unfortunate situation for all of us next May...

I am doing my utmost to refinance so that the entire issue can be paid when due, for I do not believe that any other course would satisfy Gorrell. If I fail in this refinancing, frankly, I do not know just which way to turn.

Skipper wrote in another letter on the same subject:

...Barnum said that a sucker was born every minute, there are many more. You would think that some of our bond holders who must have had a touch of Gorrell methods before now, would not be coming back for more. All bond holders should realize that the only way that the bond issue can be paid in full is for me, the largest bond holder, to have my bonds cancelled and for me to accept as security, a second mortgage. This I am willing to do providing the bond holders are good sports and show their willingness to cooperate, even going so far to extend if necessary. It was Gorrell that got them into this bond issue and then for reasons, best known to himself, left them in the lurch. It was Horton who had to take over and it is Horton

who has made the venture go during these past tough years and it is Horton, not Gorrell, who is going to pull them out with their hides if they will play the game...

...The bond holders should realize that perhaps Gorrell is playing a smart game for himself which may not be void of some spite on his part. Perhaps he would get a lot of satisfaction out of seeing me in hot water, but perhaps the bond holders would pay pretty dearly for his satisfaction...

This series of letters is rather unbalanced because we do not know Warren's side of the story. To add balance, and be fair, we must rely on Henry Stewart who in defense of his grandfather wrote:

...I am keenly aware of the manner in which Warren Gorrell sought to the extreme, to satisfy accounts and to conduct himself and his business affairs honestly, honorably, beyond fair question, and far and above the requirements legally obligating or affecting a person in his circumstances, in the winding up of the tragedy of his business affairs. As a result of this conduct with honor, the Gorrell family suffered in loss of wealth far beyond any circumstances that otherwise needed to happen...

Skipper searched everywhere for money. His letters to various potential sources of funds were revealing:

...Frankly, the terrific drought which hit us last spring and which made it necessary to sacrifice all of our livestock at a time when they were in poor condition and the market saturated, makes it necessary to work out some kind of refinancing plan...

...The HF Bar Ranch is a corporation organized under the laws of Wyoming. Practically all of the stock is held in the family. We do a general ranching and livestock business. We are more diversified than most ranches in that we run not only horses, sheep,

hogs and cattle; but dudes as well; and they are usually a very profitable kind of livestock to handle. With the exception of cattle and dudes, we consume practically everything that we produce so are not adding to the surplus problem...

In the end, Skipper was able to solve the problem. He convinced many of the bond holders to take compensation in the form of HF Bar stock. He then wrote a letter to all the bond holders which said, in part:

...For a time it was thought that it would be absolutely necessary for the ranch to ask that the due date be extended from three to five years on all outstanding bonds. I am very glad to be able to tell you, however, that by subordinating all of the HF Bar bonds which I personally own or control, that the ranch has been able to refinance so that all other outstanding bonds, including your own, will be paid on or before maturity.

That was it. In one decade, Skipper managed to survive two potentially crushing financial situations both of which placed the HF Bar Ranch in jeopardy. HF Bar was intact and now, truly, the Horton place.

The Horton Family

In the late 1920s, Gertrude and Skipper acquired a taste for California living when they paid frequent visits to Carmel to visit the area where Skipper and Warren proposed to start HF Bar West. As the 1930s came along, even though the plans fell through, Gertrude must have decided that winters in California beat winters in Wyoming for she took the boys and headed to California again in the fall of 1930.

It was a propitious time to make such a move. Both Bill and Jack had graduated from high school in Sheridan the year before and Bobby was ready to start high school. There are no family records that describe the situation but we know for sure that Jack was enrolled in Pomona College at that time.

Bobby must have been enrolled in high school in California somewhere because he does not appear in the Sheridan School Census nor is he listed in the Sheridan High School yearbooks.

Bill may have attended university briefly (two sources infer that he did) but he was not really the academic type and did not continue his university education. He stayed on at HF Bar to become a mainstay of the operation.

Jack, on the other hand, was the academic type and after his first year at Pomona College transferred to Princeton University in New Jersey. Why he transferred is unknown. As far as we know, no other family members had ever attended Princeton but Jack did.

So, the pattern was established. Everyone returned to the ranch in the summer to help Skipper, but in the winter Gertrude went to California so Bobby could attend high school, Bill stayed on at HF Bar, and Jack returned to his studies at Princeton.

In 1932, while the other two siblings pursued their education, Bill was helping his dad at HF Bar. He had a serious ranch romance with a guest which resulted in his marriage on Christmas Eve to the former Mrs. Mary Warren Hewitt. Mary, who was known to all as Sis, was the daughter of Mrs. Helene Warren of New York City and they had been guests at the ranch for several years.   After their marriage, Bill and Sis returned to HF Bar and helped Skipper operate the ranch.

In the meantime, Jack was having a successful academic career at Princeton.   His yearbook entry mentions that he was a member of the Polo team for a year and a member of the Cloister Inn. The entry also gives an account of his boarding arrangements:

...During sophomore year he roomed at 103 'O1 Hall alone; Junior year at 113 Brown with C. H. Anthony and F. G. Anderson; Senior year at 113 Brown with F. W. Lee...

The entry is interesting because it also states that he was married to Miss Josephine J. (Jody) Jahn of Milwaukee, Wisconsin, on July 21, 1933.   Unfortunately, we do not know how or where they met; nor do we know where Jody was while Jack was finishing his education at Princeton. Since they were married between Jack's junior and senior year, and Jack had boarded with another student during school, Jody may have lived with her family until Jack graduated.

Tragedy then struck when Gertrude took ill and died on March 17, 1934, at fifty-four years of age.   There is no surviving documentation or correspondence about Gertrude's death save the obituary which was published in the *Sheridan Press* on March 19th. The obituary read:

FRANK HORTON'S WIFE SUCCUMBS ON WEST COAST
Long Illness Is Fatal to Prominent Buffalo Woman

Word of the death of Mrs. Gertrude Horton, wife of former State Senator Frank O. Horton, of Buffalo, was received here by friends today.

Mrs. Horton died late Saturday in a hospital in San Francisco after a serious illness of several weeks. Funeral services are to be held Thursday at Buffalo.

In addition to her husband, Mrs. Horton is survived by three sons, all of whom live on the HF Bar Ranch near Buffalo; her father, who lives in Florida, and two sisters, one living in Chicago, and the other at Princeton N. J.

Services Here

A short funeral service for Mrs. Gertrude B. Horton...will be held in Sheridan from the Presbyterian Church, Wednesday afternoon at 4 o'clock, it was announced here by John Flint of the Flint Funeral Home of Buffalo, who is in charge of the arrangements.

The main funeral service will be held from the Buffalo Episcopal Church, of which she was a member....

The pall bearers of Sheridan services will be Dr. R. E. Crane, Dr. I. P. Hayes, R. C. Rudolph, George Scales, James D. Hart, and Roy Bedford.

The Buffalo pall bearers, who will also act as honorary escort at Sheridan, are George Heilman, Bert Griggs, Burton Hill, Wilbur Holt, Fred Dillinger and Charles P. Taylor. They will meet the body at the train and will accompany it to Buffalo after the Sheridan funeral service.

Mrs. Horton, 54, was well known here and was a member of the Sheridan Women's Club.

She was born in the state of Indiana...Mr. and Mrs. Horton were married in Chicago in 1908.

Mr. Horton brought his eastern bride to his ranch in Clearmont, Wyoming, shortly after the marriage ceremony. In 1920 (Note: This date is incorrect. It was 1911.) *he established the HF Bar Ranch near Buffalo. During the past 24 years Mrs. Horton has endeared herself to the hundreds of guests who spent their vacations at the ranch.*

She died on Saturday at the St. Luke's Hospital in San Francisco after four months of illness.

Mr. Horton and her youngest son Bobby Horton were with her at the time of her death...

Gertrude's untimely death changed the equation at HF Bar Ranch. She had always been, by all accounts, a gracious presence at HF Bar in the summer and was of enormous help to Skipper. Now that she was gone it was up to Bill's wife, Sis, to assume that role.

The death might also have caused Jack Horton to change his plans. The Princeton school annual said that Jack planned to attend Harvard Business School and then become engaged in the ranching business with his father. He abandoned the Harvard post-graduate plans and he and Jody returned to the ranch after he graduated from Princeton to help his father, Bill and Sis manage the ranch.

The management equation was that Skipper was the boss. There was never any doubt about that. Bill concentrated his efforts on livestock and the corral and Jack pretty much took care of the office. The girls, Sis and Jody, acted as hostesses and worked in the office as well.

Bobby, who was still in school in California, returned in the summer to help wherever he could. At some point in this time Bobby was dispatched to work at Paradise. The experience apparently stood him in good stead. It was referred to two years later in a letter that Al Hook, the ranch secretary-treasurer, wrote to Skipper:

...I was certainly delighted to hear about Bob and to learn that he has obtained the house managership for his fraternity. This is certainly good stuff and Bob is to be congratulated upon the sincere effort expended by him to obtain this position. His experience at Paradise will also prove to be most valuable...

The family management arrangement worked for the year it was in existence, but the equation was upset again the next year, 1935, when Bill's wife was killed. The *Sheridan Press* reported on August 26th:

Mrs. Bill Horton Killed
Mount Wheels and Kicks When Girl Falls Off
Famous Dude Ranch Near Buffalo Scene of Accident

Kicked in the head by a horse that witnesses said suddenly "went wild, and became a man-killer," Mrs. William S. (Bill) Horton, about 25, was instantly killed at the famous HF Bar dude ranch near here late this morning.

Mrs. Horton, daughter of a prominent New York City resident, had made her home at the Horton ranch since her marriage to young Horton in 1932.

The accident that claimed her life occurred at 10 o'clock as Mrs. Horton was riding from her cabin to the ranch corrals.

Daringly Dismounted

Her horse, an animal that she had only recently purchased, started to bolt as she neared the corral, witnesses said. After riding the racing mount for about 200 yards, the young woman apparently sensed the danger that confronted her and daringly dismounted.

As she did so, she fell but appeared to have escaped serious injury, H. W. Meers of Evanston, Ill., a dude, and Barney McLain, ranch employee, who witnessed the accident, told Coroner John Flint.

However, Mrs. Horton had no sooner hit the ground than the horse halted its headlong plunge and wheeled about. The animal's flying hoofs struck the woman in the back of the head.

Killed Instantly

She was dead when the two witnesses ran the 100 yards separating them from the scene of the accident, they told the coroner. An examination disclosed she died of a severely fractured skull.

Coroner Flint after a preliminary investigation said he would not conduct an inquest.

The body was taken to Buffalo this afternoon where it will be held at the Flint funeral home pending completion of funeral arrangements. Mrs. Horton before her marriage to young Horton on Christmas Eve, 1932, was the former Mrs. Mary Warren Hewitt. She is survived, in addition to her husband, by her mother, Mrs. Helene Warren of New York City.

Mrs. Warren only recently left the ranch after spending several weeks visiting her daughter.

Mother and daughter had been frequent guests at the ranch prior to the latter's marriage to Horton. Young Horton is the son of former State Senator Frank O. Horton, owner of the HF Bar Ranch.

Don King, the founder of Kings Saddlery and Museum in Sheridan, Wyoming, and a world renowned leather craftsman, has indelible memories of that day. The summer that Sis was killed, Don, who was twelve years old, lived at HF Bar with his father, Arch King, who worked as a wrangler. Arch King and his wife had divorced when Don was only five years old and he hadn't really known his mother.

Bill and Sis took a liking to young Don and Sis became his surrogate mother. Don recalls that Sis was quiet, very attractive and liked by everyone. She just had to have something to mother, according to Don, which accounted for the fact that she had two fawns and two antelope as well as some goats. Don's job was to milk the goats. Sometimes Don was invited to stay in their house, Farthest West, with them and once Bill and Sis took Don to Yellowstone on a trip. They did many other special things for him.

Saddlestring

One thing Bill did for the young Don was to let him, and another boy, Jerry Morris, the son of Bud and Norma Morris who both worked at the ranch, ride all the spoiled kid dude horses. Part of the deal was that Don and Jerry were allowed to go to the sheep pasture and practice their roping on the sheep. Don remembers that they caused that bunch of sheep to be the wildest he has ever seen.

On the fated day, which was Don's birthday, Sis and Don had been riding and were planning to go to Sheridan to have lunch in

Mary Jean Hewitt "Sis" Horton, wife of Bill Horton, had an instinct for mothering animals and children. Circa early 1930s.
(Courtesy of Don King)

Don King and Sis Horton
just minutes before Sis was killed in a tragic horse accident.
Circa 1935.
(Courtesy of Don King)

celebration of his birthday. When they got back to the corral Sis sent Don home to get ready and told him to meet her at her house, Farthest West, which was at the end of the lane from the corral. That was the last time Don saw her. Don cleaned up and was walking up the road through the cabins headed for Sis's house. She must have lingered at the corral but eventually started for her house on her horse. Don heard a commotion that sounded like a horse being ridden "over and under and hell bent for election". He didn't know it was Sis on her runaway horse. He found out moments later that it was Sis and she had been killed. It was a very sad day for a twelve year old boy and one never to be forgotten.

Don King (left) at age 12 with his friend Jerry Morris at HF Bar Ranch in 1935. *(Courtesy of the Don King Western Museum)*

In just a year and a half, the death of Gertrude and Sis must have had an enormous impact on the family, but life had to go on, and it did. Jody was now the sole Horton female at HF Bar and was to remain so for the next two years. Then things changed. Both Skipper and Bill remarried in 1937.

Bill married Josephine "Dodie" Cole. Dodie was the daughter of Ralph and Eleanor Cole, a prominent family from Canton, Ohio. Dodie and her family had been guests at HF Bar since the mid-1930s and it was there that Dodie met Bill. To Dodie, Bill was an exciting, fun-loving, hard-drinking cowboy who many called Wild Bill because he really was an exceptional roper and horseman. In fact, his roping ability was so well known throughout the state of Wyoming that Ernst Saddlery in Sheridan, Wyoming, created a roping saddle and called it "The Horton" in recognition of Bill's roping skill.

Bill and Dodie fell in love and, in 1937, were married in a huge society wedding in Canton. After the wedding, they returned to the ranch, built a new house nearby and settled in to life on the ranch.

Once again, Skipper had his two sons and their wives and Bobby, when he was not in school, to help operate the ranch. That management formula was to fail. Family difficulties were to arise and Skipper was to bring home a new bride—Henriette S. "Hank" Stuart.

Skipper was about twenty-five years older than Hank who was born in Bass, Maine on September 26, 1903. According to an article in the Omaha World Herald on July 30, 1985, Hank was the daughter of a Maine marine architect who met Skipper at a press party in Chicago which he attended as a national committeeman for the Republican Party.

Hank's early days and her introduction to HF Bar Ranch are best described by Edgar M. Morsman, Jr. the author of *The Postmistress of Saddlestring, Wyoming*. Ed wrote the book to capture the many oral ranch stories about Hank and others before they were forgotten. He was helped by Peter Constable whose extended family covers four generations of ranch goers.

Ed has a long involvement with HF Bar Ranch which gave him the perspective to write his book. Ed wrote about his family connection with HF Bar Ranch:

My father brought my mother and older sister, Julie (Mrs. John Schroeder of Waterloo, Nebraska) and me to the ranch in 1944. I'm not sure how he heard of the HF Bar. He had a friend named Tinker Gordon who owned a place on Dome Lake, and possibly he heard of the ranch from Tinker. This was during the war with gas rationing, so it was important to find a place that you could get to by train...I do remember hearing of the end of the war in the Pacific in 1945 from a radio in a sheepherder's wagon on top of the Saddle. (Note: A prominent geological formation northwest of HF Bar.) After the war, my sister and I came to the ranch with Uncle Truman who was in the Navy in the Pacific during the war. My father was a little more oriented toward Europe and luxury hotels than the ranch, although he always had fun there and enjoyed the other guests. But it was really Uncle Truman that provided our ranch experiences in our childhood.

I probably stopped going to the ranch in my high school years, as I worked summers in a bank. I never did work at the ranch. After college and the Army, I worked for Morgan Guaranty in New York where I was married. Along about 1967, the year after I was married to Beth, we both returned to the ranch in June...I think we have been back to the ranch every year thereafter. Last year (Note: 2004.) our three sons, two daughters-in-law, and one grandson were with us. They are Jim and Angela, Jeff, Amy and Tommy, and Tim. The grandson, Tommy, makes the fourth generation of ranch guests. My sister has a similar relationship with the ranch. She and her husband, John, come to the ranch every year at the same time as we do...Incidentally, my middle son Jeff and his wife Amy had a son in January (2005) and they named him Truman...

Bill and Dodie Horton with their daughter Suzanne.
Circa 1940.
(Courtesy of Suzanne Timken)

Saddlestring

In "Post Mistress" Ed captured the essence of Hank and something of her early life and her persona. He relates how:

Hank grew up in Plainfield, New Jersey, the educated daughter of a marine architect from Maine, and always retained some mannerisms of the East Coast. However, her hallmark characteristics of humor and joie de vivre were apparent at an early age. As a child, she terrorized her neighborhood by setting off a huge box of fireworks. It seemed she could not wait until the Fourth of July...

...It took a woman of some courage to pursue a career in journalism far from home in the 1930s, and Hank maintained an abundant supply of courage. She worked in radio for a time and had an amazing ability to time her writing to the second. Her soap opera dramas could be read in exactly fifteen minutes.

In the 1930s, radio was very much live time as there was no ability to prerecord. Consequently, lengthy rehearsals were required to reduce errors that could not be dubbed out. Sound effects had to be created on the spot. Hank wrote a story calling for a gentle rainfall. To convey the appropriate sound, Hank and her colleagues tried everything from crinkling paper and tin foil to dropping rice in a pan. Finally, a young page delivering mail asked, "Why don't you try water from that watering can on the shelf?"

Hank and her colleagues glanced at each other surreptitiously until one man said, "Beat it kid. What do you know! And close the door behind you." When the door closed, they simultaneously rushed for the watering can, tried it, and found the perfect sound of rainfall...

Ed describes what happened after Skipper and Hank met:

...he invited Hank to Wyoming to view the Ranch, but she

Hank Horton
A young woman who journeyed west against her better judgment
and remained there the rest of her life. Date unknown.
(Courtesy of the HF Bar Ranch)

*initially demurred. The only thing she had seen of Wyoming was
from a Union Pacific Pullman car, and she hadn't found what she
saw particularly appealing. Love eventually triumphed, and she
went to Wyoming with a carefully composed message in her pocket.
She tried to send it to her editors in Chicago on the day she arrived,
but the telegraph office in Buffalo was closed and the ranch had no
phone. After several weeks, she returned to Chicago with the message*

*still unsent. It read, "Send me a telegram telling me to return
immediately." Hank and Skipper were married in 1937, and Hank
joined Skipper at the HF Bar Guest Ranch, quite an adventure for a
young woman from New Jersey.*

Though Hank and Skipper married on September 15th, they
did not return to the ranch until sometime the next spring. While
they were away, Jack and Jody had their first child.

Jack Olgivie Horton, Jr. was born on January 28, 1938 in
Sheridan. My mother, Vesta Ringley, was hired to be Jack's
nanny when he was about two months old. Jack and Jody lived in
Farthest West at that time and my mother cared for young Jack there.
My father, Roy Ringley, was also hired to work at the ranch. My
parents were hired on the recommendation of my mother's brother,
Dean Thomas, who was to become a fixture at HF Bar and will be
discussed later.

My mother remembers Jody and Dodie, discussing the
impending arrival of Skipper's new wife. They had surely met her
when she visited HF Bar before the marriage but now wondered how
this new member of the family would affect their lives at the ranch.

Soon after Skipper and Hank returned, Jack and Jody along
with young Jack were dispatched to manage Paradise. My mother and
father went with them. At the end of the summer, Jack and Jody
wanted my mother to stay on and care for young Jack, but there was
no job for my father so both of them left the employment of the HF
Bar Ranch in the fall of 1938.

Two more Horton babies arrived before the end of the decade.
Jack and Jody had daughter, Gertrude B. "Trudy" Horton, who was
born in Sheridan on February 21, 1939. On May 5th, the same year,
Bill and Dodie Horton had a daughter, Suzanne, who was born in
Canton, Ohio.

So, at the end of the decade, there were three couples living on
the HF Bar Ranch; Skipper and his new wife Hank, Jack and Jodie and

their two children Jack and Trudy, Bill and Dodie and their daughter Suzanne. Also, Bobby Horton had by now graduated from college and somehow figured into the equation, although exactly how he fit into the family picture at that time is unclear.

It is difficult to imagine how the HF Bar Ranch could support three families or how they could all co-exist together. In the next decade, the situation would prove to be unworkable. In the setting of a looming world war, internal family problems and death would cast some members asunder, and the Horton family would never be the same again.

A rare photo of Warren "Ginger" Gorrell, Jr.
In this photo Ginger (right) is visited at his cabin in the Big Horns
by Jody and Jack Horton Sr. . Circa late 1930s.
(Courtesy of Will Dixon)

Some members of the Horton family in the late 1930s.
Front row, from left, are Bill, Bobby, and Skipper Horton.
On fence, from left, are Dodie Horton, and Hank Horton.
Jack and Jody Horton are missing.
(Courtesy of the HF Bar Ranch)

Hank and Skipper at an HF Bar Rodeo
sometime in the late 1930s or early 1940s.
(Courtesy of the HF Bar Ranch)

Ranch Operations

At the beginning of the 1930s, HF Bar was still heavily involved in agricultural production. In 1930, Skipper recorded that he had 852 head of cattle on hand at the first of the year. During the year he bought 373 more and raised 575 calves. He also sold 651 head during the year, and a few died, so that he started 1931 with 1,141 head of cattle in various categories.

For about the first five years, Skipper kept his inventory about the same but could not pasture them all at HF Bar. He ran cattle at Paradise and at the Bar 13 which belonged to Eddie Moore and Mead Creek Cattle Company. The majority of the cattle, however, were summered in Montana. In 1935, Skipper recorded in his Daybook:

> *...practically all cattle were summered on the reservation or at Allan Fordyce's on Tongue River, but they did not do well...*

He also recorded that :

> *...we killed 8 head of cattle for 1935 rodeo and for help...*

Entries in the Daybook after 1935 are limited for good reason. Basically, there was nothing to record because the cow business took a nosedive. In November 1936, when Skipper was looking for financing to pay off the bond issue, he wrote to a possible loan source:

> *...the most terrible drought ever known in the history of this western country had to come along and spoil all our plans. We were forced to ship all our livestock last spring when they were in poor condition and when the market was flooded with thin, drought-stricken cattle, and we took an awful licking...*

In another letter in December of 1936, in which Skipper sought financing from the Federal Land Bank of Omaha, he described how HF Bar operated:

...The HF Bar Ranch is a Wyoming corporation with 88% of its stock owned by my three sons and myself. All four of us give our entire time to the management of the ranch. (Note: Not quite true, since Bobby was attending university in California.) *For twelve months of the year we farm and raise livestock and for two months we ALSO* (sic) *operate a dude ranch. During these two months, as farmers and livestock men, we sell all kinds of dairy, poultry, cattle, sheep, hogs, farm and garden produce to the dude ranch. We do everything the ordinary farmer does and a lot more besides. With the exception of cattle, also poultry and dairy products during the winter months, we sell practically everything we produce to the dude ranch. During the drought year of '34 we sold 100 tons of baled hay to the government so that they could move drought stricken cattle to the road and this year have let our neighbors have 100 tons of baled hay. In both instances we received $15 per ton for the hay...*

Then, because he thought the recipient of the letter might not totally understand the dude ranch angle of the operation, Skipper drew an example to clarify the matter:

...It seems to me that our position is exactly like the Nebraska farmer who develops a beautiful lake on his farm, stocks it with bass and fish food and then sells the finest kind of fishing privileges at a good figure. He plants wild rice and scatters grain that duck and geese crave and then sells hunting privileges at a nice figure. Certainly, he has not disqualified himself as a farmer, because he still does everything that he did before. Besides, without curtailing his farming operations, he has provided additional sources of income to help meet his obligations of every kind. Of course it has

been necessary for this farmer to go to considerable expense in making his lake meet the demands of the customers, but if the revenue derived shows a nice profit on the investment, he has certainly made himself a better risk. I think you get the parallel I am trying to draw...

This same letter is very interesting because Skipper describes the land holding he has available as security for the proposed loan. This portion is worth quoting in its entirety because Skipper lays out the real land holdings of HF Bar Ranch:

...By referring to enclosed map you will find that in both HF Bar and Paradise there are some 3,680 acres of deeded land. Of this amount there are about 400 acres of irrigated land in a high state of cultivation. We have good water rights with a supplementary rights out of the Rock Creek and Piney Ditch and Reservoir Co. of which I happen to be Pres. Our lands are covered by the first ditches and small upkeep and also the first shot at water, which is an item especially in dry years. The remaining 3,280 acres of deed land are all the finest kind of grazing lands, well watered and well sodded and not too rocky. The 3,800 acres of state leased land are all fine grazing and a very valuable and necessary part of our well rounded out proposition..

The above statement from Skipper about the HF Bar Ranch holdings in 1936 supports my suspicion that his earlier declarations that the HF Bar Ranch controlled almost fifty thousand acres of deeded and leased land were inflated. Nothing had changed in the six or seven years since Skipper made such a claim except that the UM Ranch, and any leases that may have run with it, had disappeared with the departure of Eddie Moore. There was approximately a forty-three thousand acre difference between Skipper's earlier claims and reality. And, even if one considered whatever leases Skipper had on the

Reservation in Montana, or with his brother in Clearmont, or any-where else, for that matter, and the probably five or six thousand acres of deeded and leased land associated with the UM Ranch it is not likely that Skipper's earlier claims were supportable.

The sheep business followed about the same pattern as the cow business. By the mid-1930s, the sheep inventory declined from several hundred animals to less than two hundred in 1934.

In future years, HF Bar remained engaged in the livestock business, to various degrees in different years depending on the conditions, but never to the extent of the 1920s and early 1930s. The dairy did remain until the 1960s. Of course, there would always be a significant horse herd, because that supported the dude operation.

Because horses were so vital to the dude operation Skipper was always looking for suitable dude horses. Horse trading was constant. One Memo of Agreement survives from 1934 when HF Bar Ranch made an agreement with L. N. York of Sheridan, Wyoming. The agreement detailed eighteen head of horses that the ranch would convey to Mr. York in exchange for:

...16 good saddle horses between the ages of 6 and 10 years not later than the first of July 1935. These horses are to be well broken, sound and serviceable...

Skipper also left extensive comments about crop production, which certainly had its off years. He bemoaned in the Daybook in 1931 that:

...this is the second dry year in succession which has played havoc with the hay crop...figure we are 500 tons short of what we should have with good stands and normal seasons..

In 1933 Skipper recorded:

...Very wet early in season—so wet that could not get all crops in on time. When rain stopped, it stopped, season the hottest and driest on record & fortunately we irrigated all alfalfa very early so got a splendid 1st cutting...

...Secured in the way of grains for 1933—657 bu. (Note: bushels.) *wheat 166 bu. (ground into flour), 170 bu. barley, 725 bu. oats...dairy silo completely 100 tons, 250 bu. good potatos...*

The last Daybook entries for farming were made in 1937 and described what was being done with all the various acreages on the ranch. The last entry was:

...The field by Jodie's house (Note: Farthest West.) *is a little bit of everything. The old rodeo end is in wheat...the center part is plowed and in wheat...The garden for years is plowed & put in red clover to give it a chance...*

The entries in the three Daybooks for cattle, sheep and crops virtually ceased in 1937 and only resumed with brief entries in 1941 and 1942. Then Skipper, for some reason, stopped keeping detailed records.

A part of ranch operations was, of course, to maintain and improve the infrastructure that supported the dude business. The major building program had occurred in the 1920s. In the 1930s the task was to maintain and improve what was already available. Extensive records are not available for the 1930s but there is some evidence that work was done. For instance, the minutes of the stockholders meeting on November 16, 1936, contained the following entries:

...Secretary-Treasurer, J. O. Horton, called attention to the fact that certain improvements and enlargements were necessary to

the house known as Farthest West, same being the house set aside for his own use. He pointed out that since the house, as well as the land on which the house is located, are both HF Bar property, he could not put any of his own funds into the necessary improvements unless the ranch was willing to be responsible to him for money so expended. Upon motion duly made and approved, the ranch recognized such responsibility and agreed to reimburse him for all expenditures made, less a reasonable depreciation, at such a time as he no longer occupied or used the house as his domicile...

...Manager Frank O. Horton pointed out that because of lack of funds during the Depression that upkeep—especially on the main ranch house—had not kept pace with wear and tear. That, therefore, the ranch house was in poor condition and that a new roof, new dining room and kitchen floor and a general overhauling was immediately necessary. Unanimous approval was given for this needed work.

The plans must have been quite extensive for it was only six weeks later when Al Hook responded to a letter that Skipper had written about the planned improvements and commented:

...Judging from your letter, I certainly will need a blueprint to find my way around the ranch after all these new improvements have been put into effect...

People

Since the founding of HF Bar, a virtual cavalcade of interesting people has been employees. In the thirties, however, three people signed on to the pay roster and would become the mainstay of the HF Bar workforce for many years. Those three were Dean Thomas, Barney McLain and Bob Ross.

Dean Thomas was born in Sheridan, Wyoming, on October 23, 1910, to Richard and Susan DeJarnette Thomas. He was the second of four children that included his older brother Wendell and two younger sisters, Florence and Vesta. The family moved many times. Dean began school in Acme, Wyoming and attended various schools in Sheridan. The family then moved to Osage, Wyoming and subsequently to Kennewick, Washington, Idaho Springs, Colorado, and then to Denver, Colorado.

It was in Denver that Dean and his older brother, Wendell, quit school when Dean was in the tenth grade. The family was struggling, and according to my mother Vesta, Wendell and Dean had to take their lunch to school in a bag because the family could not afford to buy school lunches. Apparently, the other children made fun of them because of their brown bag lunches so Dean and Wendell simply quit school. Their father was upset but they were adamant and refused to go back.

In 1925 the family moved back to Sheridan and the family started a haulage business which was listed in the Sheridan City Directory as "Richard A. Thomas & Sons." The firm hauled coal and wood and anything else that needed hauling and guaranteed prompt delivery.

The family business ceased to exist in about 1929 when Dean's brother went to work for the Sheridan Fire Department. Dean worked around town at various jobs until he went to work at HF Bar in May of 1931.

He would die as an HF Bar employee fifty-six years later on October 27, 1987.

Dean hired on as a driver for seventy-five dollars a month. He described his early years in a *Western Horseman* article in 1978:

I drove a truck on the ranch for five years and then graduated to the passenger car. We hauled a lot of people in those days—no one had a car out here at that time. Then I went to work as a corral boy in '35...

After Dean's first summer at HF Bar he was involved in a serious automobile accident. One wintry evening in March 1932, Dean went to a party in Story, Wyoming with his friend Glenn Vickere and two other boys from Sheridan. On their way home, Glenn was driving and lost control of the car on an icy curve on what is known as Tunnel Hill. The car plunged two hundred feet down a rocky embankment. Dean, Vickere, and one of the boys were thrown clear, but one remained in the car until it came to rest at the bottom of the ravine. Glenn was killed and the two other boys were injured, but not seriously. Dean was unscathed and went for help. The *Sheridan Press* described his ordeal:

...Thomas...mounted the icy slope and ran all the way back to the Story cabin where the party was being held—a distance of nearly a mile. He collapsed from exhaustion after explaining Vickere's car had gone off the hill...

In the *Western Horseman* article Dean gave some insight about how the ranch operated in the thirties:

...When I came here, the ranch bred draft horses. They had a Percheron stud and a Belgian stud and draft mares. The draft horses were used mostly for haying and feeding in the winter. They raised

a lot of good saddle horses here too...

...We used to trail cows and calves to Montana in the spring. Skipper had some big leases up there and we'd trail the cattle up there and leave them all summer. Then we'd bring them back and take the horses up for the winter. We had someone there to look after them. In '36 none of the dude ranches had any grass because of the drought and we trailed the horses up to Garbin Basin—a big bowl. (Note: This is a misspelling. Dean was referring to the Garvin Basis which is a geological trough between the Big Horn Mountains and the Pryor Mountains. The area is well over one hundred miles from the HF Bar Ranch.) *The Eaton's* (Note: Eaton's Dude Ranch which is the oldest dude ranch in Wyoming located west of Sheridan at the foot of the Big Horn Mountains.) *had their horses there and there were horses from other dude ranches...Everyone turned out their horses in that big bowl—about 1,000 head. We'd gather them up in the spring and just drop them off at the ranches when we came home...*

In his interview with *Western Horseman* Dean does not mention his artistic talent. Dean had a natural artistic bent and loved to draw horses and people. In fact, in his first year at HF Bar he had two drawings in the HF newspaper, *Bridle Bits.* For many years thereafter, Dean drew the annual ranch Christmas card. They have been recycled countless times and are still used by the present ranch owner, Margi Schroth, to send greetings to HF Bar guests.

Dean's drawing abilities were noticed by a dude woman, who was quite a bit older than Dean. She encouraged him to develop his considerable artistic talent and offered to send him to art school. Dean accepted the offer and attended one year of school in Chicago and one in New York. Not much is known about Dean's academic art career, except that, according to my mother, one of his assignments as a student was to paint the legs of showgirls. Dean decided that he'd rather paint horses than the legs of showgirls.

Apparently, the woman who sent him to school took a romantic interest in Dean and wanted to marry him. But, according to my mother, Dean reckoned he was much more interested in her daughter and politely declined the offer.

This would not be the first time that women would take an extraordinary interest in Dean. Dean had movie star good looks and was a natural charmer. He was supremely comfortable in his own skin and had a natural ability to get on with people no matter if they were a captain of industry, a blue blood from New York, or a dishwasher from North Carolina. He had a natural grace with people and in future years would become something of an icon at HF Bar.

Another man, who would also become a mainstay of the HF Bar workforce over the years, was Barney McLain. Barney was an interesting character. He was born on October 14, 1892 at Fort Worth Texas. It was rumored that he started making his own way in the Red River country of Oklahoma at the age of eight. That is not verified but we do know for sure that he became a cowboy and went up to Wyoming from Paul's Valley Oklahoma when he was eighteen in 1910. There is a story, unverified, that when Barney arrived in Buffalo, Wyoming, he had on a scotch cap and one boot and one spur on one foot and a shoe on the other.

Barney didn't go by himself. Another young man named Greeley Hughes accompanied him. Greeley was born on October 17, 1890 in South Carolina and his family moved west when he was a boy. How Barney and Greeley hooked up is not known, but they arrived in Wyoming together and became fast friends for the rest of their lives. They were tough, rough and ready dyed in the wool cowboys in the best tradition. One example of the kind of men they were surfaced as late as 2004 in a letter to the editor in a publication called *Agri-News* published in Montana on December 17, 2004. The letter describes an episode involving Greeley Hughes.

Season's Greetings

An early Dean Thomas HF Bar Christmas card.
(Courtesy of the HF Bar Ranch)

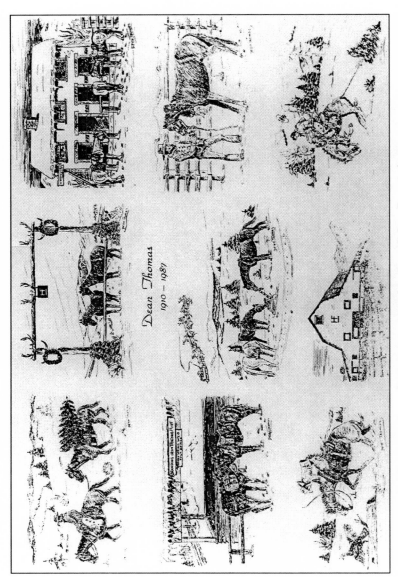

Dean Thomas drew Christmas cards for the HF Bar Ranch for many years.
After his death a selection of the drawings was published as a memorial.
Dean's drawings are still used on HF Bar Christmas cards today.   *(Courtesy of the HF Bar Ranch)*

The letter was written in response to a wolf lover who thought a certain person should be fined for killing a wolf in Montana. The wolf was the result of a wolf reintroduction program instituted a few years earlier in Yellowstone Park. Today the program presents a problem to Montana ranchers because the wolves have strayed from the Yellowstone area and kill livestock. The letter, written by Ray Krone of Augusta, Montana, read:

A real cowboy answer to the wolf problem...

Linda, the papers are full of stories about the wolf packs killing cattle. The little story I want to share takes place at a much better time, a time when there was a program in place to eradicate wolves from the Montana rangelands.

The Antler outfit (on the Crow Reservation in southeastern Montana) had their wagon out branding calves. They had hired a cowboy from Oregon (Note: Greeley was from Oklahoma.) *named Greeley Hughes to help with the roundup. Greeley had the reputation of being quite a hand with a rope. The cowboys would be on circle at daybreak, and nearly every day they would run into a wolf or two coming off a bait. The wolves would be full of Strychnine and couldn't run too fast. Greeley would jerk his rope down and fall in behind a wolf. He'd rope the wolf and turn off, breaking his neck. My dad said he never seen Greeley miss a loop, and through this summer, this man roped and killed over 50 wolves.*

I thought he had a real cowboy answer to the wolf problem...

Not a lot is known about Barney's whereabouts in the early days. We do know that he won second place in the steer roping at the Sheridan Stampede Rodeo in 1916 and that he was drafted in World War I and served with the remount but we don't know the details of his service. He did mention to me once that he had a run in with what he considered to be an overbearing Lieutenant.

Barney McLain could be hard on men and horses
but he was always gentle and kind with children. This photo was taken
by Jack Horton, Sr.
It is possible the child in front of Barney is Jack Horton, Jr., Circa 1938.
(Courtesy of the HF Bar Ranch)

Barney and Greeley cowboyed for a number of outfits around the country and worked for the Spear Ranch in Montana for several years. The exact dates are unknown.

In 1925, Barney and Greeley fell afoul of the law and made the front page of the *Sheridan Post Enterprise*, which, on August 7, 1925 carried the following headline:

Alleged Cattle Rustlers Arrested
Greeley Hughes and Barney McLain Face Theft Charges—
Officers Claim That Thousands of Cattle Were Stolen by Gang Here

The story claimed that Greeley, who at that time was range boss for the Sheridan Heights Cattle Company, was arrested in Sheridan and Barney was arrested in Aberdeen, Montana. In addition to the declaration that they had stolen thousands of cattle, the newspaper said that there was a dragnet for gang leaders and gang employees. Then on August 12th there was another story for which the headline was:

Horton Wrangler Jailed As One of Cattle Rustlers
Jack Delhart Denies Complicity For Theft

On October 23rd Barney and Greeley were convicted on charges of grand larceny in Hardin, Montana. Then, on October 26th a new trial was requested for Barney and Greeley but the charges against Jack Delhart were dismissed. On November 6th a new trial was granted on one conviction and a second conviction was appealed.

The news coverage of the incident then dried up and there was no further press coverage on the subject. However, both Barney and Greeley were eventually convicted and sent to the Montana State Prison in Deer Lodge, Montana, but not at the same time. The prison records show that Greeley was a prisoner from June 29, 1926 and was paroled on June 28, 1928. Barney, however, was not sent to prison until January 23, 1927, and he was released on January 22, 1929. Why there was such a long time span between their trials and when they went to prison is unknown.

Another unverified story, but a good one nevertheless, is that while in prison for cattle stealing, Barney received a letter from someone with a check for a stolen bull that Barney had sold to the sender.

In later years, the story about Barney's prison record was that he took the wrap for Greeley to keep him out of prison. That was not true. Greeley served time. Greeley never worked at HF Bar as far as I know, but he did work in later years as a general foreman for the Miller Land and Livestock Company at Parkman, Wyoming, and was general manager of the UM Ranch until he retired. Greeley died in 1963 in Thief River Falls, Minnesota.

Over a year after Barney was released from prison he went to work for HF Bar in May, 1931, when he signed on as a cowboy at fifty dollars per month. Barney was known to Skipper because they had met on roundups in Montana in the 1920s.

Barney worked at HF Bar for most of the 1930s, at least from spring to fall, but we don't know his work history for the winter months. The daybooks that Skipper kept often mention Barney moving livestock from place to place and I can remember Dean Thomas telling me about taking cows and horses to Montana with Barney in the late 1930s.

Barney accumulated some money as well, from sources unknown, for in 1936 he loaned HF Bar three thousand dollars, which was a considerable amount of money in those days, to buy one hundred fifty eight head of two year old heifers. The promissory note is still on file in HF Bar Ranch records. This was not the last time an employee would lend working capital to the ranch, and in fact, in later years, Dean Thomas would also lend the ranch money as well to help get through periodic lean periods. They were always paid

back with interest.

Barney never did learn to read or write, but you could not stump him with numbers. When it came to livestock and dollars, he was a pretty shrewd fellow and, as Dean told me, Barney was most likely to come out ahead on any horse trades or cattle deals.

My father once told me that during the short time he worked at HF Bar, Barney would often summon him behind the barn and pull out a letter from his future wife, Ione, and ask my father to read it to him. My father was glad to do so.

Ione Williams was born in Russellville, Arkansas in 1904. She graduated magna cum laude from Hendrix College, Arkansas, in 1924 and then obtained her library training at the University of Illinois graduate library school in 1931 from which she graduated with honors. Ione had earned her living by teaching school and working a library for many years and then she went west.

How Ione, a cultured and educated young woman would meet up with an illiterate cowboy, was described by Ione in an article she wrote for the *Denver Post* in March, 1957. The article was titled simply, *I Married A Cowboy*. Ione wrote:

...You wouldn't have picked me out for a cowboy's bride. My immediate forebears were cultured, conservative Southerners and I lived in academic circles until I was 35.

Tales of the American West fascinated me and I longed to see it for myself. Finally one summer I did come west.

It was to work at one of Wyoming's early day dude ranches. After that I returned to the same ranch for several summers.

Eventually, many years after that first summer, and when all of my family and most of my friends had decided I was going to remain a spinster, I married a cowboy...

Barney and Ione's courtship lasted for several years as they would not marry until 1942.

Another future long time employee arrived in 1935. His name was Bob Ross and he was thirteen years old. Bob was from Chicago and his father worked for the Wrigley Company. Bob was sickly and his doctor advised his family to take him to the desert for his health. Bob's father had spent his youth in Arizona and met Mrs. Wrigley there, which was how he eventually came to work for the Wrigley Company.

The move to Arizona did Bob some good. He was kept out of school and regained his health. From then on, Bob and his mother stayed in Arizona year round and his father would spend the summers with them. In 1935 they decided to try Wyoming for a change and went to HF Bar as dudes. They spent the entire summer there. From then the pattern was to spend winters in Arizona and summers at HF Bar.

Bob did not want to go back to Chicago, but his father thought it best that he finish high school there, so he did. Bob recollects that he graduated in the evening and was on the first plane out of Chicago the next morning. It was his first airplane flight. Bob would become an HF Bar employee the next year, in 1942.

Harry Huson left employment at HF Bar in 1935. His sons, Harry and Russell, offered insight on the matter. Harry got along fine with Skipper; after all, he had been with him for over twenty years. But, Skipper was absent much of the time and Harry had to put up with Bill Horton. Bill Horton was young, wild and had visions of being the corral boss. Harry, who had been the corral boss for a long time, could not get along with the boss's son and decided it was time to leave.

There was also another reason: Mae, Harry's wife, believed that the children were getting older and thought that perhaps they should not have such a heavy exposure to the dudes.

So, they left. They rented a place on Shell Creek. When their

house burned down they moved to the Hole in the Wall country near Kaycee, Wyoming, and then several other places. They ended up in Clearmont in 1943. But HF Bar had not seen the last of the Harry Huson family.

Skipper also hired his relatives to work at the ranch. Two of them were John and Charles Brockway, sons of Skipper's sister Mary Milne. Both John and Charles are alive today. John was twenty-one years old when he first visited HF Bar Ranch in 1935. He had not met Skipper before, but Skipper was very good to him. He remembers his arrival:

...When I arrived at the ranch the first day he gave me a $40.00 beaver hair hat. That really made me look like a new dude. An old sweaty, dusty hat would make me look like a cowboy I worked with...I remember he told me to eat more, and get more weight on...

John recalled some other things about his uncle Skipper:

...I hear he had a temper, but I never saw it. I believe he was a good storyteller to the guests after dinner...

John primarily worked at Paradise Ranch where, at that time, Jack Buckingham and his wife were the managers. John remembers that he worked hard hauling guests and made many trips to town for or with guests and he hauled a lot of coal and ice. His brother, Charles, worked at HF and waited tables in the dining room.

Even though there was a major split between the Horton and Gorrell families in the early 1930s, one Gorrell family member retained some connection with the area. That was Ginger Gorrell. Ginger was in the area in 1933 because he became in that year only the second person to climb Blacktooth Mountain in the Big Horn Mountain range.

At the summit of the mountain Ginger left a note for those to follow. The note was not discovered until years later, in 1949, by members of a Chicago mountaineering club. Ginger would continue to appear on the Wyoming scene throughout subsequent years and often used the mountain cabin he had built in 1924 as a base for his ramblings.

Skipper Returns To Politics

Skipper's yen for public service never diminished and he remained active throughout the 1930s even though he left the state legislature in 1931. In 1932 he was named a Republican Committeeman for Wyoming and held that position throughout the decade.

He was also active in the Dude Rancher's Association and in 1934 acted as chairman of the resolutions committee at the ninth annual convention in Cody, Wyoming. One resolution he proposed for adoption displayed his and others' concerns about protecting the wilderness areas. The resolution read:

...We learn with apprehension of roads being built to or into our primitive or wilderness areas and while such roads may at times be absolutely necessary for fire protection, we urge that in such cases locked gates be installed so that such areas may always remain primitive...

In 1938, Skipper ran for the lone Wyoming seat in the United States House of Representatives. He was prompted to run because of his strong views about President Roosevelt and his New Deal. Skipper had very strong opinions about any number of subjects. Mostly he was against big government and an ardent believer in states' rights, especially Wyoming's state's rights. In his plainspoken way, Skipper laid out his beliefs in his first campaign brochure:

FRANK O. HORTON
SAYS
THE AMERICAN MARKET
FOR
AMERICAN LABOR
AMERICAN FARMER
AMERICAN INDUSTRY

TARIFF. Save the American market for the United States. We imported the equivalent of 1,100,000 more head of cattle in 1937 than in 1932; 200,000,000 more pounds of wool; 32 million more bushels of wheat. How many acres of land would it have taken to produce these and many other farm products which the United States is now importing in increasingly larger quantities—JUST 30,000,000 ACRES! How many jobs would have been created? How much additional money would the American farmer have received?

Instead, millions of our workers are on relief or W.P.A. rolls and all of us are footing the bill through taxes. Chalk this up to the SECRET TRADE TREATIES and tariff reductions made under the name of the RECIPROCAL TRADE AGREEMENTS, approved and being defended by Mr. Greever.

W.P.A. While we have W.P.A., why is the Wyoming W.P.A. worker worth only $44 per month while those in Montana are paid $56, in Colorado and Utah $55? It looks as if our neighboring states had been getting better representation in Washington by about $10 a month per head. Our present Congressman has given Washington a pretty poor idea of what a Wyoming worker is worth.

RELIEF. Put relief funds, both federal and local, in the hands of local organizations free from political interference. You know more about the needs of your community than a lot of politicians

2,000 miles away in Washington. How much of the money appropriated for relief is going to the chain of government employees stretching from here to Washington, and how much to the actual needy for whom it was intended. Put as much of the dollar as possible into the hands of those for whom it was originally intended.

STATE WATER. The Act of Admission and the Constitution of the State of Wyoming provide that the waters of the State belong to the people of Wyoming. Congress approved these when submitted. Now the federal government has stepped in to claim ownership. Are we going to let them get away with it?

TAXES. These are Franklin D. Roosevelt's own words as expressed at Pittsburgh on October 19, 1932: "Taxes are paid in the sweat of every man who labors. If these taxes are excessive they are reflected in idle factories, in tax sold farms. Out workers may never see a tax bill, but they pay. They pay in deductions from wages, in the increased cost of what they buy or in unemployment throughout the land!"

Mr. Roosevelt admits high taxation is a dangerous thing but he runs up the national debt from 17 billion to 40 billion dollars, an all time high, in six years, (that means $40 a minute from the birth of Christ until the present time.) THE ONLY WAY DEBT CAN be paid is through taxes.

SOCIAL SECURITY. The employee and the employer are both contributing so much per week to Social Security. What is happening to that money in Washington? It is being spent by the Government for current expenses and an I.O.U. left in its place. When the time comes for that money to be paid out to the workers in the form of Social Security, the Government will have to make good those I.O.U.'s. The only way it can raise the money to do this is through taxes. THUS YOU WILL BE TAXED A SECOND TIME FOR

THE SAME PURPOSE.

This nation can never be called truly great until it drives from the heart of man the fear of poverty and misery in old age, but let's have an HONEST, WORKABLE plan.

FEDERAL LANDS. The Federal Government now controls 82% of the area of Wyoming, and it is out after more. LET'S STOP THIS FEDERAL LAND GRABBING. Wipe out government landlordism. Our game and wildlife are among our greatest assets. Let's keep them as state property.

JOBS. Wealth can be created by labor plus the product of the soil or the product of the mines. This country has plenty of land, plenty of mines and plenty of people to do the work. Industry is the agent that brings them together. Let's get rid of a government that hampers and heckles industry. Let's have a return of confidence.

IT IS FRANK O. HORTON'S belief that Congressmen represent the 48 states and NOT the President; that, under the Constitution, it is the duty of Congress to make the laws and formulate all national policies; it is the President's job to carry out these policies, not to make them. THE PRESIDENTIAL TAIL IS NOT SUPPOSED TO WAG THE CONGRESSIONAL DOG!

In the biography section of his brochure, Skipper states that he...

...came to Wyoming about 30 years ago, shortly after his graduation from the University of Chicago, where he had played football, during his entire college course, under that famous coach, A. A. Stagg...

The statement about his graduation from the University of Chicago further fuels the mystery of Skipper's academic credentials. It is difficult to imagine that a man of Skipper's intelligence would be so bold as to run for Congress on false credentials.

Skipper was elected to Congress by a handy margin and went to Washington to make his presence known. And he did that. Reticence was not a part of Skipper's make up, nor did he believe that freshman congressmen should be seen and not heard. Skipper was seen and heard a lot, and he got rave reviews for his performance. By the end of his first year in Congress, he was receiving very favorable press coverage.

In December, 1939, the local paper in Kemmerer, Wyoming carried the following article about Skipper after three prominent congressmen paid a visit to Cheyenne, Wyoming, to inspect Fort Warren. The article represented the prevailing opinion about Skipper's congressional performance.

Congressman Frank O. Horton
Held In High Esteem by His Colleagues
—Republicans and Democrats Alike

...On the word of three of his prominent colleagues, Frank O. Horton, Saddlestring dude rancher and Wyoming's lone representative in the lower house of Congress, gave a good account of himself as a "freshman" legislator...

Congressman John J. Sparkman, an Alabama Democrat, said of Skipper:

...I have been in Congress several years and I know Horton made more friends in his freshman year than any representative I've ever known. His knack of making friends and getting things done is not limited to the House. He also manages to know most of the important federal officials in Washington...

New Faces in Congress   By Sotto

HE HERDED SHEEP ON THE SLOPES OF THE ROCKIES TO EARN HIS FIRST DOLLAR. WAS A YOUNGSTER WHEN HE MIGRATED TO JOHNSON COUNTY, WYOMING, ONE OF THE LARGEST COUNTIES IN THE WORLD. . . . .

Rep.
Frank O. HORTON
Republican
CONGRESSMAN-AT-LARGE

State Seal

OF SADDLESTRING, WYOMING, WAS BORN IN IOWA, OCT. 18, 1882; GRADUATED MORGAN PARK MILITARY ACADEMY, ILLINOIS, IN 1899, AND FROM UNIVERSITY OF CHICAGO, 1903; TRUSTEE OF THE WYOMING STOCKGROWERS ASS'N.; SERVED IN THE WYO. HOUSE OF REPRESENTATIVES, 1921-23; WYO. SENATE 1923-31; PRES. STATE SENATE 1931; REPUBLICAN NATIONAL COMMITTEEMAN (WYO.) 1937-1938; MARRIED AND HAS THREE SONS.

ACHIEVED HIS BOYHOOD AMBITION WHEN HE BECAME A FULL-FLEDGED COWPUNCHER. HAS ENGAGED IN LIVESTOCK RANCHING SINCE HE WAS HONORABLY DISCHARGED FROM THE U.S. ARMY AT THE CLOSE OF SPANISH-AMERICAN WAR.

Frank O. "Skipper" Horton was recognized as a new congressman after his election in 1939. This biographical sketch by Sotto was published in several newspapers.   *(Courtesy of the HF Bar Ranch)*

Congressman Charles Clason of Massachusetts also registered his opinion of Skipper. He stated:

>...Wyoming should let Frank Horton serve in Congress as long as he wants to. He's not letting any grass grow under his feet and he's the kind of fellow that gets to the heart of most problems...

A third congressman, Thomas E. Martin of Iowa, chimed in as well:

>...Horton left quite a good record in his first term, when congressmen are supposed to be seen and not heard. I want you to know that he's got the nerve to stand up and fight, regardless of the odds, for what he feels is right...

Congressman Martin, who was Minority Leader of the House at that time, thought so highly of Skipper that he appointed a special committee to study livestock and agricultural conditions. Skipper was appointed a member of this special committee and was further recognized by being made a member of the executive committee. Skipper was given this unusual status as a freshman congressman because he became recognized early on as one of the best informed men in Congress as far as livestock matters were concerned.

Skipper's activism for those causes in which he believed, or against those matters that he opposed, brought him into the national spotlight at times, as he did not confine his speaking engagements to Wyoming. Skipper would speak wherever he was asked, and he was asked a lot. He garnered many news stories all over the United States. Skipper also published a column called *Cactus Scratches* which he used to express his views and keep his constituents up to date.

The hallmark of Skipper's congressional career, which brought him prominence on a national level, was his support of Wendell Willkie's campaign for president of the United States. Skipper worked hard at the Republican National Convention to get Wendell Willkie nominated and was a tireless worker for the campaign, especially in the western states. He also supported Wendell Willkie at home on the ranch.   Bob Ross remembers that Skipper even required the ranch employees to wear Wendell Willkie buttons at work. As Bob tells it, they didn't have any choice.

Wendell Wilkie acknowledged Skipper's support on a visit to Wyoming when he said that Skipper was:

...one of the finest batters for me at the convention...

A telling example of Skipper's fervor for Wendell Willkie is the transcript of his remarks he made for a newsreel made in Washington on October 3, 1940, for consumption by Wyoming voters.   Skipper could certainly get fired up when he was on the political stump:

Hello everybody out there in God's country:

I want to tell you something about this man, Wendell Willkie. I've known him pretty intimately for the last eight months. He's your kind of a man because he's a two-fisted fighting man. He's husky...he's rugged...and he's fearless. He would fight a buzz-saw at the drop of a hat if he thought it was crooked.

During his tour through the big cities, he and Mrs. Willkie had purposely sought out the tough spots. The spots were crooked...political and other dupes have preached the hymn of hate to the down-and-outers. He's talked with them about jobs... honest jobs...and he has made friends. He will remember the forgotten man of the past eight years. He knows work and he knows Wyoming because he has worked in the hay and harvest fields of Wyoming in order to earn money for his education. He is stressing jobs because it is jobs that build homes and make happiness possible. Ten million people without jobs and many more on relief doesn't spell homes and it doesn't spell happiness. The minimum hours and maximum wages and social security laws don't mean a thing to the man without the job. This man Willkie is going to win. He's already re-establishing faith in government and with Willkie's election, complete confidence will be the story. Willkie and his opponent are running neck and neck now. Watch them swing around the turn into the home stretch. Willkie is forging ahead. Now look at him come down the stretch. He's a great finisher because he's a great thoroughbred. He has the heart of a thoroughbred. He'll cross the line just as he did at Philadelphia with a tremendous burst of speed and plenty to spare.

Get on the band wagon. I want Wyoming to ride high, wide and handsome with this great American leader. Help save America.

To Skipper's chagrin, not only did his candidate lose the presidential election of 1940, but Skipper was unseated as well. He was shocked. All indications looked good. He had won the Primary Election by a very healthy margin and things looked good for him on the surface anyway.

The problem was that the Second World War was looming and Skipper was forced to attend to his congressional duties for longer than usual. He was not able to return to Wyoming and campaign until about three weeks before the election. When he did, he managed to cover all the bases, but not really in depth. In addition, Skipper fell victim to the democratic sweep in Wyoming. It was the third consecutive time that the state had given a majority to President Roosevelt. The state also re-elected a democratic senator, J. C. O'Mahoney.

So, Skipper's heralded congressional career was short lived. He was swept out of office in a Democratic clamor just as surely as he had been swept in by a Republican surge two years earlier. Skipper went home to HF Bar to lick his wounds and would not enter the political arena again—although he would consider it.

Birth of Saddlestring

On August 16, 1937, a United States post office was established at HF Bar Ranch. It was named "Saddlestring." A popular story is that when Skipper submitted the application he offered two suggestions for names—Deers Ear and Saddlestring. Saddlestring was selected, supposedly, because it just sounded better, but to whom, we don't know.

Saddlestring appeared for the first time in the 1939-1940 Wyoming State Directory. F. O. Horton was listed as president, J. O. Horton as vice president, and Alfred A. Hook as secretary-treasurer, Justice of the Peace, auditor, accountant and postmaster.

Forever after, though it was a post office, Saddlestring would be used interchangeably with HF Bar as a *place*. In fact, after the turn of the next century, a Wyoming novelist, C.J. Box, would use Saddlestring as the fictious name of a Wyoming town.

End of a Decade

The close of the 1930s signaled the end of a tumultuous decade at HF Bar and ended on a high note. Skipper had avoided severe financial problems brought on by the collapse of his brother-in-law's financial empire and had gained control so that the ranch was well and truly the Horton family place. Skipper had also had to deal with some of the vicissitudes of the livestock business and had kept the ranch intact, mainly because the dude business helped to offset the livestock business. By the end of the decade the dude business was the predominant business of HF Bar. Any agricultural production was supplemental.

The Horton family had suffered death—Gertrude died and Bill's wife, Sis, was killed in a tragic accident. But, the survivors recovered and got on with their lives. Skipper remarried, as did Bill, and Jack married for the first time. Bill and Jack would present Skipper with three grandchildren in two years and at the same time Skipper would be successful in his bid for a seat in the United States House of Representatives, even though his congressional career would be prematurely ended.

HF Bar had become a truly family run operation in what appeared to be an ideal situation. But, the situation would not last. Family difficulties were soon to surface, along with a World War, which would have an irreversible impact on the Horton family and HF Bar.

Chapter 7

The Forties

The Horton Family

Around the turn of the decade the Horton family became too big for the ranch—or the ranch became too small! Hank Horton, strong willed, opinionated and married to the ranch patriarch, Skipper, became involved in the operation of the ranch. She became a stockholder in 1942 when Skipper gave her twenty shares of HF Bar stock. Her presence and involvement did not sit well with all the family members and caused some problems that manifested themselves in very unfortunate ways. Supposedly, according to some old time guests, Hank was reported to have proclaimed at one time, "There is only one Mrs. Horton!"

In addition, everyone had to make a living and the ranch could not support three families plus Bobby Horton. Jack Horton took matters into his own hands and was the first to leave the ranch. He and Jody and their two children, Jack, Jr. and Trudy, moved to Sheridan where Jack took over the operation of a local Sinclair service station.

Then something traumatic happened between Skipper, Jack and Jody. What sparked the problem is unknown, but a letter from Jody to Skipper reveals that the situation was serious. Jody wrote to Skipper:

Dear Skipper—

    You're a nice guy and I'm surprised that after what I did for you and the ranch for five years you can feel so toward me. I have only one reason to suspect you've had such a change of heart. I told Hank that I was thinking of moving the children and Mrs. Teague to the ranch as I cannot stand the gaff of housekeeping and going out so much which I am obligated to do to a certain extent. We were planning to come out weekends—Take a little apartment in town and I stay in with Jack during the week—possibly even working part time somewhere. Then taking Jack away from work Saturday late and Sunday. He works too hard. It would be a very graceful way to help me out as I am no better than I was a couple years ago, and terrible nervous besides I have no intention of "working" with, for, or against you. But when Bobbie hears this—Oh, Skip, why don't you get wise to yourself before all your kids leave you. Bobbie seemed to think you liked having us at Christmas. The ranch reputation, I know, is at stake—and Henri (Hank) from what people say around here, and old dudes, is, was, and never will be the same to the outfit. Don't ever hurt Jack Horton like that again or I'll shoot you—and don't forget that all four of us have and are always devoted to you.

Jody

    Jody's undated letter was written early in 1940 because after Skipper received it he wrote to Jack on March 15th on congressional stationery. His letter refers to Jody's letter and alludes to a deep, but unexplained problem:

Dear Jack:

In response to my personal letter (Note: Contents of the letter are unknown.) *to you asking your cooperation in handling an unfortunate situation, I have Jody's "shoot you" letter which translated I assume means that she will kill me unless I do exactly what she wants done.*

Hitler is not yet surfaced and I am still doing my own way of thinking and had there been any doubt as to the correctness of my position certainly Jody's letter has dispelled same.

If you don't know, you should know that one doesn't go thru what Jody has gone through and remain quite sane and that's why I wrote you a personal letter and that's why Jody can have nothing to do with HF so long as I am connected with same and I am perfectly willing to step down and out anytime the ranch settles up with me. (Note: I do not know what Jody went through. It is possible she could have suffered a mental breakdown, since in her letter she refers to being "nervous." Possibly all this was brought about because of what must have been to her an untenable situation at the ranch. Hank's presence was most likely a factor.)

Just why you didn't exercise your usual good judgment and handle the matter yourself is more than I will ever be able to understand and your failure to do so has brought about a situation that looks pretty hopeless to me.

I feel terribly sorry for you but I don't know what I can do about it, you have only yourself to blame... (Note: I assume that here Skipper is referring to the state of the marriage between Jack and Jody which was crumbling.)

Then, Skipper refers to another lurking family problem—Bill's and Dodie's marriage:

...Regarding the Bill/Dodie affair: Both Bill and Dodie asked us to say nothing to Jody so we lied like troopers for them not

knowing until day before yesterday, when Bill returned, that he himself had told you everything and you can verify this yourself when you see Bill...

Skipper ends the letter by talking about other matters:

> ...We loved having little Jack out even if we were awfully busy at that time and we would love to have you and the kids here all summer or at anytime but please don't ask the impossible. I am taking care of little Jack's insurance and I will continue to do so but I cannot take care of the insurance for either you, Bill or Bob.
>
> Love, Dad

There it was. The family was falling apart. The rift between Skipper and Jody was permanent and the marriage between Jack and Jody was to fail and they would separate. Jack decided that the situation could not remain as it was so he decided to leave and find a way to solve his financial problems and figure out how to cope with a dissolving marriage.

Jody had already left with the children to live with her parents in Milwaukee. Jack went to New York to look for work. He summed up the situation in a letter to Skipper just before Christmas in 1941.

Dear Dad—

> Strangely enough here I seem to be in New York. Also, I have landed myself a job with Socony Vacuum Oil Co. in Venezuela with an oil survey party and am signing up with them for a period of two years.

Jack describes the details of his employment and says:

...I don't feel that I am really running away from anything as I am going to pay off every damn cent I owe anybody...

Then he discusses his personal situation:

...I have written Josephine that there was no use in our going any farther. I have made a pretty nice mess of everything so far but I'll come out of it some year if people will ride with me awhile. I'm sorry I couldn't sit down and talk this over with you before I left the ranch, as I knew pretty well what I was going to do. But sometimes its hard to talk about some things.

Incidentally, I drove straight through from Sheridan to New York in 47 hours.

I have left a pretty nice mess to straighten out on the service station books I guess but I tried to wind up all I could before I left. And I would have gone nuts if I had stayed any longer. All my station bills are paid with the exception of a note I owe First National of Sheridan and a balance I owe U. S. Rubber Co. I should have plenty coming in my accounts receivable to take care of these...

I am sorry as hell about everything and especially sorry about the kids. I guess they will have to stay over in Milwaukee and I'll send so much every month toward their support.

Well, Merry Christmas to you and Hank and hope you don't think too damn rough of me....

On January 4th, Jack wrote to Skipper again:

Dear Dad:

Thanks for your wire, which I received last Friday in New York, having spent New Years here in Princeton with the Raycrofts. The government has cancelled all Grace Line sailings for a minimum of five weeks and I am not at all sure when I will get away. At present the Company is trying to obtain Pan American reservations and I may fly down after the 15th of the month. I am also applying for a commission in the Navy and if accepted will be called in about 6 months as an ensign in special aerial map interpretation work... (Note: Jack was never called up by the Navy as the work he was doing in Venezuela was assisting the war effort.)

Jack continued with a discussion of the Jody situation:

...Jody can have any and all of the stuff at both ranches that she may send for. I believe all the things in ranch house #5 are hers, as well as in the big box in your house. All the furniture at Paradise is hers and I can't think of anything of mine up there that is important. Please do not tell anyone of the arrangements, as am sure Jody will want to make her own arrangements. Perhaps it may be possible to have the kids visit the ranch for several months next summer...

Jack wrote further about his financial problems which were brought about by his failure to make a go of operating the Sinclair Service station in Sheridan. Jack had sold the station to T. J. and E. N. Neighbors and when he left owed over five hundred dollars to the United States Rubber Company for goods he had taken on consignment as a distributor for the company. The company was concerned because he had left Sheridan without notifying them of his whereabouts or his intention to liquidate his obligation to them.

...Thanks for your offer on my Sheridan obligations. I have made arrangements for taking care of practically everything but may have some trouble with a bill I owe the U. S. Rubber Co. who seem to be getting very anxious. I'll yell if I need some help...

As it turned out Jack had to yell quite a bit for Skipper to help him out of his financial situation both with United States Rubber and several local obligations which were unfulfilled. Eventually, with his new employment and a steady source of income, and with help from Skipper and Jody's mother, Mrs. Jahn, Jack was able to take care of all his financial obligations and get on with his life. But it was a stressful time for him and Jody and the children.

At about the same time that Jack and Jody were having serious marriage problems, Bill Horton and his wife Dodie were having their own. After Bill and Dodie were married they returned to Wyoming and built a new house near HF Bar. Unfortunately, life on the ranch turned out not to be idyllic. In a tragic fire, their new house burned down and destroyed virtually all of their possessions. Dodie was devastated by the loss. In addition to that, Dodie and Bill grew apart for whatever reasons and the marriage ended.

Dodie moved back to Canton with their daughter Suzanne. The situation led her mother to believe it was best for her daughter and granddaughter to make a clean break. Consequently, all attempts from Bill to make contact with Dodie and Suzanne were rebuffed— letters and packages from Bill were returned. Suzanne was never allowed to see her father. When she was older she wanted to work at the ranch as a hasher in the dining room but she was forbidden to do so. Her mother and grandparents did not think it was the right environment for her because they vividly remembered the wild things they had done at the ranch when they were young. Suzanne would not see her father again until she was thirty years old and the mother of four children.

Suzanne's mother, Dodie, would remarry and have another family. Unfortunately, she died prematurely when she was only forty-five years old.

The next three years, 1942 through 1945, would continue to be tumultuous for the Horton family. There was the war and more death in the family.

While Jack was never called to service because he was performing war time related duties in South America discovering oil resources, Bill and Bobby did serve in the military. They both volunteered. Their service was mentioned in the HF Bar newspaper, *Cactus Scratches*, published in the spring of 1944. The article stated that:

> ...*Bill Horton is in his third year in the Coast Guard, headquartering in Seattle. Bob Horton is a 1st Lieutenant in the Engineers, now taking special training at the Adjutant General's School at Ft. Washington, Maryland, after serving a year and a half as aide to General Garlington at Ft. Leonard Wood. He hopes for an overseas assignment pretty pronto...*

In 1943, while Jack was in South America, Jody was living in Tucson, Arizona. Jody developed breast cancer and had several operations at the Mayo Clinic but to no avail. Jody died when she was only thirty years old. The circumstances surrounding Jody's death, or the impact it had on the Horton family are not known as the situation is not mentioned in any family correspondence save a letter from Jack to a friend several years later that simply mentioned the fact that Jody had died.

The situation must have been difficult, as Jack had his job in South America and now was solely responsible for two young children aged four and five. What was he to do?

A popular misconception is that when Jody died Skipper and Hank took over the rearing of young Jack and Trudy. This was not totally true. In actual fact, Jack and Trudy went to live for a time with the Fordyce family, friends of Jack.

Allen Fordyce was born May 5, 1905 in St. Louis, Missouri and first went to the Sheridan area in 1928 to work as a wrangler at Tepee Lodge in the Big Horn Mountains above Sheridan. He married Ethel

Marian Roberson in Vancouver, British Columbia. Over time, Allen became more involved in the Tepee Lodge operation and eventually bought it. He also purchased and operated several other ranches in the Sheridan area and southern Montana. Two of his ranches were the NX Bar and the Bar 13, both well known ranches, even today.

Allen was active in local and state politics and served in the Wyoming House of Representatives and on the board of trustees of the University of Wyoming. At one time he was president of the Dude Ranchers Association.

Marian Fordyce was an active member of the community as well. Among other activities she served on the Sheridan Memorial Hospital Board of Trustees for twelve years and was active in the Red Cross. Allen and Ethel had one daughter and two sons: Helen and Allen Jr. (Ike) and Mike.

The Hortons and the Fordyces were friends. Somehow Jack prevailed on the Fordyces to take on two more children until he could make arrangements to look after them himself.

The addition of two more children did not faze the active and vibrant Fordyce family. In fact, the Fordyce family became very attached to the children. In August, 1945, Phyllis Jones, to whom the reader will be introduced later, wrote her friend, Marian, and asked about the children. Marian replied:

...To answer your questions: Mollie (Note: For some reason they called Trudy "Mollie.") *and Jackie have been with us for two years now and I cannot remember what the house was like without them. Jack is still in South America but is returning in October to marry Eleanor Gibson of Sheridan. He seems to have no intention of taking the children for some time which is grand for us. I do not know what we will do if they are taken away as they are completely part of our family. Our children are devoted to them and being so close in age they are just like brothers and sisters...*

Jack Jr. and Trudy Horton with the Fordyce family in the mid-1940s.
From left are Ike Fordyce, Trudy Horton, Allan Fordyce, Helen Fordyce,
Jack Horton, Jr., and unknown boy. Man in back also unknown.
(Courtesy of Martin McCarty)

But there were occasional challenges. Pam Dixon, who in later years became Trudy's friend and who was to marry Trudy's husband Mike Dixon after Trudy died, recalled in an interview that:

> *...Apparently young Jack got really creative while staying there—he painted the interior of a car—that may be about when they called Jack senior and said, "Come back soon!"...*

How long the Horton children stayed with the Fordyces is not certain. The Sheridan School Census shows that Jack went to school in Big Horn Wyoming in 1945, but after that he is not listed. The School Census lists Jack as "Jackie Horton" aged eight, and his guardian is listed as Allen Fordyce. Trudy Horton is not listed in the census. Neither Jack nor Trudy is listed in the 1946 census.

Jack and Trudy's whereabouts from about 1946 to 1948 is unclear. There has always been a storied rumor that Hank and Skipper raised Jack and Trudy. That is not true, but Jack and Trudy may have stayed at the ranch for a year or two while Jack Sr. was getting his life organized. Also, supposedly, Jack and Trudy attended Rock Creek School and made the three mile trip by horseback. Unfortunately, the school records have disappeared and their attendance cannot be verified. However, Jack once described the trip to his friend Bob Montgomery. Bob Montgomery believes, from Jack's description of the trip, that they may have attended Shell Creek School which was a few more miles down the road. At any rate, by 1947 or 1948 Jack and Trudy were probably in South America because their father had a new wife and could provide a home for them.

On October 13, 1945, Jack married Eleanor Gibson. Eleanor was born in Douglas, Wyoming, but her family moved to Sheridan early on and Eleanor was schooled in the Sheridan School System. The profession of Eleanor's father, Lawrence Gibson, is not known, but her mother was a teacher in the Sheridan school system.

Eleanor graduated from Sheridan High School with the class of June, 1934. Eleanor was a diminutive young lady. In fact, she was described in the high school yearbook as:

> *...A gay, modest, demure little lass*
> *Handle with care! She's delicate as glass.*

Eleanor was active in high school. She was a class officer, a member of the French Class and the National Honor Society and participated in class plays among other things. After she graduated, she must have attended higher education courses because in the city directories of 1935-36 and 1942 she is listed as a student. However, by 1945, Eleanor was living with her mother and was employed as a saleswoman at Totman's Frontier Shop in Sheridan

How Jack met Eleanor is not known. But, after their marriage, Jack Sr., and Eleanor returned to South America where they, and the children, lived for several years. It must have been an exciting prospect for Eleanor to fly off and live in South America and a daunting one, too, to suddenly be the stepmother of two young active children.

Often in this period the children would return to the States when school was out and stay at HF Bar, and occasionally visit with their other grandparents, the Jahns. It was not unusual for Jack and Trudy, young as they were, to be put on an airplane to make these long trips by themselves.

While Jack was reorienting his family in South America, Bill and Bob finished their war service with the end of the war and returned to their Wyoming roots. It was not to be a particularly successful return for Bill. Bill and Hank did not get along too well before the war, and after the war the rift must have widened. Hank had been one of the mainstays of the ranch during the war years, and Skipper's helpmate, while Bill had been far removed from the scene on duty with the Coast Guard.

Bill chose to opt out of the HF Bar Ranch Corporation and sold his stock, which had been given to him by Skipper, to Hank in 1945. The records show the payment of $20,000 to Bill for two hundred fifty three shares of the HF Bar Ranch stock which was transferred to Hank in October of 1945. Bill was given two thousand dollars in cash and a note for the balance. Also he owed HF Bar Ranch almost four thousand for:

...cash advances, tradesmen's bills, insurance premiums, maids' wages, etc. paid by HF Bar...

This money was deducted from the stock sale transaction amount and in addition, Bill took part of his payment in exchange for fifteen horses worth $2,010 and a John Deere baler valued at $1,000.

Bill took off for parts unknown but returned to the ranch in 1948. By then, because of his drinking, he had joined Alcoholics Anonymous (AA). He worked at the ranch for awhile and that fall bought four hundred two year old steers with Skipper and trailed them from Clearmont to the ranch.

That fall, Bill remarried to Harriet Stuart who was a cousin of Hank's and who must have had considerable resources. She purchased a sizeable ranch for Bill between HF Bar and Buffalo. Today, it is known as the Steerhead Ranch. According to Bob Ross, they stayed there for one year and the next year, 1949, sold out and moved to Arizona where Harriet bought another ranch called the Rosetree. In all of Bill's ranching endeavors, he was heavily involved in the horse business and bought, sold and raised many race horses. He had a reputation as an excellent horseman and a good judge of horseflesh.

Bobby also came back after the war and worked at HF Bar. But, by 1948, Bobby had left the ranch for good and was living in California with his partner with whom he was apparently attempting to start up some sort of inn keeping business. On June 21, 1948, Bobby wrote a letter home. It is one of only two letters from Bobby in any of the ranch records and says something about Bobby and his relationship with his family. He wrote from Los Gatos, California:

Dear Folks:

Have been lousy about writing but can't say that any of you have been as good. However, that is typical. With all the noise over the radio this morning from the GOP convention, I'm wondering if Dad is there. As yet haven't heard Wyoming mentioned but will probably hear one of these hours.

All goes well here but wouldn't go so far as to say that we are making millions as yet. Thanks for sending along the last check for

Saddlestring

$500. I never really realized how fast money can dissipate itself until I started to keep the books for this small place. Our greatest expenses have been met for the year—linens, stocking the commissary, insurance, booklet, etc. Business looked good at the beginning of the month, but we got fouled up by bad weather for two weeks and didn't do as well as expected...

My partner's mother has been here all month and will be here 'til fall I think. His father died recently and she is sort of at loose ends at this point.

The climate here now is just about perfect. Long hot days and cool nights. Is always cool in the shade and no humidity. Should be like this until December or so now. The place is a riot of color with roses, etc., all over the place. The pools are a lot of work to keep up—but are full of clear water and look mighty fine. Have been living off the produce of my garden—lettuce, beets, turnips, artichokes, etc. Here again a lot of work to keep going.

Hope all goes well there and that you have a successful summer. Miss you all and the ranch—but feel I have made a wise move and I'm much happier and feel like a million bucks here. Still trying to figure out a way to finance this place. At this point there are 3 or 4 people who want to help out so it may be that we can incorporate the place.

Give everyone my best regards and do drop me a line one of these days—so I won't feel that I'm too much of a heel and in the doghouse. Love to you both.

Ever, Bob

While all the children were coming and going and having their various encounters with life and its vicissitudes, Skipper and Hank operated HF Bar. Hank assumed more and more of the responsibility. In "The Post Mistress," Ed Morsman wrote that:

...Hank had learned to manage the ranch through on-the-job training. Hank said that Skipper let her make her own mistakes as long as she fixed them, and this approach proved to be a good management training program...

Skipper and Hank even went to dude ranching conventions together. They went to one in Billings, Montana in November of 1943 and the local paper carried this amusing story.

...Loads of hogs that accompanied several dude ranch parties to Billings for their annual convention Friday and Saturday reiterated the streamlining of the dude business in favor of increased food production, which was emphasized throughout the convention program.

Frank O. Horton, former congressman and Republican national committeeman for Wyoming, arrived Friday, chaperoning a shipment of hogs from the HF Bar Ranch at Saddlestring, Wyo. He was accompanied by Mrs. Horton, for 10 years a newspaperwoman in Detroit and Chicago, who, at the beginning of her career, flipped a coin to decide whether journalism or law was to be her profession...

It was just as well that Hank learned to manage the ranch, for sometime in 1946 Skipper got sick. Little is known about his illness other than it must have been long and lingering. As early as November 4, 1946, Skipper's sister, Bertha, referred to his illness in a personal letter:

...we were so sorry to know you had not been so well. I wish you could take more than two weeks vacation...

Saddlestring

In the same period that Skipper's illness appeared he was corresponding with Jack, Sr. Jack must have expressed an interest in coming back to help run the ranch, perhaps because he knew his father was sick. Skipper must have written back to tell Jack that he did not support the idea at that time. Then Jack wrote the following letter on November 16, 1947 from Caracas, Venezuela. Excerpts from the letter explain the HF Bar state of affairs at the time and illustrate the plaintive wish of Jack to return to the ranch. It could have been the last letter Jack wrote to his father:

Dear Dad:

Glad to get your letter of November 5th with your figures on the ranch and your views as to what is best to do about it. It has, needless to say, been the cause of considerable serious thinking on my part. Your figures on the reduced income and the increased expenses of last summer's operations were no great surprise as I had not been overly optimistic over the outcome. If anything, I expected both payroll and food costs to be higher.

We agree, at least, that the situation is bad. I concur one hundred percent. It is definitely bad. But I do not entirely agree with your statement that we are necessarily facing the toughest times we have ever faced. The international crisis is pretty grim and I expect the ranch will stand or fall as does the country. As far as the ranch's immediate financial status is concerned, I think that the record for the past 15 years will show that we were operating on borrowed money by January on most of these years, plus the fact that our indebtedness was a great deal higher than it is today. I do not of course have the figures before me, so check me if I'm wrong. Our interest payments are certainly lower and our credit position much better than our average status quo since 1930. Of course, we cannot continue indefinitely to show a loss and decrease our net surplus year after year. But that is something that you are not going to permanently cure in a single season. The slow building up of our surplus figure, and of course with it the slow reconstruction of the run-down condition of the ranch, may take nearly as long going up as coming down. I am convinced that the ranch has an excellent future and I think that I have the ability to make that future a reality. If I am right in this premise then the time for me to get started is right now as much, or more so, than would be true a year from now. I say more so because a year lost is a year gone. If I am wrong in this premise and I do not have the ability to make a go of the ranch I would rather find out now than wait a year before moving to the ranch, and then finding it out.

Labor costs and food costs especially, as well as increased costs of all kinds, I agree present a traffic problem and I agree that we are going to have to watch our pennies very carefully in all branches of ranch operations and that all unnecessary expenses must be cut out. If I come under the latter classification and am a luxury that the ranch can afford only in good times I had better stay where I am and now is a good time to find it out.

But I don't think that I am.

For one reason, I am conceited enough to think that I can dig up, draw or otherwise find enough new business to bring in several times over my salary in income to the ranch. But I can't do it by arriving the middle of July and leaving the middle of September. That angle is out anyway, because transportation plus State income tax on such a basis would cost me close to $2,000. This drumming up additional business is a year round job. It's a question of keeping in touch with old friends, of maintaining a personal touch with recent guests, of seeking new contacts and new markets. Most of it can be done by correspondence...

Jack continued his discourse and wrote about how there were many wealthy people searching for a good place to spend their holidays and how they should be found and cultivated. He continued:

Saddlestring

...but we haven't touched the possibilities and I have some good connections with the oil and allied industries, through my work. But I haven't time to do much about it from here.

In addition to the usual winter Christmas card and the usual spring letter, I think that a revival of the old Bridle Bits, rejuvenated and with one or two good pictures and a paragraph or two of ranch news and published say in November, March and May would be well worthwhile. But you can't lock up the ranch the middle of September and leave that for Ed Winther to do. You have to be on the ranch and on the job damn near the full year to do and do the right multitude of things, big and little, that add up to the sum total of getting everything out of the year that the ranch has to offer. I am not referring to you personally and I am not attempting to criticize you or Hank in the least particular because I know you have to get away for your health and I know you have done a swell job and have earned the right to take it a little easy. I am just airing my views for what they may be worth...

Aside from the dude business, we shouldn't forget that we are supposed to be an operating stock ranch as well. It may well be that in future years the ranch may depend on income from livestock operations as much as from resort for survival. I realize that most years we don't have feed enough to run many head of stock, in addition to the horses, on the HF. These are the two alternative courses: one, to run a limited number of quality stock—say 25 to 50 head of good registered Herefords, buy good bulls, show at the shows, maybe sell a few bull calves at fancy prices and top the market with your steer calves. The alternative is to be on the lookout when prices are down and the opportunity presents, to pick up some good leases and get into the cattle business on a big scale. I would think a combination of the two would be ideal. Of course all this takes financing and can't be done in a day or maybe a year. Cattle prices are out of sight at present, but buying in at the right time I think year in and year out the ranch would average a good profit on calf crop plus maybe running feeders, or what looked best...

September business may be the profit after July and August have paid the expenses. I would write about September in every letter and talk September all summer and plan to stay open, on a reduced scale of course, during September and as far into October as people would stay. Let it be known that we are there the year around, with a winter proofed steam-heated ranch house and I'll venture it will pay.

Don't think for a minute that I am not aware of the problems, the drawbacks, the difficulties in the way of every idea I have mentioned. I repeat that I firmly believe that they can be overcome and that the ranch has a future as great as the past. But it's a fulltime job and it's a man's job and you've reached the point where you've got to hand part of the load on to someone else because you can no longer carry it all. You can do the planning and the supervising, sure, but you can't be there the year around and you know that the only way you can see that the job gets done is to get out and do half of it yourself.

You ask me in your letter to consider waiting a year before coming back to the ranch, because times are bad. How much better will times be in another year? In some part at least, they will be as much better as we make them so far as the ranch is concerned? Who is going to run the ranch during that year: Bob was not very keen on coming back the last time I talked to him. You won't do yourself much good if you tackle it alone.

Insofar as the actual drain on the finances of the ranch is concerned, I would, as I said at the meeting, draw only what I needed and leave the balance with the ranch. Don't forget that at the time when you were making a salary of $400 that prices were down and that amount won't buy more than $200 in equivalent living today. When I sever relations with Socony I will have enough in bonus, annuity and sale of our furniture etc. here to pay in full my balance with the ranch.

To bring all the above verbosity into the form of a practical recommendation: I hereby propose, as a compromise, that instead of January we plan to come to the ranch in March; to live in Farthest West until the dude season and to move into something smaller during the season so as not to decrease revenue from Farthest West; I to make the salary formerly agreed upon ($400 a month) but to draw only what I need. At the end of one year, or earlier by mutual consent, to call a meeting of the stockholders to decide on future continuance of this arrangement.

So I'll leave the above for your consideration and I'll be looking forward to hearing your views. Otherwise, we are fine and fat. Eleanor joins in best to you and Hank. How's the dairy and chicken ranch? Ever do anything on the fish pond location?

Love, Jack

That was the proposed deal. Jack Horton was ready to leave his position in South America and come home to help his father get the ranch back on its feet.

Skipper's reply to the proposition, if there was one, is not available, but if there was one it was obviously negative for Jack never returned to help operate HF Bar Ranch. It would not be the last time Jack expressed an interest in coming back but it was the last time he made the proposal to Skipper—for Skipper died the next year.

Skipper died in Sheridan, Wyoming, on August 18t, 1948, after a prolonged illness. His death was marked by an editorial in the *Sheridan Press*:

For more than 25 years, Frank O. Horton was active in the public life of Wyoming, serving in the state legislature, as a trustee of the Wyoming Stockgrowers Association, as congressman and as Republican National Committeeman.

In addition, Mr. Horton took a prominent part in community life and in things concerning his colleagues in the livestock and dude ranching business. Throughout these years he devoted his conscientious efforts to the advancement of his state.

Although there were times when everything Mr. Horton said or did were not popular, he tried sincerely to serve to the best of his ability and as his convictions dictated. He did not fear criticism and did not hesitate to say or do what he felt right. His prompt movement to head off a clash between stockman and the dude ranchers at the last state stock growers' convention last spring despite his failing health was evidence of his intellectual courage.

Wyoming is fortunate in having enjoyed the devoted services of such a man as Frank Horton. Hs death is an unfortunate loss.

Two years before he died, Skipper prepared a handwritten will. It was vintage Skipper, for it began:

...If and when I kick in, the following are the things I want done..

Skipper's will is curious. He ordered that his shares in HF Bar Ranch, of which he only owned twenty-two, be equally divided between Hank and Bobby. He also left a small five acre Arizona holding to Bobby as well as half of his furniture, guns, fishing tackle and other sporting equipment. The other half he left to Hank as well as his government bond and other securities.

What is curious is that Skipper expressly explained why he did not include his other two sons in the will:

...I am not leaving anything to my sons William S. Horton and Jack O. Horton because they are no longer associated with the ranch and because long ago I gave each of them a big percentage of my stock in the HF Bar Ranch...

Actually, Skipper had left each son an equal number of shares. I suppose that in 1946, when the will was prepared, the fact that Bobby was the only son still around made the difference.

Agricultural Pursuits

In 1942, HF Bar only ran about 300 head of mixed cattle which consisted mostly of yearling steers including a number of Mexican steers. There is no evidence that Skipper had any kind of breeding program in operation. If he did, it had to be on a very limited scale. In addition to the primarily steer operation the ranch did maintain the Holstein dairy herd but the number of animals involved is unknown.

The sheep operation was diminished as well. By all accounts there were not more than three or four hundred sheep on HF Bar Ranch in 1942.

In 1942 Skipper recorded plowing and planting of wheat, barley, oats and alfalfa but gave no production numbers. Crop production was only sufficient to support the needs of HF Bar Ranch.

Even though agricultural production was not anything like earlier years, the ranch was still productive. Skipper heralded the production in an article he placed in the 1944 spring edition of the ranch newspaper, *Cactus Scratches*:

HF PRODUCTION AT PEAK LEVEL

Every department on the ranch is just bustin' itself in the effort to produce more. Six hundred head of fine white faced cattle are kicking up their heels at the first signs of green grass. (Note: I assume the cattle were steers and not cows. Rather than raise calves, the ranch was by this time into the practice of buying yearling steers, feeding them hay all winter and grazing them in the summer and selling them as two year olds in the fall. This practice would continue into the 1970s.) *A good many of them will be kept at HF Bar all summer and the rest will be sent to Paradise.*

Most of the plowing is done and the grain is being put in.

Carl's vegetable garden is still in the hot bed stage but it promises to be a dandy.

There's a regular stork derby in progress among the livestock. The hogs, naturally prolific, are always a safe bet to win this but we can't say the sheep haven't tried and so far have turned out a 120% crop.

Fifteen hundred baby chicks recently moved into the brooder houses and the older hens are dutifully turning out 30 dozen eggs a day. A few Holstein calves have already made their appearance and there will be twenty or more of them within a month.

The palomino stallion, "Golddigger" becomes a proud papa every few days and a good many of his colts bear a strong resemblance to him.

In the same issue of the ranch newspaper, Skipper also made mention of new additions to the ranch dude horse herd:

ARMY PONIES MUSTERED OUT

Several hundred fine young horses have been released by the Army for service on the home front. At a recent sale at the Remount Station at Ft. Robinson, Nebraska, we bought a carload of well broken ponies particularly well suited to our needs. We've sold our HF Bar raised colts to the Army for many years so we know something of their standards and we feel we've made a real addition to the saddle horse cavvy.

The minute the newcomers stepped into our corral they were christened with appropriate new names—military ones, of course— Corporal, Sergeant, Captain, Major, Pistol, Musket, Bayonet, Reveille, Brass Hat, Bombardier, etc.

Ranch Operations

During the 1940s, particularly the war years, not many improvements were made to the ranch. Basically, it was a struggle to maintain what already existed. But Skipper put a good face on it when he discussed the subject in another article he put in the 1944 spring edition of *Cactus Scratche*

ALL SET FOR COMING SEASON

Plans for the coming season are pretty well set up. We've lined up what looks like a competent staff. (Note: Many of the Ranch mainstay employees were still away at war.) *We're sure we can still give you plenty to eat, a good bed to sleep in, a horse to ride, a stream to fish in, plenty of scenery and plenty of fun. A few of the pre-war frills may be missing but the essentials of a really restful, healthful, and thoroughly enjoyable vacation remain intact.*

It's tough not to be able to make a sensational announcement about some splendid, shiny new addition to the ranch. For years we tried to improve the place each season—a new tennis court, a fish rearing pond, a new building or two or an old one remodeled. In these times the materials and labor can be put to much better use elsewhere, in the war effort, so we content ourselves with such slight improvements as can be made with a few cans of paint, and a hammer. About the only new equipment we can boast of is an old but well preserved buggy which we expect to see burning up the HF Bar boulevards after a few minor repairs.

There will also be a new croquet set (unless the mail order catalog is kidding us). The croquet ground has been the hottest spot on the ranch for the past couple of seasons. Many a fierce feud has had its inception there. By the end of last summer it was obvious that the contestants were badly in need of new weapons. We're doing our best to supply them.

HF Bar stayed open during the war but it was not easy. The HF Bar Board meeting minutes of April, 1943, reflect the general situation and concern.

...The president indicated that a great many ranches were being sold at this time and suggested it might be wise to dispose of some of the holdings of the HF Bar Ranch. The president pointed out that the war had greatly handicapped the resort business and that we should either sell part of our property or run many more cattle than we had been running. After a thorough discussion the president was advised by the stockholders to use his best judgment in either buying more cattle or selling part of the ranch..

At the December meeting in the same year, the minutes reflected:

...The president stated that 1943 had not been a good dude year largely because of the difficulty of transportation. He also stated that while the ranch owned a large number of cattle that only a few had been sold, hence that the ranch income was considerably reduced. He also pointed out that since the dude business had been greatly reduced it had been necessary to temporarily change our business to stock cattle in order to carry on at all. He further pointed out that 1944 would show a large income from the sale of cattle and that all indications pointed for a better dude year for 1944...

Even though it was tough going during the war HF Bar still received good notices in the Chicago area. In one of the war years, the following article was published in the *Chicago Tribune* Society Column:

...The tire shortage doesn't mean a thing to the more than 200 saddle and pack horses at the HF Bar Ranch in Saddlestring, Wyo. devotees of the ranch have been told. The horses have been fitted out with sets of puncture proof shoes and are full of high test oats and rarin' to go, the ranch announces. Among the early arrivals at the resort are Countess Ruggero Visconti Di Mondrone and her young son, John, who will spend the summer there...

Many dude ranches in the area closed their doors for the duration including Paradise which was used for no more than a picnic spot for HF Bar guests. Two other ranches that closed down were Tepee Ranch and the Pass Creek Ranch.

Marian Fordyce, in her 1945 letter to Phyllis Jones, provided an interesting commentary on the local dude ranch situation and gave Phyllis the lowdown on some of their mutual acquaintances in the dude ranch business and her own personal situation:

...We have not opened Tepee for three years now. Allen has been so involved here with registered and range cattle, registered and range sheep, hogs and horses not to mention the endless farming that we felt we could not do a decent job at Tepee and here (Note: The Bar 13 ranch in Big Horn.) We plan on opening next summer and it will be fun in many ways but a headache in others. All the things that we have been unable to buy for this place we have just moved down from there and it will take months, I am sure, to find them all again. We have missed the mountains sadly and all our good friends that used to come out....The Jacques ranch has been closed for about four years so there are not too many dude ranches going in this section these days. Eatons has had a very full summer. They are nice as always. We were over there not long ago. Patty was feeling miserable and is tired out but full of fun. Bill is as large as ever and still playing dirty tricks on me. Last summer I stayed there for three

weeks. *I had been ill and went for a rest, but the three weeks could hardly be described as restful as it was steady parties all the time. However, I had a wonderful time and no responsibility and came away feeling years younger...*

Wartime changed things a lot but sometimes brought about humorous situations. One relates to Hank's wartime duty and it is best described by Ed Morsman:

...Undoubtedly, because of her natural leadership qualities, Hank was...also appointed the air raid warden for Sheridan, Wyoming, during World War II. I think Hank accepted because she was given a droll hat to wear and an armband. The duties of an air raid warden were not particularly onerous because even the most ardent booster of Sheridan could not have put the little town high on the enemy's priority list.

In case of enemy attack, the plan approved by the appropriate civil defense authorities was for the citizenry to jump into their cars, race up the Red Grade, and disburse into the forest. Unfortunately, cars and gasoline were in short supply owing to rationing. More important, the Red Grade, aptly named for the color of the dirt and gravel, was, and is, a narrow, rough road that climbs in tortuous hairpin curves up the foothills into the Big Horn Mountains. Frequent turnouts provided spring water for overheated radiators.

Knowing that if bombs ever fell, the citizenry would be far safer in their beds than converging en masse on the Red Grade, Hank performed her duties as an air raid warden but kept the master plan to herself and a few friends with a good sense of humor. She did enjoy the hat...

People

Beginning in 1942, the war began to take its toll on the HF Bar work force. Bob Ross remembers that well. It was the first year he worked at HF Bar. Skipper approached Bob and allowed that as Bob had been coming there for many years as a dude and knew his away around then he might as well work in the corral. So Bob and a man named Alvin "Hawk" Schaffer became the corral crew. Bob and Hawk took turns being the corral boss because the boss got to rope the horses.

The next year, Bob would be called to service as well. Skipper used *Cactus Scratches* to pay tribute to all the ranch employees that had gone off to war. In 1944, he wrote:

HF BAR RANCH SERVICE FLAG

We're mighty proud of our representation in the armed forces and we're betting on the boys to make it pretty tough for the Japs and the Jerries whenever they get a crack at 'em...

The Navy is keeping Lt. (jg) Al Hook busy in San Francisco, doling out payrolls (that's one item of government expenditures we feel we don't have to worry about).

Dean Thomas served a year in the ski troops, where he spent most of this time praying for a Chinook. (Note: Bob Platt noted that Dean was assigned to the ski troops only because he was from Wyoming. By Dean's own account he did not ski well and never really skied in the ski troops.) *Now he's a sergeant and with a horse and mule pack outfit. Item for the small world department: he rides a horse that carries an HF Bar brand, one of the many raised on the ranch which have been sold to the Army.*

Jerry Morris—remember Bud and Norma's "little Jerry"—

recently received his commission in the Air Corps and was one of the top twenty selected for further training as a B24 bomber pilot.

Tommy Barker was stationed in Alaska for several months and back in the neighborhood for a brief furlough before being shipped off again. Johnny Scott, Elmer Gibbany, Buck Metcalfe and Bob Ross are some of the others in Army uniform. Bob, incidentally, is keeping in shape to step back in the HF Bar corral after the war. Almost as soon as he had gotten located "somewhere in Australia" he wrote home for his jeans and his spurs and announced that he had bought himself a horse.

Billy (Annabelle) Cook is a Wave. The navy also has Gene Keuny and Garner Trusty. The latter paid a brief visit to Buffalo recently, flying back from the Far East by the China Clipper.

We have been able to keep track of the ones mentioned here because they come from this neck of the woods, but there are a good many others too—all those hashers for instance. We hope they are as tough on the enemy as they were on the HF Bar crockery.

Not many details are known about the war service of the HF Bar employees but some of the exploits of Dean Thomas and his eventual service with the 10th Mountain Division were captured by Ed Morsman. Ed wrote:

...In its infinite wisdom, the army assumed that everyone who was drafted in Sheridan and Johnson County would know how to pack animals.

Consequently, Dean and his friends were sent to an army packing school where they had to unlearn everything they already knew and begin packing mules the Army way.

In later years, Dean exhibited a great deal of respect, and even fondness, for mules, which was strange as familiarity in the army often produces the opposite effect.

Apparently, the army did not think that the Germans could be defeated with only mule packing aptitudes, so the Sheridan inductees were sent to Colorado to learn winter survival skills. In fur-lined chaps, caps, and overcoats, Wyoming cowboys have survived winters quite adequately for over a century. In army-issued winter gear, the inductees almost froze to death.

By all accounts, the worst part of the training was learning how to ski. Although Dean was well coordinated and athletic, try as I will, I cannot imagine this bow-legged cowboy swishing down a ski slope. Apparently, most recruits were somewhat skeptical of their ability to learn this art, and perhaps it was this defeatist attitude that caused such a disaster.

Army ski equipment was little better than boards strapped to boots, and the accompanying instruction was neither subtle nor elucidating. Dean described a line of freezing recruits at the top of a hill being told to descend when the signal was given. Most launched themselves unquestioningly at the appropriate time, and the recalcitrant, and perhaps rational, ones were pushed.

The smart ones fell down before they reached bone shattering speeds. Because the bindings were little more than straps, it was virtually impossible to maneuver, so many soldiers just crashed into each other. Anyone who got beyond the initial mayhem could only pray that he was heading in a direction without obstacles. As the injuries mounted, the army concluded that the cowboys had been converted to maximum readiness, and they were shipped overseas.

Dean did relate some of his experiences to me as well. He said that some of the recruits were from the east and were adept at skiing. Dean called them "slope dopes."

1946 corral crew.
Back row, from left: Dean Thomas, Bob Christian, Louise Evans, Bob Ross and Bill Hackert. Front row, from left, "Tex" Ewing, Bob Gearhart, and Bill (last name unknown). Missing is Jack Buckingham.
(Courtesy of the author)

While the boys were away at war, Barney got married at age fifty to Ione Williams. They were married in Hardin, Montana in 1942. Ione described those days in her article, *I Married A Cowboy:*

...As you can see I was far from young and he was ten years older than I. He was Scotch and Irish. He had a perfect pair of bowlegs. His language was salty.

But he was honest, upright and thrifty. He had common sense and, except when riled, instinctive good manners.

He was suspicious of my background and I suppose he thought I couldn't do anything but read books and sew a fine seam. And he was sure I couldn't ride very well. He and his friends could see that plainly.

But we were married and Barney, for that's my cowpoke's name, first set me down in town to sew my fine seams and, in due time, to bear our baby.

The baby died.

I was lonely and heartbroken, and it was then I decided that, tenderfoot though I might be, I was going to take to the sagebrush and live with the man I had married.

This particular sagebrush was on a dirt road more than 20 miles from a post office. It grew on a ranch that was in no respect modern. For years the ranch had been a bachelor outfit and a sheep ranch at that and everything was dirty and run down. But it was bigger than the county I had grown up in.

Barney was the ranch foreman, but there was no use on the ranch for a useless woman, even though the woman was the foreman's wife. If I was to be there at all, I had to be the ranch cook.

I took along a cookbook, a wedding present. I thought: I can read very well; therefore, I can learn to cook very well.

My cooking improved quickly; my horsemanship never. Overnight, I was ranch veterinarian, nursing sick baby lambs, calves and colts, kittens, pups and chickens.

I made friends with everybody. Barney and the ranch cowboys taught me that the code of the West was one of friendliness and hospitality. They taught me their horsey lingo and they showed me a lot about treating sick animals and sick men. And they didn't forget to teach me to cook—their way...

Ione's article further describes her life with Barney and her impression of him and others of his ilk. She ends the article by stating:

...It may seem strange, but after many years of being married to a cowboy, I like the species, eccentricities and all, and I'll be honest enough to admit that I've been told my cowboy is zanier than most...

I do not know which ranch Ione described in her article but I assume it was somewhere in the area where the Montana and Wyoming borders join near the Crow Indian reservation. Nor do I know how long they were there. At some point in the late 1940s or early 1950s Barney and Ione moved to Sheridan where Ione was to become the librarian at Sheridan College and Barney returned to summer work at HF Bar where he helped in the corral. In the wintertime, Barney helped move livestock at the local sales barn. When he wasn't doing that he hung out at the Ritz Pool Hall in downtown Sheridan.

When the war was over, many of the boys came back and resumed their former lives. Bob Ross was one of them. When he was discharged he returned to live in Buffalo with his mother, Helen. He worked in the corral at HF Bar in the summer and during the winter he played drums with local bands. Bob maintained this routine for many years.

Dean returned after the war as well My first memory of Dean is when I was five years old at the end of the war. My family lived in Sheridan, but toward the end of the war my father was drafted and my mother, sister and I went to California to live with my grandparents.

One day my mother was giving me a bath when she happened to look out the window and exclaimed, "You'd better hurry up and get out because here comes your uncle Dean." I looked out of the window and saw this figure in uniform with a duffle bag slung over his shoulder striding up to the house. I didn't have time to get out of the bath and dried. Dean burst into the house and grabbed me, dripping wet, out of the tub and gave me a big hug.

After that, I saw Dean only periodically, usually once a year, when he would come by wherever we were living. Following the war he picked up the pattern he established before the war. He worked at HF Bar in the summers and then went to warmer climes for the winter. Before the war he worked in California in the winter, but in post war times he worked in Arizona mostly at the Silver Bell Ranch near Tucson. One winter he ran a riding stable in Palm Springs. I remember going to visit him there and riding a pony around a ring. Dean would continue his annual north-south work pattern up until the mid 1950s. It was interrupted one year when he became the owner of a ranch in Arizona. The same woman that sent him to art school bought him a ranch. Dean ran some cows there and spent one year on the place but sold out after one year because he said, according to Bob Ross, "it was just too damn lonely down there." The woman who bought the ranch for him let him keep the money from the sale of the ranch.

It was on his way, to or from each place that he would stop and see his family. Whenever he did come and visit, it was always a treat. He always had his horse with him and hauled it in a one-horse trailer. On the front of the trailer, he had painted the phrase *Rancho No Tengo*, which in Spanish meant, "I don't have a ranch." While he may have had several trailers over the years, each one carried

that inscription.

Dean's arrival was always an event in the neighborhood. First, this cowboy would arrive and he cut a pretty dashing figure. Then, he would unload his horse and let it graze on the lawn. When Dean was in town, I definitely had bragging rights and got a lot of attention from the neighborhood kids.

The history of dude ranching in Wyoming is replete with a legion of romances between dude girls and cowboys—it is a natural phenomena. Some of the romances lasted only until the girls left; but many resulted in marriage. The lineage of many families in Wyoming today includes a dude ranch romance. The subject is worthy of a book in itself.

HF Bar Ranch was no different. I asked one descendant of an HF Bar romance to provide me with information about his family's dude ranch romance. Thomas L. "Tee" Barker wrote an account which is quoted here in its entirety because it sheds such an interesting light on how these things could come about:

Margie (Brown), 19 years old and her father drove to Ethete, Wyoming from New York City about 1937. Barrett Tyler, Margie's uncle, was a pastor at the mission where they visited for a few weeks and then they stopped at Horton's on their way back. Margie returned as a guest with her sister Joan in 1939 or 1940 and at the end of her visit became acquainted with Tommy Barker who was a dude wrangler.

On March 3, 2005, Joan (Brown) Aitkin still had vivid memories of several circumstances. She was about 14 years old when she and Margie were at HF Bar and too young to date glamorous cowboys. But she knew Connie Thurlow who, along with the other girls, thought Dean Thomas "quite dashing" and although Connie had dated Lex Barker she was quite taken with Dean. One evening Connie convinced Joan to sleep in her bed and when Dean appeared sometime during the night and recognized Joan, it was quite horrifying for both. Connie later married Lex Barker. Joan remembered Hank, Skipper, Bill and Bob Horton and Bob Ross who at 15 was already an accomplished drummer.

Margie had been seeing a guy named Jerry that summer but during the final few days met Tom and became very disappointed that it was time for Joan and her to return to New York. Margie was "cross" the entire drive back, not stopping when Joan needed a restroom. Margie would say "We are getting home as fast as possible and we are not stopping."

Margie was hired as secretary/bookkeeper the following summer and dated Tom with plans to marry. Tom entered the Army in late 1941 and they were married on July 11, 1942, at Fort Sill, Oklahoma with Freckles Brown as best man and Don Bard and perhaps Ed Adler as witnesses. Freckles Brown rode bulls professionally for several years after the war.

Margie had married a man with an interesting history. He was born on November 8, 1915, and went to first grade at the Ohlman School about five miles south of the Montana border. His father, Arthur Jarrett Barker, grew up in Kentucky, moved to Illinois where he married and then arrived in Wyoming in 1903. Mr. Barker began acquiring homesteads near Parkman, Wyoming, and by 1920 he had accumulated several thousand acres, including large amounts of irrigated land. He raised grain, well bred horses, cattle, and hay and was a respected community leader, serving on the local school board. The Barker house was one of the first to have indoor plumbing.

Wealthia Layton, a long time Sheridan resident, recalled that the Barker barn dances were popular events in the Ranchester and Dayton area. Guests would often stay for several days.

The combination of grasshoppers and a precipitous drop in

agricultural prices after World War I caused Mr. Barker to go bankrupt, losing the ranch to a bank in 1922. He was able to keep a saddle horse, a two horse team, and a wagon on which he constructed roof and walls. He packed cooking utensils, food and clothes for the 150 mile trip to Acton, Montana, north of Billings. Eight children, including seven year old Tommy, walked and rode for several days until they arrived at a small parcel of land that Mr. Barker rented. Arthur Barker died about a year later in Billings, leaving Pearl on the family farm. She and Ted, one of the older sons, moved the family to another rented place near Luther, Montana.

Rudy Frankovic grew up in the area and remembered Mrs. Barker struggling to support the family the only way known, by raising pigs, chickens, one or more milk cows and a garden. After graduating from the eighth grade, Tommy left to make his own living. He returned to Wyoming and worked for Sandy Jacques at the Pass Creek Ranch for several years. He then joined Dean Thomas as a wrangler at Hortons.

Like Dean and the rest of the corral crew, Tommy went to war. His combat unit went to Kiska, Alaska, expecting fierce Japanese resistance, to find that the intelligence was faulty. The Japanese produced the misleading information as a diversion and had never planned to invade the USA across the Bering Strait.

Tommy then received glider training and landed in France during the Normandy Invasion. The Germans anticipated that gliders might try to land at that particular location and flooded the field causing Tommy's glider to spin out of control in the mud and hit a tree. He had been shot in the leg during the descent and was knocked unconscious by the impact. The wounded were placed in a barn where Tommy's watch and other personal items were taken before he regained consciousness. After several months in London recovering from his wounds, he rejoined the 10th Mountain Division *for the invasion of Italy. He traveled with the mule pack from the southern tip well into central Italy. Red Rideout told me that the mules would start early every day before the tanks and trucks left camp and arrive last every night. Tommy recalled one night when the mules had just arrived at camp when the order was given to move on because the Italian Army was approaching. So the very tired U.S. Army reloaded the mules and moved through the night.*

While Tommy was away, his son, Thomas L. Barker, was born on July 12, 1943, in New York City where Margie lived with her parents until Tommy's discharge in 1945

Tommy and Marge worked for Wales Wolf on his Rotten Grass Creek Ranch from 1945 to 1947. Their house was a few miles from Bill and Jane Yellowtail's ranch and the three of us (Note: Tommy, Margie and young Tom.) *would travel by horse and sleigh in the winter for overnight stays. On one trip the two horse team suddenly began stumbling in the deep snow. Tom got off the sleigh and discovered that the horses had walked into a row of feed bunks.*

After a relatively pampered childhood with nannies and other helpers around the house, and membership in the prestigious New York City Social Register, Margie quickly found herself cooking for a husband, a three year old child, and unpredictable numbers of Indians who were constantly dropping by. Her house lacked running water and was many miles on a dirt road from Wyola, the nearest town.

Margie stayed by herself at the Historic Sheridan Inn for about two months before having Helen on September 1, 1946.

Margie and Tom purchased the Bydler place (Note: Between the HF Bar Ranch and Buffalo, Wyoming.) *for $20,000 in 1947. There was a large barn and garage, which are still in use, and a small home on the 400 acre property. The home remains as it was remodeled in the 1950s. Tommy Barker had a mild heart attack in 1965 and passed away on January 1, 1969. Margie still lives on the ranch...*

(Note: Very soon after Thomas L. "Tee" Barker provided me the above information about his family he met a tragic and untimely death at aged sixty-two. He is missed.)

Many families began long term associations with the HF Bar Ranch in the late 1930s and early 1940s. One of them was the Jones family.

The Jones family, which consisted of Hoyle "Buck" Jones and his wife, Phyllis, came to Wyoming country in about 1934 when Hoyle Jones, Senior, purchased the Red Rim Ranch for his son and daughter-in-law in about 1936. The origin of the Red Rim Ranch is unknown, but it was listed as an operating dude ranch as early as 1927. The ranch was thirty miles west of Wyola, Montana and at the head of Rotten Grass Creek and along the foot of the Big Horns.

In the late 1930s, Buck and Phyllis were invited, along with the owners of other dude ranches in the area, to the HF Bar Ranch to get acquainted. Thus began a long association between the Jones family and HF Bar which continues to this day.

The Jones family and various members of the Jack Horton family, mainly Jack, Trudy and Jody, even spent some time together in Arizona in the wintertime. The Jones' first son, Hoyle Clay "Bronco" Jones was born in Sheridan in 1938, coincidentally in the same year and same hospital as Jack Horton, Jr. They were even delivered by the same doctor—Doctor Crane.

The Joneses had a second son, Phillip, who was born in Arizona in 1942. Six months after his birth, Phyllis and Buck divorced in 1943 and Phyllis and the boys returned to her home in Tulsa, Oklahoma. However, Phyllis visited the ranch as a guest and worked in the ranch store for two summers in the late 1940s.

Today, Phyllis is ninety-six years old but still remembers those days. She remembers one thing about Skipper: According to her son Phillip, she told him that Skipper had a reputation for a fierce temper and most people tried to steer clear of him. Phyllis, however, got along with him fine.

Phyllis was working in the store the summer that her future husband from Tulsa, Hugh Long, visited the ranch to see Phyllis, and they were married in 1949.   Phyllis and Hugh would have two daughters, Elsa and Margaret (Margie).   Various members of the family frequent HF up to the present day as guests and employees. As the reader will find later, Bronco worked at HF Bar as a hasher and wrangler and Phillip (who changed his name to Phillip Long when he was twenty-one years old) worked several years as a hasher. Three of the children, Charlotte, Elliot and Elisha, have worked at the HF Bar Ranch for the last five years. Today, they are regulars every summer and definitely a major part of the extended HF Bar family.

Another family that would become very close to the HF Bar Ranch was the Taylor family from Kirby, Montana. Shirley Hopkins had been a guest at HF Bar Ranch as a teenager from Lake Forest, Illinois in the mid-1930s . She loved the ranch but would not return until 1948 after Skipper died. Then she would return not as a guest, but as a neighbor.

Shirley married Walter J. Taylor in 1944. Walt was born in New York City and attended Yale University but his education was interrupted by World War II when he enlisted and served in the U. S. Navy in the Atlantic and Pacific theaters. Walt was discharged as a first lieutenant in 1945, but a year earlier married Shirley in Lake Forest.

Walter worked for Standard Oil of New York for a time but wanted to move west. He and Shirley found a ranch in 1948 near Kirby, Montana, and settled down there to raise their family which, in the end, consisted of four children; James, Walter "Watty," Susanna and Margie all of whom would be raised on the ranch, the W Lazy T.

When the Taylors moved in, Shirley really didn't know anyone, so she visited HF Bar Ranch and met Hank. That was the beginning of a lifelong friendship between Hank and the Taylors. Hank and Shirley played bridge together and even, at one point, shared an apartment in Sheridan which both ranches used as a base whenever they were in town. In later years, the Taylors would visit HF Bar often and used it as a place to celebrate birthdays and anniversaries. Their daughter, Susanna, even chose HF Bar over New York as the venue for her debut.

It was in the early 1950s that Harry Huson reappeared on the HF Bar scene after an absence of many years. His family had lived in Clearmont for about eight years from 1943 so his son Russell could finish school and then they moved to Buffalo, Wyoming. Harry's wife, Mae, went to work for the county agent, and Harry worked at HF Bar. He performed a variety of jobs, like irrigating, but also took dudes on pack trips in the mountains he knew so well.

Ed Morsman was a very young man, but he remembers going to the mountains with his uncle Truman and Harry. Truman and Harry got along famously and reveled in finding forgotten trails and blazing new ones. Ed remembers that his uncle Truman was always fearful that Harry would keel over because he seemed so old. (Note: Harry would have been seventy two years old in 1951.) Harry was far from feeble at that age. In fact, his son Harry, recalls his father taking him on a strenuous elk hunting trip in the Big Horn Mountains when he was seventy nine years old!

But, Harry didn't die in the mountains. Rather, he died indirectly from smoking. Harry always lit his pipe with a farmer's match.   One day, he lit his pipe and discarded the match, but somehow it ended up in his boot. He had on a pair of nylon socks which caught on fire and Harry's foot was burned so badly that he had to be hospitalized. Harry wasn't one to abide by hospital rules, like calling for a nurse when he needed assistance, for instance. So, when Harry had to go to the bathroom he got up himself but fell and broke his hip. That was a setback for Harry and he began to decline. Harry died of natural causes in 1966 at the ripe old age of eighty-six.

End of an Era

Skipper was at the helm of HF Bar Ranch for thirty-seven years—a remarkable era which closed when he died on August 17, 1948.

It was only happenstance that he and his brother-in-law Warren discovered the future site of HF Bar Ranch when they rolled off Stone Mountain that day long ago in 1910; and it was surely fate that caused the death of William Robbins so that his widow had to sell out to Skipper and Warren.

But it wasn't happenstance that for twenty years Skipper, with help from his brother-in-law Warren, developed HF Bar in the way that he did. Skipper was ambitious and had big ideas. He was bold in his vision and relentless in the pursuit of that vision. He was successful.

Skipper was also a survivor. He endured repeated financial crises and coped with all the vicissitudes of Mother Nature and the ranching business. He came out on top and kept the ranch alive.

Skipper was a family man, too. But the family eventually was torn apart by circumstances: Skipper's strong personality and unwavering convictions; his remarriage to Hank which changed the family dynamics and altered the equation forever; the lifestyles, interests and personalities of his sons and their wives, and the reality that either the ranch was too small for the family, or the family was too big for the ranch, caused the family to be something other than close knit. But, as he demonstrated repeatedly, Skipper was usually willing to help when needed.

Skipper was also a promoter. Prone to exaggeration if it served the purpose to promote HF Bar Ranch or himself as a public figure, he could even engage in deception.

As a person he was interesting. Bob Ross said of Skipper that he was:

...a likeable guy...didn't take crap from anyone...big bluffer...good con man...could talk anybody into doing anything...

Skipper was not above exploiting the guests. Jim Niner, of Big Horn, Wyoming, who worked at HF Bar Ranch for a time, remembers Dean telling him how Skipper could get double duty from the cabins at HF. Skipper would send HF Bar guests up to stay at Paradise Ranch for an "adventure" for a few days. Of course, there was a fee for this "adventure." While they were off having fun, Skipper put their things in temporary storage and rented their cabin out to other guests. Apparently, they never knew the difference and Skipper was able to collect double rent on a cabin.

Skipper would also, according to Bob Ross, get up at lunch in the dining room and absolutely lay down the law to the guests about ranch rules. Typical rules were that there would be no alcohol in the dining room and absolutely no smoking on horseback. Period.

In spite of his autocratic nature, maybe because of it, Skipper gained a great measure of respect through his bent toward public service and participation in local, state and national politics. Skipper was a problem solver and a man with which to be reckoned. He was respected for that.

Skipper was also somewhat of a mystery. I suspect he was one of those people that you never knew what he was thinking or what he might do next. Skipper's unpredictability, coupled with his temper, most likely caused people to keep him at arm's length. If you were close to Skipper, it was probably best to stay on his good side.

In the end, Skipper and the HF Bar Ranch had seen some halcyon days and some bitter ones, as well. He must have been justly proud of his accomplishments. One cannot help but wonder,

though, if he did not regret that he could not keep his immediate family more involved in his legacy. Regardless, Skipper left his mark in the world and a legacy that exists today—the HF Bar Ranch.

Hank was left to carry on.

Part III

A Thirty-Two Year Continuance
1949-1981

Chapter 8

The Horton Family

The Horton Boys

After Skipper died, Jack, who was still in Venezuela, expressed his interest in the ranch to Hank, much as he had done with Skipper. He was always eager for information and harbored ambitions to return in some capacity. Unlike his brothers, Jack wrote Hank frequently and asked all manner of questions about the ranch operation. And Hank must have asked Jack's opinion about certain matters. In December of 1950, Jack wrote Hank from Venezuela in answer to one of her letters:

...I meant to answer your letter of some time back, regarding the Milo Buckingham cows. Actually, it is hard for me to voice an opinion from down here; not knowing your plans for winter help or

your hay and feed situation. I am of course in favor of anything that will bring in extra income for the ranch, other considerations being equal...

To express his long-standing desire to be a part of HF Bar Ranch, other than just a minority stockholder, Jack wrote further:

...It occurs to me as being within the realms of possibility that sometime you might care to get married again and, if so, that you might not want to be tied down to the ranch all or even part time. If so, I just want you to know that, with advance notice, I can always arrange to terminate with the company here. I have a good job here and am gradually getting ahead, but the tropics do not compare to Wyoming. Within another year, it will not be possible for either of the kids to be with us here, due to the school situation.

Hank did not open the door to his return. It was not to be. But Jack's interest in the ranch continued. In fact, just a few months later he wrote Hank another letter to thank her for some Christmas presents and to inquire about the ranch:

...Am anxious to see your statement of last year's operations, when ready. About hay baling vs. hay stacking, I would think that the main factor will be the man-power situation. If ranch help is going to be as hard to get as during the war, a one-man baler would certainly have an advantage over a four-man stacking crew. What did you do with the Milo Buckingham cows? ...

As has been mentioned earlier, Jack and Eleanor and the children, Jack and Trudy, were all together in Venezuela for the latter part of the 1940s. Trudy stayed in Wyoming during the winter of 1951-1952 because she required extensive dental work. It was then that Trudy's maternal grandparents, the Jahns, invited her to spend

Trudy and Jack Horton Jr. with their stepmother Eleanor.
Location and date uncertain, but it may have been in California in 1950
when Jack Horton Sr. attended graduate school at Stanford University.
(Courtesy of the HF Bar Ranch)

Jack, Jr. and Trudy Horton
at various stages of their lives at the HF Bar Ranch.
(Courtesy of the HF Bar Ranch)

Christmas with them in Milwaukee. They apparently made the request through Hank, who then asked Jack. It didn't sit too well with him, for he replied to Hank:

> ...Margaret has written of Trudy's invitation to go to Milwaukee for Christmas and of your kind offer to take or send her there. Thanks for your offer, but we don't want Trudy to go this time. Maybe later—next summer or such—it might be possible. Actually, they should not have bothered you with this at all, but should have communicated with us...

Something of the family life was also revealed in a May, 1951, letter Jack wrote to an old friend, Mr. Warren Perry of New York, whom he hadn't seen for some time:

> ...I'm married again. Jody died in 1943 and I remarried in 1945 and have my family down here with me with the exception of Trudy, now 12, who had to stay in Wyoming for orthodontic treatment this year. We all were in California last year, for nine months. The company sent me back to school (Stanford), for a year's graduate work. Jack, Jr., now 13, is with us in Venezuela. We will have a States vacation coming up next summer, 1952, and would sure enjoy seeing you at the HF Bar for a Willow Park trip...

In fact, in 1952 Jack and Eleanor returned to the United States permanently. Jack gained employment with the Wood Company which dealt in oil and gas leases and had an office in Sheridan. Jack and Eleanor bought a house which they lived in with Jack, Jr. and Trudy who were enrolled in Sheridan High School. In 1954, Jack received a job offer to be the general manager of Vitro Minerals Corporation. He accepted and the family moved to Salt Lake City, Utah. He worked for the company for a few years and then established a geological consulting business.

Jack and Eleanor were living in Salt Lake City when Eleanor suddenly took ill and died within a few days on September 11, 1962.

A few years later Jack would meet Margaret (Maggie) Keyser of Salt Lake City. Maggie was born in Salt Lake City and was the daughter of Paul Keyser, a wealthy real estate developer. Jack and Maggie fell in love and married in San Francisco in about 1966. Jack's daughter and other family members were present.

According to Maggie's daughter, Leila Javitch, her mother had been married before, but:

...her happiest marriage was certainly with Jack. He was a great guy...wonderful wry sense of humor...

Jack, at that time, worked for City Services as a geologist and his work took him and Maggie to Santa Fe, New Mexico, and Cuernavaca, Mexico as well as Salt Lake.

According to Leila Javitch, Jack developed lung cancer sometime in the late 1960s and was operated on. He seemed to recover and worked for a few more years. Jack and Maggie were in Argentina for some time and while there Jack suffered severe headaches. They returned to Salt Lake for medical consultations and Jack was diagnosed with brain cancer. Jack underwent a course of treatment and Leila Javitch remembers that:

...Jack was very stoic and dignified during his last months. My mother was able to take care of him up to a week before he died...

Jack died on June 26, 1973 at age sixty-one.

Leila has fond memories of her mother, Jack and HF Bar Ranch. She wrote that:

...I didn't really live with them after their marriage although I did visit a couple of times a year, and we had some wonderful trips to the ranch. I am sure you have heard the story about the friends designing the crazy cabins on napkins one drunken evening...I also remember wonderful horse trips...earlier where we would ride out; Jack would catch fish, my mom would shed her clothes and jump in whatever creek or body of water was there, and then we would have a delicious lunch, the fish being cooked by Jack in a coffee can.

About her mother, Leila said:

...My mother by the time she married Jack had stopped drinking completely...so I think that aspect of the ranch did not appeal to her, although she was always very tolerant of others' habits. She had great charm and good humor herself...She remained devoted to Mike and Pam and Anne and Will, Ezra and Sophie (Note: Mike and Pam's children). *She died of cancer in the mid 1990s at age 77...*

After her mother died, both Jack and Maggie's ashes were scattered in Red Canyon on the ranch. Leila recounts that:

...We all made a trip up there on horseback to do that and it was a very moving experience for me. Annie Dixon started singing, "The woods are alive with the sound of music..." and she had a beautiful voice...

The details of Bobby Horton's life after he left HF Bar in the late 1940s are vague. No one living seems to know what he did for a living or everywhere that he lived. About the only information available was provided by Pam Dixon who remembers that Bobby had a partner named George Gordon and they had a long and happy relationship.

Pam recalls that Bobby was a:

...wonderful guy and seemed to have a warm relationship

with Trudy (Note: Jack's daughter and Bobby's niece) *He was blond and really handsome with movie star good looks...The last time we saw Bob and George was when our son Ezra was brand new—so about April 24, 1972...*

Bobby's life had been troubled at times, in fact at one point in time he attempted suicide while at HF Bar Ranch. In the latter part of his life, after he last saw Mike and Pam Dixon, Bobby became despondent. His partner George Gordon died and Bobby was left alone. He wrote a letter to his nephew, Jack Horton, Jr. who was then in Washington, D. C. The date of the letter is June 23, but the year is unknown, but it was written probably about 1974 or 1975.

The plaintive letter, written from Sedona, Arizona, explains his condition at the time:

Dear Jack:

Certainly news from or about you personally very scant— though I do see your name and activities in the papers from time to time. Wish we could become closer together, somehow. I do keep in contact constantly with Maggie who seems to be keeping busy and somehow appears happy.

The news here not good and I may need your help—at least moral support. I spent two months in California visiting old haunts and friends with an idea that maybe I belonged back in Monterey— but that seems out as prices, taxes, etc. higher than I can afford on my limited income. Returned to find Bill in poor condition. He went into the hospital last week to have a simple prostate "ream-out"—no complications, but he was worried about his wife Ann (as well about the prospect of possible cancer) and had a bad flare up of his ulcer which really kicked up and set him back considerably. In the meanwhile Ann started worrying and since she has always been "ill" and unstable she worried herself into a bad state. No one (sic) can do anything for her. I was with her as much as possible, though we are not friends, and over to see Bill in the hospital every day. They live ten miles south of Sedona... Ann is in the hospital too...in intensive care and very critical condition. Bill is completely (sic) dependent on her financially and since she lives on a trust fund, if she dies he will not have a "pot to piss in." I do not have enough to support him.

To make matters worse (or in the future possibly better) I am in the process of finding out whether I have been suffering from Hypoglycemia or diabetes—which (or something) has made life all but unbearable for me the last 12 months. I am on a rigid low blood sugar (hypoglycemia) diet now but not reacting well yet—worry and unsettled conditions probably the cause. I had a 6 hour glucose tolerance test Monday but will not know until next Monday. My strength and energy and moral sapped.

Whatever your hidden sorrows and fears are, at least you have unlimited energy and drive, which I never had. I don't know if it is the result of "low blood sugar" or if I am just plain nuts and should be committed.

Sorry to be so gloomy—but that's how it is...

...Will be looking forward to hearing from you and hearing of your activities and future plans for HF Bar. The one bright spot in my life is that I may someday go back there—fit in in some small way and maybe find at least a little peace of mind. I can't do that as long as Hank is there, unfortunately.

Best of everything to you,

Always, Bob

In later years, Jack, as well as Trudy, had a warm relationship with their uncle Bob and Jack met him frequently in California at Mike and Pam Dixons. Pam Dixon remembers how they kidded around with each other and called each other "Horton." Whether or not Jack responded to Bobby's plea is unknown.

It was in his precarious state of mind that Bobby decided to take his own life, which he did on November 20, 1976. In his will he made provisions to provide a small trust for his older brother, Bill. He also made provisions for Jack Horton, Jr. and Trudy's children Will and Anne Dixon.

Sometime after Bill and Harriet moved to Arizona, they divorced and Bill was alone again. He remained in Arizona but often returned to the ranch for visits. I remember one summer in the late 1950s when Bill arrived unannounced. I had no idea who he was other than a Horton. Bill drove up in a new 1958 Chevrolet and made himself at home. He made an impression on me because of his concern for the employees. Bill often ate with them in their dining room (fondly known as the "Zoo") in the back of the ranch house. At that particular time, the kitchen was having problems and Bill was appalled at the quality of the food served to the employees. The next day he went to town and purchased a huge box of steaks for the kitchen staff to prepare for the help. The help ate the steaks with gusto.

That same summer, Bill met Ann Norris who, with her daughter Wendy, was a guest. Bill and Ann developed a relationship and left together for Arizona where they were married and lived near Sedona. Occasionally they would return to the ranch for a brief stay.

In 1974 Bill's daughter, Suzanne, whom Bill had not seen since she was two, was thirty years old, married, the mother of four children and living in Canton, Ohio, when she got an unexpected telephone call on her birthday. It was her father.

When Suzanne answered the telephone the caller said, "Hi, this is your dad." He told her that he wanted to meet her after all this time and Suzanne wanted to meet him, too. As it turned out, she planned on being in Arizona anyway and they set up a time and date to meet in Scottsdale.

Bill told Suzanne, "Go to Trader Vic's. I'll be sitting in the bar

at six o'clock on Saturday night." Suzanne kept the appointment. When she entered Trader Vic's she peered into a long dark hall with no idea of what her father would look like. It could have been anyone in the room. But, down toward the end of the hall she saw a figure in a big cowboy hat. It was her father. Suzanne and Bill greeted each and visited for about three hours. They had a wonderful time together. Suzanne did ask him why he had not been in contact all those years and he told her about the family restrictions that had been imposed on him.

After their initial meeting they agreed to meet again at HF Bar and they did for three years in a row—1975 to 1977. Suzanne's family was able to meet her father and they had three great reunions.

At the last meeting in 1977 they were in the Horton House one night having drinks with Hank. Bill declared that he wasn't feeling well and left for his cabin. Suzanne did not go with him but had a strange premonition that something was wrong.

When she finally left the Horton House she had to walk past Bill's cabin, Corral, to get to her own. There was a strange eerie glow around the place. Suzanne, who had had no experience with death, felt very strange and did not go in to check on her father. Rather, she skirted around the cabin and went to her own.

The next morning she got up and went riding. When she returned Hank was waiting for her at the corral to tell her that her father had died. Suzanne had to leave but Hank made all the funeral arrangements. Bill died on June 19, 1977, at age sixty-seven.

Suzanne recounted how Bill's wife, Ann, had died before he did and in his last years he was all alone. He had been a hard drinker all his life, but, of his own volition, stopped drinking for the last eleven years he was alive. Bill once asked Suzanne if she drank and she told him that she did. After Bill's death, Suzanne stopped drinking. Her father's resolve served as a model for his daughter, and Suzanne considers her father's example as a gift to her.

In hindsight, Suzanne believes it was probably for her own

good that she was not allowed near HF Bar during her formative years because it was a wild place. It could have had a less than desired effect on her.

Today, Suzanne is divorced and lives in Naples, Florida, and has what she describes as "four super children" and five great grandchildren. She has fond memories of her father, Bill Horton, who she only knew for a few brief years. But, she harbors no regrets. The years she did have were "memorable."

Trudy

Ed Morsman knew Trudy and wrote about her in *The Postmistress of Saddlestring.* He described her as:

> *...lithe with the unconscious fluid movements of a natural athlete...*

And Ed lumps Trudy and her brother Jack together when he writes in "The Postmistress" that:

> *...Both were highly intelligent and quick witted, and each had an ingrained curiosity. They were both somewhat introverted in the psychological sense of deriving energy from within as opposed to through other people. If other members of the ranch staff got together for a beer and songs, Jack and Trudy would probably not be there. Far from appearing aloof, this introversion enhanced their magnetism, and their contemporaries were more attracted to them. If there was a significant difference between the two, it was that Trudy accomplished her objectives with more visible enthusiasm and exuberance than Jack, who was equally effective but in a much more understated and laid-back way...*

Ed Morsman provided other anecdotes about Trudy which illustrate that she was an extraordinary person even at a young age:

> *...Trudy was highly competitive. When my cousin and I were about ten we found an old shoeshine stand in the tool shed, so we started a shoe and boot shining business with the catchy motto, "You scuff 'em, we buff 'em." Sooner or later, all footwear on a ranch is covered with dust, mud, manure, or worse, so the money started rolling in, particularly on the evenings when dances were held. With*

a new source of discretionary income, we became pretty big spenders at the candy counter in the ranch store and soon attracted Trudy's interest.

Typical of Trudy, she started a business that not only made money but had a positive effect on the environment as well. In the days when the spaces were truly wide open, people seemed to feel that dumping a little refuse would have a negligible impact...

Fifty years ago, some people thought nothing of tossing empty bottles from their porches into the creek, and many of these bottles were worth several cents in deposits. Dressed in tennis shoes and shorts, Trudy would skip from rock to rock collecting bottles in a huge sack. She could make a run from Frontier, the furthest cabin, to the store in no time at all, sort the bottles into trash and returnables, and cash in.

Trudy made the business look so easy, I thought I would horn in and diversify my sources of revenue. After all, she was several years younger than I was. I donned shorts and tennis shoes, slung a sack over my shoulder, and plunged into Rock Creek to seek my fortune. Less than 100 yards downstream, I emerged, scratched, bruised and exhausted. The sedentary ways of the shoeshine business took on a new allure. To this day, I am not sure how Trudy did it. Maybe she could walk on water when out of sight. She was incredibly athletic and occasionally would do things such as walk to Willow Park carrying nothing more than a sandwich and return before dark, thinking nothing of it...

Trudy had a remarkable ability to organize people. In her teenage years during the summers at HF Bar she played a major role in organizing the dude rodeos. Before that event, her skills were apparent. Again, Ed Morsman, provides a telling anecdote:

The little boys and girls pulling decorated wagons and carts or skipping and running across the lawn in front of the ranch house ranged from about five to ten. Although a first glance suggested they were off somewhere for organized play, a closer inspection revealed that they were imitating a rodeo parade. In fact, a rodeo queen led the group of floats, clowns and contestants, some carrying homemade flags representing unknown territories.

After watching this fair imitation of the parades preceding rodeos in Buffalo and Sheridan, the bemused adult would rightly conclude that the instigators were Jack and Trudy Horton, more likely, Trudy. Naturally, a reader might guess that Trudy would be playing the role of the queen, haughtily leading her charges along the proscribed route. Actually, Trudy played many roles, none of them queen. At times she was a contestant waving a banner. Or she might run up and down the line giving orders and holding the group together. Or she might drop by the side to be an enthusiastically applauding spectator.

If not Trudy, then who was the queen in the lead position? Actually, it was Jack made up and costumed by Trudy who had more important things to occupy her talents. What kind of power and leadership must a person have to dress up an older brother ranch kid as a rodeo queen and then organize an unruly bunch into a parade: Whatever it takes, Trudy had it in abundance as did Jack...

Trudy's stay in Wyoming for dental treatment in the winter of 1950 was not temporary. The Sheridan County School Census shows that Trudy attended sixth through eighth grades in Sheridan elementary schools. For the first two years she lived with Eleanor's mother, Margaret Gibson, a Sheridan schoolteacher. So, in the winter Trudy stayed with her maternal step-grandmother and spent summers with her paternal step-grandmother.

By the time Trudy reached the eighth grade, Jack and Eleanor had returned with Jack, Jr. and purchased a house. Trudy, of course, lived with them while she attended the eighth grade and her first year of high school.

While attending high school in Sheridan, Trudy and her classmates were asked to write a paper on the subject of their choice. Most students selected a topic along the lines of what they did last summer. Trudy already had a well-developed social conscience that was unusual not only for her age but for the age in which she grew up. Her topic was alcoholism, which flabbergasted her totally unprepared teacher. Hank, of course, took this choice in stride and remarked, "You certainly are in the right spot to do your research."

The Sheridan High School yearbook, *The Bronc* also recorded that Trudy was a member of the Stutter and Strut, a drama club. She was also a member of the freshman Glee Club.

When Trudy completed her freshman year in Sheridan, her father Jack and stepmother Eleanor moved back to Salt Lake City. Trudy was enrolled in a private girls day school, Rowland Hall. Rowland Hall was founded in 1880 as an Episcopal school that provided an education to daughters of miners and ranchers in the intermountain West. Many years later it was to merge with St. Mark's, a boys day school, and is now the Rowland Hall/ St. Mark's School.

While a student at Rowland Hall, Trudy, as usual, was active and popular. She was in the French Club and was a member of the student council and a member of the Rowland Hall chapter of the National Honor Society. She also served on the staff of the school newspaper and was active in athletics.

The caption for her graduation photo in the Rowland Hall yearbook proclaimed:

Trudy is a girl with great talent and interest in many areas.

Trudy gets help donning her chaps from Bob Ross in 1957.
This photo was used as a cover for an HF Bar Ranch brochure.
(Courtesy of the HF Bar Ranch)

She accepts praise graciously and leaves a vivid impression. Her high grades and wonderful sense of humor have won her the respect of all who know her.

Virtually every summer Trudy worked at HF Bar Ranch as the bookkeeper and hostess. One exception was the summer of 1957 when she spent the summer as a Missionary Social Worker in Saskatchewan.

During her high school years, Trudy took a great interest in her second cousin, Ginger Gorrell. Even though the Gorrell and Hortons relationship had dissipated because of the difficulties of the 1930s, Ginger kept a link to HF Bar through Trudy. Trudy was attracted to Ginger because he was bright, amusing and different. She also had great empathy with him.

Ginger's life was described in an article in the Buffalo Bulletin in 1993 by Jane Wells, a staff writer. The article was written in conjunction with action by the UM Ranch to fix up Ginger's old cabin, which had been deserted for years, so they could use it as a cow camp. Jane Wells's article is anecdotal. While all of the information cannot be verified it certainly captures the essence of this unusual man:

There are two types of cabins.

One exists only in our imagination. Made of restless dreams, these inner fortresses appease our longing to be different than we are. They are usually simple structures, mental asylums built to escape the complexity of life.

The second kind is made from the earth and related to reality. Their wood and stone tranquility is shared with whomever possesses the key.

Both cabins are shelters. And occasionally both are the same.

Trudy Horton
on her graduation from Wellesley College in 1961.
(Courtesy of the HF Bar Ranch)

One such oasis lies northwest of Buffalo, tucked behind the UM Ranch. Accessible only by foot or horseback, it is almost 30 years since anyone called this cabin home.

Built high in the timber by a long dead eccentric, the story could someday add substance to local folklore and legend.

Known as Ginger's Cabin, it was named by the townspeople for the person who lived there. Not a red- haired, calico woman, but a man with a nickname, a man with a history. A man with the burden of being unable to accept mediocrity in himself or others. (Note: According to Ed Morsman, this was the second cabin built by Ginger. The first was built in a place now called Ginger's Meadow. When the Forest Service removed it he built another one further upstream on the south fork of Rock Creek. He even assembled a water-driven generator to provide electricity for the cabin.)

He called his place "Trio." Surrounded by aspen and towering lodgepole, the cabin was Ginger's compromise with a frustrating world.

Unable to exist under society's bondage for long periods of time, Ginger needed the solitude of his secluded life.

He was not a hermit. Ginger chose to restrict his contacts to only those he considered meaningful.

Journal entries tell of his trips to Buffalo for supplies, of visitors welcomed; his enthusiasm for ideas, projects, and the people he loved. Children "adored" him and followed him around. He encouraged them to learn, he taught them, and he monitored their lives with a mentor's enthusiasm...

Those who knew Ginger said the loss of the HF Bar was a life long struggle of resignation for him.

Ginger was educated at Northwestern University, Amherst College and the University of California. Eventually he was employed at the White Sands Proving Grounds in New Mexico. A practical joke involving a stick of dynamite on a co-worker's chair caused his dismissal.

The dynamite exploded.

During employment at the HF Bar, Ginger loaded a magpie with dynamite to see how much weight the bird could carry in flight.

Another explosion. Another job lost.

Often called a nuclear physicist, his obituary said he had degrees in mathematics, physics, and astronomy, besides several honorary degrees. He was fascinated with photography, astronomy, rock climbing, writing, and immersed himself in the challenge of learning. Ginger was a guide and mountain climbing instructor at Long's Peak in Colorado.

While in the U. S. Army, Ginger suffered an accident causing epilepsy, which he endured for the rest of his life.

He also battled the bottle and wrote often of disciplining his drinking. Experimenting with prunes, he learned how to brew his own wine. Believing self-control was within his power, Ginger berated his binges.

His love of photography included a darkroom he built in his cabin. Ginger also rigged a trip switch outside his home for night photography of curious animals.

Being a doer and not just a thinker, Ginger designed and built telescopes. He shared his knowledge of astronomy with several children, and some of his telescopes are treasured today by local citizens, now adults.

Jane Wells concluded her article with the following:

...This past summer, the crew at the UM Ranch decided to restore Ginger's cabin. For years it had been used as a cow camp for summer grazing, and was in need of repairs. Pack horses hauled supplies for the project up the mountain, and carried the debris down.

Logs were oiled, flooring and roof replaced, and the memories resurfaced, along with an interest in the original owner.

The people who remembered told different stories about Ginger. Waves of the past surfaced: childhoods spent in the Big Horns; a pied piper; a brilliant, driven man; a bitterness toward a lost fortune; a drinker, a loner, a fine sense of humor; a man who dared himself to be all he believed he was...

What Jane Wells does not mention is that at one point Ginger was married to a woman named Virginia. Who she was or what happened to her or the marriage is not known.

Ginger died on January 15, 1963. It was rumored that he froze to death in his cabin, but the obituary said he died in his home in Buffalo of natural causes. The funeral home records state the cause of death as "Status Epilepticus—3 hours"—a seizure which could have been brought on by alcohol or epilepsy.

Trudy carried on a correspondence with her unusual cousin over the years, and she occasionally visited him in his cabin. Once, Trudy and I took some dudes on an all day picnic ride to Paradise. As we rode by Ginger's cabin she told me how Ginger had "practically invented color photography" and was a genius. She also described how the cabin was jam packed with equipment from floor to ceiling, but Ginger, when he needed something, would literally bury his arm in the clutter and unerringly retrieve the item he needed.

When Trudy graduated from high school in Salt Lake she matriculated at Wellesley College in Massachusetts. Supposedly, according to Phillip Long, Trudy, on a lark, wrote an essay for a Betty Crocker scholarship contest—and won! No details are available about these circumstances.

Trudy had a sterling academic career at Wellesley. She majored in philosophy with a minor in biblical history. Trudy received freshman honors and was named a Durant Scholar. In her junior year she was made Phi Beta Kappa and then was named a Senior Durant Scholar. In her senior year she won a Woodrow Wilson

Scholarship which provided her with one year of graduate work.

Socially, Trudy was very active in the Wellesley College Community Chapel and was chairman of religious forums of the Chapel. She always wanted to help others and so it was only natural that she would be active in Vil Juniors which was a group of young women that took freshmen under their wing and eased their transition into college life.

At other times Trudy served as a campus guide, helped with college theatrical productions and participated in the social programs of her house. Once, she traveled to Norway to work for the American Field Service.

When Trudy graduated from Wellesley College she returned again to HF Bar Ranch to work for the summer. It was there that she met her future husband, Mike Dixon. Mike was an accomplished artist and musician who had studied at the Art Students League in New York and Cornell University as well as the Brooklyn Museum School. He was the nephew of Barclay Morrison who had been a friend of Jack Horton, Sr. at Princeton. He made the contact that led to Mike's employment at HF Bar that summer.

That fall, Trudy used her Woodrow Wilson Scholarship and enrolled in the graduate school at the University of California at Berkeley and began to study for her master's degree in philosophy. To supplement her scholarship Trudy worked for a short time as a waitress in a Rathskellar restaurant in San Francisco.

The next summer both Mike and Trudy were at HF Bar again and fell in love. Mike had taken to the West and when fall rolled around he and Trudy left for California where Trudy continued her graduate studies and Mike began to establish himself as an artist.

Mike and Trudy were married the next spring in April of 1963. During that spring, Trudy, in addition to her studies, worked for a few months as a part-time physical education instructor for the Marin County Day School.

Mike and Trudy's first child, Anne Butler Dixon, was born on

October 30, 1964. When she became pregnant, Trudy was still working on her graduate degree but she ceased her studies because, according to Pam Dixon, a friend of Trudy's:

...At that time having a child was the kiss of death for a woman graduate student; it showed you were "not serious enough!!!"...

Pam also commented that:

...Trudy's interest in Zen Buddhism emerged and supplanted her desire for an MA—it was something she followed to her death...

Unfortunately, Trudy's death was imminent. In June of 1966, Trudy was pregnant with her second child, Willard Christopher Dixon, when she was diagnosed with breast cancer. Willard was born on October 1, 1966, and Trudy had to undergo a mastectomy both before and after his birth.

Trudy suffered the lingering illness until July of 1969 when she died at age thirty. It was a remarkable coincidence that thirty years before, her mother, Jody, died at the same age from the same cause. It was a sad untimely ending for such a vivacious, intelligent and vibrant young woman.

A few days after Trudy passed away her brother Jack wrote a tribute to his sister. Part of the tribute contained the following lines:

Beyond the almost hypnotic sadness of the funeral
    I found an extraordinary awareness developing
    that superimposed upon itself
    beauty sympathy awe and humility
It restrained and clarified the silence
    as it did a great message in our lives

# Saddlestring

That all of us both close and casual
  were privileged to have known someone whose life
  has essential meaning
  because it had relevance
We had known in a way that could never be lost
  a beautiful spirit fulfilled...

During the last part of Trudy's difficult illness, Anne and Will were sent to live with their paternal grandparents in New Jersey where they lived from 1968 to 1970. In 1970, Mike married Pam Fore who had been a friend of both Trudy and Mike. Mike was then able to have his children back with him. Pam recalls that:

...the children arrived to make a family three days later. Mike was eager to get everyone into one house and move forward. We worked hard to make things good for them...

Mike and Trudy's daughter, Anne, when she grew up, obtained her undergraduate degree in French from Vassar College and then her graduate degree in journalism from the University of Colorado at Boulder. She later taught English for three years in France.

Anne has had an eclectic writing and performing background. She has written features for National Public Radio and documentaries for television including the nationally broadcast *Dude Ranches Out West: Then and Now* which won the Wyoming Historical Society Video Award. Anne also performed in improv/sketch, comedy troupes, musicals, and acapella groups and this sparked her interest in writing for the stage. She wrote sketches for the comedy troupe *Head Games* and for the show *Friends and Lovers* at the Bovine Metropolis Theater in Denver. Anne also wrote the book for the musical comedy *Virtual Love* which received a grant from the Longmont Arts

Commission and was produced at the Longmont Theater in Longmont, Colorado.

In the winter of 2004-2005 Anne studied in New York. She works as a freelance writer in Colorado

Anne's brother, Will, went to Midland School, a small boarding school near Santa Barbara, California and then to Washington State University, where he received his Bachelor of Architecture and Bachelor of Science in Architectural Studies. Today, he practices architecture in Oregon and lives near the Willamette River with his wife, Lynn and their two sons, Ben and Miles.

Mike Dixon and Pam had children of their own. Today, Mike is a very successful artist with numerous exhibitions and commissions to his credit. He has a gallery in San Rafael, California where he lives with Pam.

Will and Anne Dixon strike a pose
similar to an early photo of their mother,
Trudy Horton and their uncle, Jack Horton, Jr.
(Courtesy of Anne Dixon)

Jack, Jr.

Jack returned from Venezuela with his father and Eleanor when he was fourteen years old to enroll in Sheridan High School. During his years at Sheridan High, Jack was active. He was on the Student Council as a sophomore and also one of the managers of the Bronc football team. He was also a member of the basketball team and won second place in the school intramural tennis tournament.

Jack's junior year in high school is somewhat of a mystery. Jack definitely left Sheridan High School after his sophomore year according to the county school census and the high school yearbooks. He might have gone to Salt Lake City with his parents and Trudy to attend high school there, although I have been unable to verify this. But we do know that he attended Deerfield Academy in Deerfield, Massachusetts for his senior year (1955-1956). Ed Morsman, a classmate, takes up the story:

...Like everyone, Jack had his dreams, but he also had the courage, talent, and energy required to turn them into reality. While in high school, he decided he wanted to go to Princeton as his father had. He also concluded that he probably could not get there with his current educational background, and he knew that his father would not pay the tuition of a first rate Eastern prep school. That would stop most people. Jack, however, wrote the legendary Frank Boyden, the headmaster of Deerfield Academy, and Mr. Boyden was so impressed, they struck a deal.

Jack and I were classmates at Deerfield, both graduating in 1956. At that time, most of the students had never been west of Philadelphia, if not the Hudson River. Coming from Central High School in Omaha, Nebraska, Deerfield was a major culture shock for me. Imagine what it was for a ranch kid from Saddlestring, Wyoming. Jack was involved in the usual mix of athletic and cultural activities. *He was on the varsity track team where he focused on the broad and high jump. He was in the chess and music clubs and was president of the ornithology club. He always was an excellent birder and could easily identify anything that nested at or migrated through the ranch.* (Note: The Nassau Herald, the Princeton yearbook, also states that while at Deerfield Academy Jack played football and basketball and was on the yearbook board as well).

Living along Rock Creek in Wyoming, Jack was an excellent fly fisherman and brought those skills to the Connecticut River, which ran through Deerfield. Fly fishing was unheard of at Deerfield, and Jack was probably the only practitioner within miles. It certainly was not a topic of discussion on Park Avenue or Darien in 1956. Jack managed to land a very nice rainbow that he showed to a student on the bank before releasing it. The student was so impressed that when his mother came to visit him, he introduced her to Jack saying that he had caught a huge fish in the Connecticut River. The matron looked totally mystified and finally, in a puzzled tone of voice, said, "What in the world were you doing in the river?" It was a different world.

Ed Morsman also gave an account of graduation at Deerfield:

...After a rather gloomy spring filled with torrential rains and flooding, graduation finally arrived. My parents came and were able to kill two birds with one stone as my sister, Julie, was graduating from Smith down the road to the south. My dad was beginning to show considerable signs of strain at having to be nice to so many people he did not know and would never see again when who should he bump into but Hank who was there for Jack's graduation. Hank was dressed in New England style tweeds, and except for the deep tan and signs of weathering, looked like she could be the president of the garden club in Greenwich.

Dad was overjoyed at not only seeing someone he knew but

someone he liked, and said to Hank, "Let's go somewhere where we can say 'shit' and have a drink. Finding a place like that near Deerfield in 1956 was not easy, but my parents and Hank disappeared. When the three finally reappeared, Dad was in an expansive mood and much more tolerant of his fellow man, at least through the graduation ceremonies....

Jack's strategy to attend Deerfield Academy so he would have a better chance of getting admitted to Princeton University worked. He was admitted to the class of 1960. While at Deerfield Academy, Jack applied for a Naval Reserve Officers Training Corps scholarship. He was awarded one, and in exchange for summer duty and classes while in school, and a service commitment after graduation, the United States Navy paid for Jack's Princeton education.

Jack's time at Princeton is summed up by an entry in *The Nassau Herald*, 1960:

...At Princeton, this versatile native from Wyoming concentrated his studies in the field of geology, writing his thesis on "The Geology of Southern Lake Valencia, Venezuela." He played a variety of sports including crew, skiing, soccer, football and lacrosse. He was a star defenseman on the lacrosse team for three seasons. He was also a member of the Undergraduate Schools Committee and a keyceptor during his junior year. His senior year he was awarded a Rhodes Scholarship for study in England.

As for the future, Jack plans to attend law school at Oxford after completing service in the United States Navy.

Cactus Jack's home address is the HF Bar Ranch, Saddlestring, Wyoming...

Jack Horton Jr. on the lacrosse field.
(Courtesy of the HF Bar Ranch)

After Jack graduated he was selected as a member of the All American Lacrosse Team. That was the summer of 1961 when Trudy, Jack and I were all at HF Bar. I remember Trudy walking out of the office with a telegram that Jack had received to inform him of the honor. Trudy was incredulous about how nonplussed Jack was when he read the news—apparently the award was no surprise!

Following graduation, Jack negotiated an arrangement with the Navy so that he could attend one year at Oxford University as a Rhodes Scholar before he began his service commitment. During his year there, he continued to play lacrosse and was named to the All England Lacrosse Team, and was, perhaps, the only American to receive that distinction.

After his first year of study at Oxford, Jack was sent to navigator school by the U. S. Navy and then to the Far East where he served for four years and flew 175 combat missions over the South China Sea. Senator Malcolm Wallop, then a United States senator from Wyoming, stated in the Congressional Record, in 1981 that:

...Living off base in Japan, he explored the Eastern philosophy, produced a more than credible Japanese meal, and became fluent in the language...

When Jack was released from the Navy in 1965 he returned to Oxford University and in 1967 received an MA degree in politics and economics. His intention, upon graduation, was to return to HF Bar and assume his rightful place in the operation. He did do that, for a time, but then other forces came into play.

A man with Jack's background did not go unnoticed in a place like Wyoming. And it was not probable that he would settle at HF Bar with no outside interests. In that regard, Jack followed in his grandfather Skipper's footsteps. He was interested in politics and he also wanted to serve. It was no surprise that he had been back in

Saddlestring

Jack Horton Jr. receives his naval aviator wings.
(Courtesy of the HF Bar Ranch)

Wyoming for only a few months when he was named as executive director of the Wyoming Republican Party.

While Jack served in that position, he was also engaged in helping Hank and Dean run the ranch. But it wasn't long before another opportunity beckoned that caused prolonged absences from the ranch.

In April, 1969 Jack was named assistant to the undersecretary for the Department of Interior, Russell Train. He then began what was a rather meteoric rise through the ranks. In May, President Nixon established a Federal Task Force on Alaskan Oil Development and Jack was named executive director and then later served as special assistant to former Secretaries of the Interior Walter J. Hinkel and Rogers Morton.

Senator Malcolm Wallop commented in the Congressional Record about this phase of Jack's life, and about Jack:

...His professional life began in Wyoming—a stint as executive director of our Republican Party. Horton's commitment to Republican principles and goals was evident throughout his many years of public service. He was a partisan. He did not, however, allow that partisan commitment to impede his communications with the very diverse people and interest groups of the West.

Horton played a very important role in the inventory and allocation of Alaskan resource lands. He was the first chairman of the Federal-State Land Use Planning Commission for Alaska—the Department of Interior's effort at resolving Alaskan land issues which ultimately reached this Congress as the controversial Alaskan Lands bill.

From 1973 to 1977, Horton was assistant secretary of the Interior for Land and Water Resources—a new assistant secretaryship which was largely designed to facilitate a major policy role for Horton in recognition of his commitment to preserving the quality and ways of life in Alaska and the western states. Jack was unwavering in his belief that a balance could be achieved in the West's production of energy and natural resources without irreparable damage to the environment. It is a balance this nation has not yet achieved, but his accomplishments moved us much closer to an effective multiple-use program.

Horton served as Assistant Secretary throughout both the Nixon and Ford administrations. With the change to a Democratic administration, he continued these same efforts as a private consultant in natural resources, counseling industry, public interest groups, and political leaders...

Jack Horton Jr. with President Gerald Ford.
(Courtesy of the HF Bar Ranch)

During Jack's federal career he spent a year in Alaska as chairman of the Alaskan Land Use Commission. He told the *Western Horseman* magazine in 1978 that:

...while there, hunted moose, caribou, Dall sheep, and bear, but admits that he spent more time fishing than hunting.

The article went on to say:

...If you ever meet Jack Horton, ask him about the time he encountered an Alaskan brown bear at 15 feet when armed only with a fly rod...

While in Alaska, Jack also took advantage of the opportunity to climb Mt. McKinley. Apparently he carried in his backpack the flag of then Bicentennial Chairman John Warner and later presented it as a memento of the successful climb to the White House. Mt. McKinley was not the only mountain Jack climbed. He also is reported to have climbed Killimanjaro, Fujiyama, Mount Ranier, and the Matterhorn.

Jack took every opportunity to return to HF Bar during his federal career, often with his boss. He served under two Secretaries' of the Interior, Walter Hinkel and Rogers Morton, and both visited HF Bar. Jack took advantage of one of his sojourns to HF Bar to train for his forthcoming climb of Mt. McKinley.

Ed Morsman described Jack's training in the *Postmistress of Saddlestring*:

...To condition himself for the trip, Jack began a regime whereby every day he would don hiking boots and shorts, fill a backpack with rocks, and walk up to the top of the Speedway and back. The climb is steep and takes thirty to forty-five minutes. Although vigorous exercise, it is still short of the McKinley summit by about 14,000 feet. Nothing can totally prepare a person for a trip like McKinley, so basic endurance and courage are required.

Jack realized that most of the ranch hands would think he was nuts and he particularly wanted to avoid Dean. Like most cowboys, Dean was not lazy but could be considered economical in terms of energy expended. To Dean, energy was for work, and the idea of exhausting oneself for pleasure was nonsensical. Consequently, Jack went out of his way to undertake his exercise when Dean was not around.

Of course, the inevitable happened. Jack was rounding the corner of the barn in his hiking attire and ran almost literally into Dean, who was coming from the opposite direction. Dean eyed Jack's clothing skeptically and asked, "What do you have in the pack?"

Jack Horton Jr. at summit of Mt. McKinley.
He made the climb during the year he spent in Alaska
as chairman of the Alaskan Land Use Commission.
(Courtesy of the HF Bar Ranch)

Jack replied somewhat sheepishly, "Rocks."
"Where are you going to take them?"
"Up to the Speedway."
"What are you going to do with them once you get up there?"
"Bring them back down."
Dean walked away incomprehensibly muttering to himself
and shaking his head. Jack knew that explanations would be futile....

Even with prolonged absences Jack remained engaged in the operation of the ranch. For instance, in September of 1971 he sent a memorandum to the HF Bar Ranch Board of Directors, who were scheduled to have a board meeting soon, and made suggestions:

...Since my return to the ranch may be delayed beyond the next couple of weeks, herewith are four points for consideration on the Agriculture for next year...

Jack then continued with the suggestion they develop a master plan as to what should be done with each field to improve production and how they should get the tasks accomplished. His specific recommendation was that they hire Lindy Shattetz, a past employee, as a paid consultant. The actions taken are unknown.

Jack also tried his hand at marriage. He married Grace Espy Ford of Savannah, Georgia in the late 1960s. Grace was a guest at HF Bar with her mother. Other guests who were there describe Grace as easily the most beautiful girl at HF Bar. Apparently, according to some on the scene, Grace's mother thought Jack Horton Jr. would be an ideal match for her daughter and set about to do what she could to influence the relationship.

She threw a huge party for Jack and Grace that is still talked about. What most people remember is that the party featured brandied peaches, champagne and salmon. That was the first year that Bronco Jones brought his new wife, Botsy, to HF Bar. Botsy was expecting a pretty primitive western frontier scene, perhaps even with some Indians. She was startled to find herself at this amazing party— Peaches? Champagne? Salmon? She soon learned it wasn't typical HF Bar.

Some of Jack's friends were skeptical about the marriage idea and gave it no hope of success. While Jack and Grace were both stars in their different worlds, the fact is that their worlds were different. Grace was thought, by many, to be totally unsuited to the kind of

rugged, western, political, adventurous high flying life led by Jack, and Jack was ill suited for Grace, a southern beauty but used to southern gentility. In fact, one of Jack's friends, and a long time guest of HF Bar, when he learned of Jack's intention to marry Grace, called Jack to inquire, "Jack, are you crazy? Why are you doing this?"

Part of the answer to his question was provided by Margi Schroth, who later became Jack's fiancée and the owner of HF Bar. According to Margi, Jack told her that Trudy was a major influence. She loved her brother, she was dying, and she wanted to be sure that Jack had someone to look after him.

And so Jack and Grace were married in California at Trudy's home. And as many predicted, the marriage was short lived and Jack and Grace divorced.

While Jack was still in Washington, there was much speculation as to whether Jack would run for the United States Senate in the 1976 election against the three term incumbent democratic Senator Gale McGee. For reasons known only to Jack, he chose not to run. Instead, his friend, Malcolm Wallop of Big Horn, entered the fray and defeated Senator McGee.

Jack left Washington in 1977 and returned to the ranch. He was glad to get back. The *Western Horseman* magazine article reported that:

...Someone asked him what his title was at the ranch. His comment: "I'm tired of titles. I came back here to be untitled."

When Jack returned to life at the ranch, he assumed his rightful place in the operation. He inherited a small amount of stock from his father, Jack Horton, Sr., and Hank had given him small stock gifts at various times. Jack, on his own, acquired stock from other major stockholders. By the mid-1970s Jack was the majority stock owner in the HF Bar Corporation and Hank held the second position in terms of shares owned.

While Jack became involved in ranch operations, he still had to cope with the fact that Hank had operated the ranch for many years and had strong views on certain matters. Jack gave her full credit in the 1978 article in *Western Horseman* magazine. He stated:

> ...*Hank has been the overall manager, financial wizard and* tour de force *behind the ranch since 1948. The success of the ranch and indeed the fact that we still have it are very much her doing. She is both very tough and very generous and has that wonderful flair for both understanding and entertaining people and bringing them together. Her presence here is that extraordinary blend of strength, character, and dedication that together constitute the real institution that is Saddlestring today...*

Hank had an equal amount of respect for Jack, and stated in the same *Western Horseman* magazine article that:

> ...*I've always received a great deal of pleasure out of the things he does. I can talk like this since he isn't my child or even my grandchild. You would hate to boast about your own children that way...*

As much respect as Jack and Hank had for each other they didn't always agree. Both were intelligent and strong willed and had the courage of their convictions. Neither one held back when it came

Jack Horton Jr. (far right) gives his boss, Secretary of the Interior Walter Hinkel (second from left), a tour of the HF Bar Ranch with his father, Jack Horton Sr. (far left) and Dean Thomas (second from right). Circa 1970.   *(Courtesy of the author)*

to speaking their minds. Their positions were sometimes poles apart.

Hank had been around for a long time and had just about seen it all. She was ultra conservative when it came to spending money for improvements. Every project, to her, had to pass the practical and common sense test and had to be really needed. She put the same practical test to new ideas, even if money was not involved. Hank was not one to push the envelope with new ideas for HF Bar.

Jack, on the other hand, was of a different bent. He had lots of ideas and was bold about putting them forward. While Jack knew a lot about the ranch operation, his ideas were not always bound by convention and practicality.   Plus, I suspect, Hank sometimes harbored resentment towards some of the ideas and suggestions that drifted her way from someone whose management involvement and presence at the ranch was basically part-time.

Nevertheless, Jack did have an influence and he and Hank reached agreement on many things.   One of those was the hunting operation: Jack told *Western Horseman* magazine:

...I feel that important revenue base of the ranch should be hunting. We have truly outstanding deer and elk hunting. We have a herd of 900-1,000 elk located here in the Big Horns. I ran the hunting program before I went to Washington, and I'm just starting it up again. I think hunting is important for two reasons. We have so many animals that the herds need to be broken up. The other, of course, is that the elk eat a lot of our alfalfa and knock over a lot of our fences. We are trying to concentrate on providing very high-quality personalized hunting experience so that we can select a relatively small number of hunters. We would provide not only elk and deer hunting, but pheasant hunting, fishing, skeet, and trade out with adjacent ranches for antelope hunting...

Jack's background and interests spread his energy further afield than just the confines of the ranch. When he left Washington *Time* magazine ran a short piece which expressed Jack's view of his role in the world:

>*...After four years as assistant interior secretary, Jack Horton is back on his 10,000 acre ranch in Wyoming's Big Horns...hopes to use his Washington experience as an environmental consultant. Says he, "You owe the world much more than to just go back and lock yourself into a ranch..."*

Jack did start a consulting business. It was mentioned in the *Washington Star* society column written by Betty Beale at the time that Jimmy Carter was inaugurated as president and Jack Horton was in the process of leaving Washington for Wyoming. Betty Beale wrote:

>*...Jack Horton, the personable bachelor who was assistant secretary of Interior for Land and Water Resources until last Tuesday, incorporated his own resources and environmental consulting firm this past week. It is called Horton and Co., will have an office here and possibly one in Denver. But Jack, who is the co-owner of the 15,000 acre HF Bar dude ranch in Wyoming at the foot of the Big Horn Mountains, will live there he says, come April. Right now there's no water there, only ice. Has he a girl in mind, he might take with him? "Maybe..."*

Another Washington columnist, Lee Catterall, wrote about the new company as well and commented that:

>*"...consulting firm" is Horton's term. Others pronounce it "lobby" but Horton insisted that lobbying congressmen won't be in the outfit's repertoire...*

Jack put out his own press release on February 9, 1977:

Formation of a western resource and environmental consulting firm was announced today by former Assistant Secretary of the Interior Jack O. Horton.

The company, to be headquartered in Saddlestring, Wyoming, will provide consulting and government-relations services in the fields of land, water, timber, coal, upland minerals and environmental analysis.

Through its own offices and agreements with other firms, the company plans to assemble and offer a "total service" package of assistance from community impact and environmental analysis to resource development, as well as individual services within these areas.

The firm will also focus on the emerging interests and capabilities of state governments in environmental protection and resource management.

In addition to the central office in Wyoming which will open immediately following the spring thaw, the company has established a Washington office which is now in operation...

So, Jack returned to Saddlestring. What with his consulting business and constant travel, and his involvement with the operation of HF Bar, he was a busy man—and he was satisfied. Two years later, his life would change. A woman entered his life. Her name was Margi Schroth from Pawling, New York.

Margi came to Montana in 1973 after working as a magazine editor in New York City. She had attended Briarcliff College with Margie Taylor, the daughter of Walter and Shirley Taylor. Margi worked as an irrigator on the Taylor family ranch and spent much time with the Taylors at family gatherings. At these events, Margi became acquainted with Hank, Dean and Jack.

Margi eventually took a job with the public relations department at a hospital in Billings where she worked for a time until her life became difficult. For one thing, her house was struck by lightning which prompted her to return to New York. No sooner had she returned than she got a telephone call from Jack Horton in July of 1979.

Jack told her that the ranch storekeeper had quit and they needed a replacement. Would Margi be interested? Jack told her that if she accepted the offer the ranch would pay her five hundred dollars a month and she could have her own cabin and her own horse to ride. It didn't take Margi long to decide that the offer was too good to pass up. With some dispatch, she went to work at HF Bar.

Margi related to me that she did indeed go to work as the storekeeper, but wryly noted that the promised five hundred dollar salary actually turned out to be three hundred dollars; the cabin turned out to be a room in the ranch house; and her own horse turned out to be Jack's roping horse, Buck, that needed exercise.

Margi loved her time there. She became friends with many of the multi-generational guests and became a really good friend to Jack Horton. In fact, they became romantically involved.

That fall, Jack needed a reason to keep Margi at the ranch and he had a convenient one. He was on the road a lot with his consulting business and needed someone to coordinate his business affairs while he was traveling. Margi filled the bill. She was hired.

Margi's presence during the winter was a slight culture shock for several reasons. First, Margi was given a tiny two room cabin, Outlaw, which, incidentally was built in the late 1920s or early 1930s by a man named Vincent Corbett. The cabin was known by the old timers as Corbett's Cabin.

It was pretty spartan, with no heat. Margi kept warm by burning wood in the fireplace.

The other culture shock was for Dean. Hank always spent the winter in her apartment in Sheridan, or traveling, and Dean was used to being the only one living on the ranch in wintertime. It was his territory, and here was this woman living there! Nevertheless, Dean and Margi became friends. He would take her out to dinner and introduce her around to all the locals.

For Margi and Jack, the months from October of 1979 to February of 1980 were good times. Margi remembers them fondly. For the first time in many, many years, Christmas was celebrated at HF Bar Ranch.

But the good times ended in March when Jack began to feel ill. He called Margi from a road trip once and complained that after he ran a mile he felt like he had run five. He couldn't figure out why he had no energy and felt so tired. Margi suggested that he stop in Boulder, Colorado and see a doctor, which he did. The doctor examined him and did blood tests.

On April 4th, Jack received the fateful news. He was diagnosed with acute lymphocitic leukemia which is, as Margi described it, an "impossible disease."

When Jack discovered he had a really difficult disease, he knew he had two problems. The first, of course, was to survive. But, he was also concerned about the survival of the ranch. What would happen to it?

Since it was a corporation, Jack did not own the ranch, but he did own over sixty percent of the stock. He wanted to devise some way that the ranch could be kept intact. The best approach, he thought, was to leave his stock to the Nature Conservancy so it could, in the words of Jack's will:

...be operated so as to protect, preserve, propagate and provide a refuge for all wild game and birds and all hunting thereon may be prohibited...

...Provide for meetings, studies, and seminars for groups, organizations, and individuals interested in conservation, preservation, and study of the geological, botanical, and ecological

resources not only of the Horton Ranch specifically, but also of the Big Horn Mountain range...

...When appropriate provide the ranch as a location for study of interested people from all of the United States to assess and evaluate policies relating to the quality of the environment and the protection of the ecosystems of the United States...

Jack then wrote Hank a very poignant letter informing her of his decision. On April 28th, just over three weeks after his medical diagnosis, Jack wrote:

Dear Hank,

In my will I have left my shares of the ranch to the Nature Conservancy to establish a "Horton Natural Reserve" in honor of Skipper and all members of the Horton family who over the years have contributed so much to the ranch.

I am hoping very much that you will see fit to do likewise, donating your shares as early as you find prudent to this cause in the Horton name. I have left both security and flexibility in the timing, leaving it to you essentially to call the shots.

I feel my disease has let you and the ranch, and, of course, myself down tragically, but we must face life and its travails as it comes.

You should also know that despite our tiffs about the ranch, I love you very deeply and wanted nothing more than a really warm and affectionate working relationship between us as I think Skipper would have wanted.

God Bless,
Jack

What Jack did not mention to Hank was that his will also assigned a secondary position to the University of Wyoming. His will provided that if the Nature Conservancy failed to accept his bequest, then it should be offered to the university under the same terms.

The basic terms were that HF Bar would continue to be operated as a dude ranch for two or three years and that Hank be provided a permanent place to live at the ranch for as long as she desired, and that Dean be kept under employment for as long as he desired.

I don't know if Jack and Hank ever discussed this matter. I suspect not. What is known is that Hank did not accede to Jack's wishes. She kept her stock intact.

Jack and Margi were extremely aggressive and determined to combat Jack's illness. Their search took them to Denver, to Boston and to Houston. They did intensive research of the disease and its treatment as well.

Jack wanted to spend as much time at the ranch as possible so they bought an IV pump with which they could administer the prescribed drugs themselves. Margi put the IV pump in a backpack and, while she and Jack took long walks together, Jack received his medication. Jack received the prescribed drugs through trips to the Sheridan Hospital and agreements with the University of Colorado Health Sciences Center where his main treatment was being given.

Jack and Margi were so determined to keep Jack fit and get him well, that when Jack was in the hospital, they measured off a course around the hospital corridors. They walked miles each day, pushing the IV drip stand in front of them.

Their determination, and Jack's courage and the medical treatment he received seemed to pay off. In October the disease was judged to be in remission and Jack and Margi were able to return to the ranch late that month.

They celebrated by having a great elk hunting season. Many of Jack's friends came to be with him and celebrate including former

Wyoming Governor Stan Hathaway; one of his oldest friends, Chris Farrand; Hugh Duncan from Casper, also an Interior Department buddy, and two other old department acquaintances Brent Kunz and Jack Speight from Cheyenne and Bill Eikenberry.

The celebration was short lived. A blood test in late November revealed that the dreaded disease was back. Jack and Margi then drove to Denver where Jack was admitted to the hospital. They had friends in Denver who made sure that Margi had a place to stay. For a time she stayed in the residence of Peter Dominick, Sr., former ambassador to Switzerland, and with his son Peter, one of Jack's best friends. Doctors Sandy and Mike Shasby, old friends of Margi's from Billings, were living in Denver and working at the Colorado Health Sciences Center in pulmonary research. They were incredibly helpful in finding Margi other places to stay. She was able to prepare meals and take them to Jack in the hospital.

In December, 1980, Jack and Margi heard of a new treatment available at the M. D. Anderson Clinic in Houston. Jack was admitted and underwent a six week course of treatment. But Jack was anxious to return to the ranch once more and so they prevailed upon the doctors to let them return to Denver as a staging point for a quick trip to HF Bar.

Sadly, Jack was not able to have his last time at HF Bar. A serious fungal infection had set in. The doctors did everything possible. They gave him massive doses of antibiotics and performed surgery to save him—but, to no avail. By February 28th, the doctors determined the infection was too widespread. The situation was hopeless. Jack then went into a coma, suffered respiratory arrest and was placed on a respirator in intensive care. Respiratory arrest then occurred a second time and Margi made the decision, on advice of the attending physicians, to remove Jack from the respirator to see what would happen.

In the meantime, Hank had been summoned and was present with her close friend, Shirley Taylor. At 10:10 that evening, Jack

Horton died with Margi at his bedside. Another young life cut short, as with his mother, Jody, and his sister, Trudy.

All were devastated by Jack's death and returned to Peter Dominick's home to make plans. Jack had specifically requested that he be cremated, that there be no service, and that his ashes be scattered on the ranch. Margi was helped at this trying time by Susannah Taylor Meyer, Shirley Taylor's married daughter and family friend, who traveled to Denver to help Margi make the trip back to the ranch with Jack's ashes and their belongings. It was a difficult trip.

While Margi was enroute to the ranch a highway patrolman stopped her because her license tags were out of date. Margi believes that was probably that patrolman's worst day. She was emotionally distressed anyway and was pretty animated when she explained her circumstances including the fact that she was carrying Jack's ashes and "just trying to get home." The patrolman did not give her a citation. When she did get home, she went to Farthest West, where they had not been for some time only to discover that a skunk had taken up residence inthe living room.

Margi complied with Jack's wishes to the letter. She scattered his ashes and did not have a memorial service. After twenty-five years of reflection, Margi wistfully regrets that she did not schedule some kind of memorial service, because Jack's friends had no way to find closure, no way to say goodbye to him. But, on the other hand, Margi reflects, even though Jack was extremely personable and funny, he was really a very private person. She honored his wishes.

Jack's death was noted nationally and obituaries ran in newspapers across the nation. Senator Malcolm Wallop, a good friend of Jack's, read an extensive tribute to Jack into the Congressional Record. Probably the tribute Jack would have most enjoyed was the Memorial Minute adopted by the Trustees of Princeton University on June 8, 1981. The touching tribute ended with the words:

...Jack is gone now. His ashes are scattered in the magnificent Wyoming countryside which was his home. But surely if there is a Heaven, Jack is now pestering God, persistently and effectively lobbying on behalf of the things he loved—the land, wildlife, and Princeton...

Margi assessed her situation. There she was, thirty years old with absolutely no career plans. What was she to do? During her deliberations she unexpectedly received a call from Jack's attorney, Henry Burgess, in Sheridan. He wanted to talk to her. Margi agreed and went to meet him. He had some startling news.

Unbeknownst to her, Jack had, on November 24, just a few months before his death, instructed his attorney to change his will and include Margi. The revised will changed the nature of his bequests. The revision stated that the Nature Conservancy and the University of Wyoming, in that order, were to be given the option to purchase Jack's stock in HF Bar. If neither of them elected to purchase Jack's shares, the proceeds were to go to Margi. He also made some provisions for others. However, if both agencies declined the bequest, then Margi was to inherit Jack's interest in the ranch.

In the end, both the Nature Conversancy and the University of Wyoming declined the offer. Margi, a thirty-year-old woman with exactly one year of ranching experience, became the major shareholder in one of the most historic ranches in Wyoming.

Interesting times lay ahead.

Hank

When Skipper died Hank was forty-five years old. She had spent ten years in a place in which, just ten years earlier, she never could have imagined herself. But, HF Bar had become a part of her.

The thought of selling the ranch did occur to her but it wouldn't have been that easy to do. She was not the majority stockholder. Two of her step-sons, Jack and Bob, together owned more stock than she did. They would have had to agree. Additionally, what would she do if she could sell out? Get back into her old career after an absence of ten years? At any rate, Hank decided to keep the ranch intact and carry on the enterprise her late husband had worked so hard to build. For the next thirty-one years she was to be the *force majeure* of HF Bar Ranch.

Many years later though, in a 1978 article in the *Western Horseman* Hank was quoted as saying:

> *...But sometimes I regret that I couldn't dispose of the ranch after his death. When Jack was graduated from Princeton, I suggested that we sell the ranch. When you consider the value of this property, it isn't very productive. No ranch is; especially a dude ranch that operates two or three months out of the year. You've got too much invested in equipment, facilities and horses; and there is always the horrible problem of hiring help. But Jack said he would just work until he could get himself another ranch for that is what he wanted. So I kept the place...*

Even though Hank committed herself to the ranch for the rest of her life, it did not inhibit her yen to travel. Ed Morsman described this penchant in *The Postmistress*:

During the winter, Hank would say that she got terribly homesick meaning she was sick of home. At the first sign of snowfall, she would reach for an atlas and go anywhere warm, and preferably exotic. On one of her trips deep into Africa, she was on a river boat that included a group of pink hats. They debarked while some scantily clad native porters unloaded their bags in the intense heat. As one would expect, there was some confusion in getting the correct luggage to its appropriate owner that generated considerable and incomprehensible discussion. One of the pink hats berated a struggling porter by saying, "No, no! Not the Louis Vuitton. The Gucci." Hank was incredulous.

No one knows every one of Hank's destinations but they were many and far flung. When Jack was stationed in Japan with the United States Navy, Hank took advantage of that and took at least two trips to the Far East; one to Japan, to see Jack, and one to Thailand where she met up with Jack. She also spent a lot of time in Mexico and South America. Very often she was accompanied by her close friends, one of whom was another inveterate traveler, Maggie Wolfe.

Hank also spent a great deal of time in the East visiting friends of HF Bar. Often friends would organize HF Bar reunions when she was in town. HF Bar Ranch aficionados all over the United States loved to gather and talk about "the ranch."

When Hank wasn't traveling in the winter months, she hunkered down in her apartment in Sheridan and took care of ranch business. She'd had several different apartments over the years. For several years, she shared an apartment in the Keenan Building with her good friend Shirley Taylor. It was a convenient place to meet people, use the telephone or stay overnight after a late night on the town. Often the ranch driver would take a nap there while waiting to pick up dudes on a late plane at the Sheridan airport.

In April or May, Hank would move to the ranch for the dude

season. She lived in the Horton House, as she had with Skipper, which Ed Morsman described as the:

> ...multilevel stucco and wood structure that everyone called the Horton House. Although no architectural marvel, it radiated charm because it soon reflected the personality...of its occupant. From the Harrisons' yellow rosebush on the verandah to the books, newspapers, western art work, and Native American artifacts, everyone could tell that an interesting person lived here...

Some of the parties that occurred in the Horton House are legendary; some of them maybe best forgotten. But they were always fun. Often, Hank would use her love of hats and costumes to liven up the gathering. She kept a chest full of them in the Horton House. Ed Morsman provided a vivid description of one of Hank's parties:

> ...Whenever a gathering reached a certain momentum, which usually meant that the libations had attained critical mass and a retired admiral was powering the piano with tunes that only could have been learned in a bordello, Hank would open the chest and distribute the hats and costumes. Pandora would have been proud. Only a person walking into the room stone sober found the hats unusual for people who were prominent citizens and highly respected in their various communities. Hank usually reserved the grass hula skirt for the moment when most inhibitions had run for cover, and the chosen wearer would perform enthusiastic bumps and grinds to a mixture of cheers and cat calls.
>
> Hank's hat of preference was a multicolored beanie with a propeller on the top. When importuned by the assemblage, the piano player would strike up Down by the Old Mill Stream, and the gathering would burst lustily and occasionally tunefully, into song. With the propeller fluttering, Hank would pantomime the words,

rotating her forearms for the mill, using a flowing motion of her hand for the stream, and performing other highly original, if not amazing, interpretations.

No matter how many times people saw this performance, it always brought down the house. The guitars would come out next, and the songs would range from tearjerkers like Little Joe the Wrangler *to limericks that would make a muleskinner blush. Finally, people would say their long overdue goodbyes and exit through the patio into pitch darkness. There were a number of stone steps descending to the road, and at that hour, the descent was always precarious. People would argue about how many steps there were and on which foot you should start and then launch themselves into space. The inevitable thuds, crashes, "Oh, my Gods," and shushes followed...*

The only person who didn't have to go down the steps was Dean. His abode, Virtues Reward, was only a few yards up the hill from the Horton House, so he had only to stumble up a narrow path.

Occasionally, members of the ranch dude families would visit in the off season for various reasons, and even then humor was the order of the day. Ed Morsman described one such incident that involved Tom Baird, an old friend of Hank:

...Tom Baird spent many an evening in Hank's living room chatting amicably about issues as wide ranging as their diverse interests and backgrounds. One year, Tom was at the ranch during the off season doing some research for a novel. While chatting with Hank, the phone rang and Hank asked Tom to answer. Tom dutifully complied saying "HF Bar Ranch" into the receiver. A voice apologized for a wrong number and hung up. Sensing a unique opportunity, Tom carried on a one-sided conversation as follows:

"Rome?" Pause.

"Il Vaticano!" Longer pause.

"Why yes it is, Your Holiness."   Very long pause with intently furrowed brow.

"Beatification! No, I'm afraid you have the wrong Horton."

So it went at the HF Bar.

Life was not always fun for Hank. In addition to the constant burden of managing the HF Bar year in and year out for decades, she had to cope with all the family deaths. Though Hank was not particularly close to Skipper's three sons, they were, nevertheless Skipper's sons, and so she must have felt some sadness when they died at relatively early ages, although she never would have expressed it.

And then Trudy died. And then Jack. Hank was closer to them than any other family members and had been a constant influence in their lives from their earliest years. How did Hank cope with all the death? Hank was a very stoic woman. She showed much strength, but not sadness, except to her closest friends.

The answer to the question comes from Margi Schroth. The day after President Ronald Regan was shot in 1981 Margi went to Hank's apartment in Sheridan to watch the television broadcast. Margi was still feeling very sad as Jack had died only a month earlier.

Margi sank down into a chair and said, "Oh, Hank, how do you get rid of this feeling of loss?"

Hank replied, "After you lose a husband and two sons you learn to take losses a little bit differently."

It was then that Hank told Margi a story that few people, other than her closest friends, had ever heard. Hank revealed that she had been married before she had married Skipper.

She had married a man from Syracuse, New York and they had two sons, Billy and Stuart. For a time they lived in Palm Beach, Florida. One day, the family chauffeur drove the oldest boy and the nanny to a doctor's appointment. On the way, there was an accident

and the boy was killed. A tragic event.

Hank and her husband took their son, Billy, to Syracuse to bury him. They left their youngest son, who was only a few months old, in the Palm Beach Hospital nursery where a virus ran rampant and their youngest son, Stuart, died suddenly. In just one week, Hank and her husband lost both of their young sons. Then, less than two years later, Hank's husband died of a heart attack and Hank was left alone. Such an experience would indeed give one a unique outlook on death and loss.

Chapter 9

Three Decades at HF Bar

Ranch Operations

Not only did Hank have to cope with Skipper's death but also with the stark fact that she alone was now responsible for the management of the HF Bar Ranch. Unlike many of the earlier years which were marked by a continuous expansion and improvement, Hank's level of expectation was to maintain the status quo: in other words, just manage to keep the place going and "if it ain't broke, don't fix it!" And that's what she did for the next thirty-two years with a lot of help from Dean Thomas.

In the beginning it didn't take Hank long to realize she had her hands full enough with the management of HF Bar. She didn't need the added burden of Paradise Ranch, so, she sold it in 1950. The buyer was a flamboyant character called Wyoming Jack O'Brien and a partner, Jack Chase. The ranch was sold for $55,000 which included $40,000 cash to HF Bar and the assumption by Wyoming Jack O'Brien of a $15,000 mortgage to Mabel Hayden. This was the last known land transaction made by HF Bar.

As Hank assumed the management of the ranch, her game plan was to just get through each year. She never placed new construction or infrastructure improvement on her agenda for a number of probable reasons. The main one was pure economics. It was difficult enough financially to just keep the place operating from year to year. Often she had to borrow money just to do that and

sometimes the lending source was Dean Thomas. Hank personally told me that one-year she had to borrow $40,000 from Dean to keep going. He was paid back with interest. There were probably other instances as well.

Hank was used to the place like it was and saw no need for change or improvement. It was what it was—rustic with a character all of its own. After all, what brought generations of guests back year after year? Status quo was good.

An article in the *Omaha World Herald* in 1985 summed up Hank's philosophy. It said:

> *...As the years passed, post-war America boomed and the automobile and interstate came to dominate vacation plans.*
>
> *The dude business changed to resorts with many guests who demanded tennis courts, hot tubs, gourmet food and three-day package deals.*
>
> *Mrs. Horton resisted the trend and kept the slower pace of HF Bar. Meals stayed hearty, wholesome and down-home. The cabins remained rustic, the activities casual...*

So, the modus operandi was generally to maintain what was already there; paint when needed, remodel when needed, and sometimes maybe add a room to a cabin. In 1960 the ranch did make some improvements. Mrs. George "Freddie" White, who at the time was a stockholder in the ranch, described them in her annual ranch newsletter *Hosstalgia*, 1961, which was written from the viewpoint of Dean's horse, Sac:

> *...It was the 50th anniversary of the ranch, and everything was sure shipshape. We have a new heater for the swimming pool*

and everybody was dunking like mad.   Also we have a new bathhouse with showers and tubs for the employees and it was so popular that even the dudes took to going there for showers—so we're looking to install a bunch of showers in the cabins to go with the tubs. It seems sort of silly when people could just stand outside in a nice rain—but the longer I live the more different I realize people are from horses.   We're going to get lots of new beds, too, and we're working on some kind of filter system for the North Fork because last summer the whole state of Wyoming was so dry that the ranchers below us needed their water from the Willow Park Reservoir even early in July.   The poor old North Fork was really riled up and people's bath water looked like café-au-lait. *I don't speak French myself but I am told this is a polite word for "muddy."   One thing that is great for us horses is that a sprinkler system is going to be put in, to keep the dust down in the corrals, and along "horse alley" so we won't be coughing so much, and neither will the dudes.   And if the ranch house roof leaks enough, they're going to put on a new roof!*

For infrastructure systems, like the plumbing, the general strategy was to fix it when it broke which in the case of the ancient plumbing system, was often and caused no end of grief in the summer months when it was used in full flower.

Guests, at least the new ones, were not aware of the fragility and crankiness of the system. Foreign items, like socks and other unmentionables, inevitably caused the system to balk and back up. The system was made of ancient ceramic pipe installed in the 1930s, some of it possibly in the 1920s, and was not buried deeply. In places it was even exposed. There were few built-in access points, so when there was a stoppage somewhere a shovel and hammer were usually needed to first expose the pipe and then bash a hole in it so a plumber's snake could be inserted to break up the stoppage. The improvised access areas were then simply marked with a large stone

for future reference.

One man, Dean Thomas, of necessity, became the plumbing guru and knew all the nuances and secrets of the system. He coped with most of the plumbing problems, which usually occurred at the most inopportune moments, like just before lunch or a cocktail party. They annoyed him intensely. I have vivid memories, when I worked at HF Bar, of Hank trudging up the hill to the corral where we were saddling horses for the morning ride to tell Dean that a toilet had overflowed in one of the cabins. Often, the bad news would be delivered by a guest who when they came to ride, would say, "Oh Dean, we have a little problem in our cabin." He was always outwardly gracious, but grumbled on the inside and muttered a lot while he labored to fix the problem.

Dean's problem solving techniques were often unique. Ed Morsman described one incident in *The Postmistress*:

...Dean had an uncommon, but pragmatic approach to plumbing. A guest informed Dean of an overflowing toilet that could not be stopped and was flooding the bathroom. The bathroom floors in cabins that may have been started around the turn of the century are not always plumb. In this case, over an inch of water was accumulating on the floor. Dean sloshed into the bathroom, fixed the faulty plumbing, and then sloshed out to his truck.

At this point, the guest assumed he would return with a mop and a bucket. But Dean was not your ordinary plumber. He returned with a brace and bit, surveyed the floor with a critical eye, and drilled a hole in the correct spot. As the floor drained, Dean sloshed out, returned with a knife and a piece of wood. When the floor was dry, Dean whittled a plug, popped it in, and declared everything as good as new...

So, for many years Dean was the resident in-house plumber and Hank liked to be as self-sufficient as possible. Ed Morsman summed up her attitude accurately in *The Postmistress*:

...Although not a native Westerner, Hank shared the sense of self-reliance that distinguishes the breed. She felt that virtually all maintenance could be handled by ranch personnel. Calling in and paying for a professional was a mark of failure, and if the truth were told, Hank could be a little tight about maintenance...

Sometimes her attitude was reinforced by experience such as the one documented by Ed Morsman:

...The cottonwood is the predominate tree along water courses in Wyoming, and the trees can grow to huge proportions. Because the cabins are nestled along the north fork of Rock Creek under cottonwoods, there is always the threat of a dead branch crashing down on an unsuspecting roof. And so it was not surprising that an extremely large and heavy limb eventually grew over a cabin with the unlikely name of the House That Jack Built. The limb began creaking ominously, even in moderate winds, and Hank spent days surveying the obviously dead limb and discussing it thoroughly with anyone who could handle a chainsaw. Finally, biting the bullet, Hank called an arborist from Buffalo to trim the tree without damaging the cabin.

Why is it that professionals always look like teenagers! The arborist who greeted Hank looked very young and inexperienced. Although Hank did not ask to see his credentials, she did ask if he had done this before and if the branch could be removed without consequence. His reply was yesterday's equivalent of "no problem."

The arborist scampered up the tree and after tying off the limb, jerked the chainsaw to a roaring start. Fortunately, the house had been evacuated and there was quite an assemblage of onlookers eager to watch a professional in action. The saw bit into the wood, the ropes snapped, and the limb crashed into the roof of the cabin causing considerable damage. While this turn of events would have sent most people into a towering and justifiable rage, Hank said resignedly, "We could have done that."

Toward the end of the 1960s the need to update and improve the HF Bar plant was addressed again. The minutes of the stockholders meeting in September of 1968 reflect the situation at the time. Present for the meeting were Hank, the president, Jack Horton, Jr., the vice president and Dean Thomas, the treasurer. Following are the items that were discussed:

Mountain Camp: Mr. Horton noted that the new roof on the two cabins at Willow Park had been completed, and that the next improvement would be the installation of a wood heating stove which had been on order for several months and had just arrived on the ranch.

Agriculture: The virtues and disadvantages of "contracting out" the haying was discussed in light of the 1968 experience with Ed Moore of Big Horn. (Note: I don't know what kind of experience they had with Ed Moore of Big Horn. This was not Eddie Moore who gave Skipper financial assistance in the 1930s.) *As against the decreased efficiency and increased unreliability of contracting, it was pointed out the savings to the ranch in terms of capital investment, personnel management, and repair time. Mr. Horton felt that unless the ranch could acquire an experienced farm manager that it would be best to contract out, particularly if this could be arranged with nearby neighbors...*

Resort: During the two weeks preceding the stockholders meeting the officers and members of the Board conducted an extensive examination of all cabins and resort facilities. A detailed

list of repairs was prepared in triplicate; one list to be posted on the
outside of each cabin and one to be retained as a master. Extensive
discussions followed concerning the best method of accomplishing
all the needed repairs. It was finally decided to concentrate all ranch
efforts this winter on this task, and not to re-invest in cattle until the
spring.   The repairs were to be divided into two groups: those
requiring technical carpentry to be managed by Ed Winther, with a
possible assistant to be employed by the ranch; the rougher repairs to
be managed by Dean Thomas and Bob Ross. It was also decided to
investigate the feasibility of renovating Cupid's Flair or the small
cabin to the north of Plunge for use by Mrs. Pete. (Note: Mrs. Pete or
"Miz Pete" whose real name was Ilah Peters, was the office manager
for years. In the wintertime she worked at the Silver Bell Ranch in
Arizona.)

Mr. Horton requested permission from the stockholders to
use $5-7,000 to start the construction of a new water system. This
was granted and a professional engineering study was to be arranged
on this proposal...

This was the first time, to my knowledge, that the need to do
a wholesale upgrade of the water system for HF Bar was addressed.
From the beginning, ranch literature advertised the purity of the
water. The 1912 brochure boasted that:

...The ranch is the first habitation on Rock Creek, a rapid
mountain stream having its source in the melting snow and ice of
Cloud Peak (13,323 elevation). This insures an abundance of pure
cold soft water, and pure ice.

For decades, the water was as advertised. But increased people
and livestock traffic in the Big Horns and other traces of

civilization began to take their toll until in the 1950s and 1960s the purity of the water was suspect. In fact, it was an accepted condition that new arrivals to HF Bar would become afflicted with the "Wyos Trots." The ranch store stocked a good supply of Kaopectate.

The water system was upgraded, and has been upgraded several times since so that today the water plant produces a product in compliance with the Environmental Protection Agency standards. The system is now a far cry from the good old days when there was just a pipe in the creek with only a wide mesh screen to "keep the big stuff out."

Most years the ranch bought yearling steers and/or heifers in the fall, fed them hay throughout the winter, put them on grass in the summer and sold them in the fall. The hay was produced on the ranch as well as occasional crops of oats and barley. If more hay was produced than was needed it was sold if there were buyers.

The dairy and chicken operation that Skipper established in his quest for self-sufficiency continued, but on a smaller scale. A small herd of Holstein dairy cows provided milk for summer guest consumption and there was always excess which was sold to the creamery in Sheridan. Some was used to produce pig slop to feed the few pigs that were kept around to eat the garbage produced in the kitchen. Sour milk mixed with barley in a big drum and allowed to ferment makes a real treat for pigs.

Eventually, this operation became impractical and more trouble than it was worth. Times were changing and it became increasingly difficult to find reliable help to look after the dairy and chickens. It turned out to be a worse headache than even the plumbing, especially in those times when the dairyman was too drunk to take care of business or didn't even bother to return from town for the morning milking. Finally, sometime in the 1960s, Hank decided it was easier and more cost effective to buy milk and eggs in town and the dairy cows and chickens became history.

Two other traditional programs dwindled over the years as

well. One was the garden. During Skipper's days the ranch had a sizeable garden; at one point five acres. Such a large gardening operation was necessary in the beginning because fresh produce was hard to come by due to transportation and availability. Besides that, for Skipper, the bottom line always was about self-sufficiency.

After Skipper, Hank maintained a large garden for many years, but not five acres worth, through the 1950s and 1960s. But, as in the case of other fading operations, the garden was phased out because of labor problems (one summer I remember the ranch went through three different gardeners) and the fact that it was easier to buy produce from wholesale outlets in town.

Farming was the same. The effort dwindled as the years went by. In the 1950s and 1960s, the ranch had a farm manager named Lindy Shattetz. Lindy put up all the crops—hay, oats and barley—with the help of college boy crews, often from Princeton. There was also a full time summer irrigator to get water to the crops.

Eventually, Lindy left and it became more difficult to get irrigators and hay crews. There were a series of people hired to do the farming but finally it declined. The course of action then was to contract the crop harvest, mainly hay, out to the neighbors. This practice met with varying degrees of success, but eventually the farming operation became a very minor component of the HF Bar operation.

One program that will never be phased out is the riding program. The corral is the hub of the ranch and has operated the same way since the first days of HF Bar. The routine never varies. Dudes on their arrival are assigned a horse and saddle. They can ride twice a day, morning and evening, unless they go on an all day picnic or a pack trip or it is Saturday, which is "Horse Holiday" in the afternoon and there is no riding in the evening.

To maintain this program, the ranch needs on the average about one hundred fifty horses. Finding the right types of horses for the different riding abilities of the guests at affordable prices was

always a challenge, and it still is, to an even greater extent today.

Dean was the horse buyer. Ed Morsman described Dean's horse buying exploits:

> *...Although Dean had many talents, the HF Bar dudes thought of him primarily as the corral boss, and certainly, horses did occupy a significant part of his time. Because of constant attrition through age, injury, or winter, replenishing the herd was a constant challenge. It was in this capacity that Dean met the original Marlboro Man who was a horse trader from Riverton...Over the years, Dean knew about everyone in the horse business and was always able to find animals, even when others could not...*

> *...The price of horses can fluctuate significantly depending on quality, fads, supply and demand. On one end of the spectrum, the canners and cutters set somewhat of a price floor as horsemeat continues to be a main ingredient in dog food. Dean had also been known to deal in that end of the spectrum because some of the guests preferred a slow moving animal with low elevation in case of a fall.*

> *Dean occasionally bought retired race horses, but the results were never optimal. Because of their rather narrow purpose training, they were not particularly sure footed on mountain trails and did not seem to get along well with anyone, man or animal. They were also high spirited and incredibly nervous. Nevertheless, the racetrack was one of many unusual sources of animals that Dean scouted and frequented...*

Anyone who has ever worked as a wrangler in the corral at HF Bar can recount humorous episodes. Ed Morsman in the *Postmistress of Saddlestring* recounts one such typical story:

> *...One of Dean's many challenges in the corral was assigning*

horses to guests of wildly different, often overestimated or unknown, riding skills. The assignments often gave the horses attributes they could not possess in a million years. One experienced guest brought her grown daughter to the corral and assured Dean the young woman was an excellent rider. The daughter was quite tall, so Dean brought out a huge and spirited animal. A wrangler saddled the horse, and the woman hiked a left foot to the stirrup, bounced several times on her right foot, and launched her right leg and remaining body with great gusto over the high cantle. It would have been a mounting demonstration worthy of a western film stuntman except that her momentum was so great, she somersaulted off the other side of the horse and landed on her back in corral dirt and excrement.

Dean watched this performance with a barely perceptible widening of the eyes and then suggested that a shorter horse was perhaps more appropriate. He roped a small, lethargic animal who followed him docilely to be saddled. Dean assured the woman that this was a horse of great heart and stamina and would be perfect for someone of her experience. And he was...

Dean, and Barney McLain and Bob Ross could be a bit scornful and vindictive if the occasion warranted it. In *The Postmistress of Saddlestring* Ed Morsman described an incident in which Dean surely assigned an unsuitable mount to a woman who was employed at the ranch but arranged to go on a pack trip with her husband and his parents who were guests at the ranch. Dean was probably a bit resentful that the woman was taking time off from her ranch duties. Ed Morsman writes what her husband wrote thirty-six years later:

...I initially expressed doubt that Dean would do such a thing, but as I thought back over the years, I wasn't so sure.

I recalled that when they deemed it appropriate for any of a number of obscure reasons, Dean, Barney and Bob Ross, and others, with the barest hint of a smile and talking in a cowboy code that only other cowboys can decipher, would load some poor soul on an absolutely inappropriate horse. The big-talking, know-everything "expert" macho horseman might just as well find himself on Dynamite, a real bronc that would only run, as on Jasper, a plug who could only walk. Nothing was ever said about this, and although one can never be positive about such things, I think it likely that my wife was the butt of some cowboy humor. By not complaining, she thinks she fooled Dean. My guess is that Dean knew better...

Until the middle of the 1950s the horse herd had always been moved to Montana pasture in the fall and rounded up and returned in the spring. It finally became increasingly impractical to do this, one reason being the construction of a freeway across the route, and the ranch began wintering the horses on Shell Creek, the country on the opposite side of Castle Rock north of the ranch. The horses were turned out to forage for themselves until they were gathered in the spring for their summer duty.

In the winter, when all the guests were gone and leaves had fallen from the trees, there was work to do in preparation for the next dude season. Since the beginning of HF Bar, two tasks had to be accomplished every winter; cutting wood and cutting ice Even though the guest season was in the summer months and early fall, Wyoming evenings can be chilly and the guests need a source of heat in their cabins. Besides that, a fire in the fireplaces is cheerful and adds to the ambiance, especially during cocktail parties after the evening horseback ride. And for cocktail parties, ice is needed!

In the early days, wood was cut by hand, but in later years the wood was cut with a rotary saw blade mounted on an old car chassis. The wood was foraged from fallen trees around the ranch and scrap lumber.   One year, 1958, a road was constructed from Story, Wyoming, to Willow Park, the HF Bar summer camp, to be used for transporting materials for the construction of Willow Park reservoir. The road construction uprooted hundreds of lodgepole pine trees and created a good source of wood for fence poles and HF Bar fireplaces. HF Bar sent workers and trucks to gather up the trees and bring them back to the ranch. I was involved in this project. I can remember that when the ranch stock truck had been loaded to the gills with trees, which extended well beyond the end of the truck bed, some of us had to sit on the front fenders of the truck as it descended down the steep road to keep the front wheels on the ground. HF Bar obtained several years' worth of firewood from this operation.

The wood cutting process had one critical by-product— sawdust. Sawdust was used for two things; to make "dynamite" and to act as an insulator for the ice in the ice house. Guests needed a convenient way to start their fires, so long ago someone came up with the idea to mix sawdust with kerosene. This concoction, easily ignited with a match, was delivered to the guest cabins in a coffee can with a big spoon and the guests used it to start their fires. They still do, except now the mixture is made with diesel fuel.

The other use for sawdust was to preserve the ice that was cut in the winter. Every year the winter crew went to a pond on the neighboring UM ranch to cut ice. As with the wood, in the very beginning the ice was cut by hand but in later years mechanization came to the fore and the ice was cut by a big circular blade driven by a gasoline engine mounted on a skid that could be pushed across the ice. The whole rig was pushed along the ice first in one direction and then the other to make a crisscross of cuts which created eighteen square inch floating ice cubes that had to be guided with long poles with hooks on the end to the edge of the ice. Each block of ice was then pulled up a wooden ramp and loaded into a truck and transported to the ice house at the main ranch.

The ice house was a simple wooden barn. The first ice house

was down on the creek below the ranch, but in later years another barn up by the main barn was used. The ice was off loaded from the truck and stacked in the ice house with about a two foot gap between the ice and the walls. Once all the ice was stacked, the gap between the barn walls and the ice was packed with sawdust and the top was covered as well. This created a natural insulation that would preserve the ice all summer.

Ice making was a labor intensive operation and was cold and wet work. The ranch never had a large enough crew to do it all by themselves and had to rely on help from the neighbors. So on ice making day, the neighbors showed up with their trucks and equipment and the job got done. It usually took about two days to cut, transport and stack the ice and another day or so to shovel all the sawdust in to cover the ice. But the neighbors got fed, and there was always a bottle of whiskey beneath the seat of one of the trucks to keep the chill off, so a good time was had by all.

In the summer, the wood and ice were delivered to guest cabins by the "HF Express" a horse drawn wagon which was also known as Ben Hur. Ice delivery was a wet and dirty job. First, the sawdust had to be scraped from the top of the ice stack and the blocks of ice were loaded into the wagon. Of course, one had to replace the sawdust to keep the remaining ice from melting. The load of ice was then taken to the bridge over the creek in back of the ranch house where it was hosed down to get rid of any clinging bits of sawdust before it was delivered to the iceboxes that were on the porch of every guest cabin. Of course, the trick was to deliver sawdust free ice, which, depending on the thoroughness of the ice boy, was not always the case.

Like the chicken, dairy, and gardening operations, the ice making operation became too difficult and was replaced by an ice maker that produced giant ice cubes. Mind you, the ice is still placed in the ancient ice boxes on the porch of every cabin, but it's now free of bits of sawdust.

Every fall the HF Bar Corporation held their annual meeting and discussed the past year and made plans for the next. The meeting of 1970 was typical. The people present at the meeting were Mrs. Frank Horton, Mrs. Wesley Frame, Mr. Jack Horton, Mr. Jack Horton, Jr., and Mr. Dean Thomas. (Note: It is interesting that Jack Horton Sr. was in attendance and that he still took an interest in the ranch. He may have been able to take more interest since his son, Jack Horton, Jr. now held a major stock position in the corporation.) At that meeting:

...The stockholders then addressed the overall operation of the ranch by the following categories:

MOUNTAIN CAMP:
New Forest Service regulations prohibit the long established use of garbage pits in the mountains. Garbage must now be returned to the ranch for disposal. This policy was commended at the meeting. The old privy was moved to a new location during early summer....

RESORT:
It was decided to raise resort rates from $160.00 a week to $175.00 for the 1971 season. The renovations independently undertaken by the Nelsens and Mrs. Wakeman will be accomplished without preferential rate agreements. The number of dude days in 1970 was 3,016, the average revenue per guest per day was $22.60.
Costs were higher for this season. The chef was paid more, but justified this with much-improved culinary performance. The kitchen help was also satisfactory.

HUNTING:
The ranch received a good number of hunting inquiries, largely, however, from camper-hunters. Only one party was firmly

booked, and it was thought that the Ely party had cancelled out. It was noted that the UM lands under the State Fish and Game Department would be hunted this fall. The various possibilities of leasing hunting rights was (sic) also noted, and it was clear that further advertising and booking would be required before the ranch hunting operation could be completely successful.

CATTLE:

Both steers and heifers were purchased in 1969 on the dates indicated below:

Date	No. of Animals	Price
11/30/69	70 steer calves	$10,080.00
12/31/69	101 steer calves	
	114 heifer calves	$26,365.20
Total	285	$36,445.20

Seven animals were lost during the year; three from water belly in the winter. The herd was sold on October 5, 1970 to T&G Cattle Co. (Taberna)......the total net revenue (excluding feeding and net costs)was $19,577.80

AGRICULTURE:

Bob Jones put up the hay this summer, estimated to be 200 tons total.....South Fork was not irrigated or cut because of ditch leak problems. The remedy to this problem, either by a new ditch flume or pump, was decided to be of the highest priority if adequate hay is to be harvested during the 1971 season. None of the fields were fertilized in 1970.

Castle Rock produced 1,487 bales of oats (to be fed to the steers) and will be seeded in oats and alfalfa next spring.

IRRIGATION:

The ranch was unable to hire an irrigator until late June. All the reservoir water was used, though not all the stream flow.

SPRAYING:

No weed spraying was conducted in 1970.

HORSES:

Sixteen horses were purchased during the year. No new saddles were purchased, but future replacements will be required. Jim Duke is said to have some for $100.00 a piece.

CAPITAL EQUIPMENT AND EXPENSES:

New purchases during the year were a Paddy Wagon, (Note: Suburban.) Chevrolet Station Wagon, freezer and bed linens. Ed Winther renovated Garden Spot and two rooms in Roaring Forks for an approximate cost of $1,500. A new water heater was decided upon for Outlaw, and the roofs of the ranch house and saddle barn will be painted for the 1971 season. The ceiling in the ranch house living room must be replaced and the walls of the dining room repainted. A list of the smaller necessary repairs will be prepared during the spring.

WATER MAIN:

Work had not commenced on digging a trench for the new water main, pending an estimate by Jay Walker. It was estimated that the trench from the intake to Farthest West could be completed in three days.

The Sheridan Iron Works was identified as the probable source of new pipe. It was emphasized that an integrated plan for the construction of a new settling tank, the delivery of the pipe, and the excavation of the trench was essential. It is important that an individual or concern be responsible for the entire project.

TREES:

Several trees near the swimming pool and Branding Iron need to be cut down. Further, the stump man was expected to come out to treat decaying stumps around the ranch.

The stockholders meeting was concluded at 3:30 and followed immediately by a board of directors meeting. The board agreed that the employees accounts receivable would be reduced to zero as soon as possible, and the account eliminated from the ranch books.

Henceforth no employees account would be extended longer than one year.

It was also decided to employ a Resort Manager who would have the jurisdiction over the entire gamut of resort administration from cabin inspector, to trip schedules, to phone messages and ice water deliveries. (Note: This was never accomplished. The same subject was brought up in the 1973 meeting. It wasn't accomplished then, either. Hank maintained the managerial burden.)

The meeting was concluded on a note of optimism for the successful 1970 resort season and the conduct of business.

So it was in the HF Bar Ranch operation.

The Staff

Dean Thomas, actually, became more than just "staff." He had been the corral boss since he returned from the war in 1946 and replaced an older man named Jack Buckingham. Jack had operated the corral during most of the war and his wife, Babe, was in charge of the cabins. Jack and Babe are still fondly remembered by Ed Morsman and his sister Julie Schroeder.

Dean, until 1951, spent the winters at a ranch in California, the B Bar B, but beginning in 1951 he worked winters at the Silver Bell in Tucson, Arizona. According to Dean, he started working full time at HF Bar in 1956. The story is that Hank was in Europe and called Dean at his winter job and asked him to work full time at HF Bar. He accepted and was the ranch foreman from that day on.

Even though Dean had only worked during the summers at HF Bar, he had worked there for twenty-five years, minus, of course, the war years, and had become a ranch staple. Hank showed her appreciation in 1954 when she made Dean a HF Bar Corporation shareholder by issuing him five shares of stock.

Hank expressed her feelings about Dean in the 1978 *Western Horseman* magazine article when she was discussing the ranch:

...But we are lucky in many ways. Dean Thomas, our ranch manager, is marvelous. He's a fine horseman and a terribly good cattleman. For example, he can spot pink eye a mile away. Even the bank calls him to appraise cattle. He handles the entire horse end of the business, buys and sells cattle, and handles the plumbing and maintenance on the ranch. The number of things he can do is amazing. Not that he doesn't have his moments of being a little cranky, but it's marvelous that he can keep his disposition with the horses. The guests adore him. The kids love him. The fan mail he

Dean Thomas with one of his favorite horses, Sac.
Circa mid-1950s.
(Courtesy of the author)

Dean Thomas and Hank Horton share a light moment in a doorway of the saddle barn at the HF Bar Ranch.   Circa early 1950s.
(Courtesy of the author)

gets is enormous. And he's never too tired to take some little kid up in front on the saddle. He was here years before Jack was born and he now serves as secretary-treasurer of the corporation. It adds up to good management and I think that is why we have been successful. And that is why 80 percent of our guests have been previous visitors to the ranch...

Jack Horton, in the same *Western Horseman* article also expressed his opinion of Dean. He said:

...But apart from the scenery, location, and geography of the ranch, our horses would be among the strongest attributes that we have, thanks to Dean Thomas. He's got an eye for really good riding horses and replaces them often. He also has a unique ability to match a rider to a horse. He's really of fundamental importance to the whole operation of the ranch...

Dean had a natural charisma and made an impression on all he met. Ed Morsman, who knew Dean well, wrote in *The Postmistress* how George White, Jr. first met Dean in 1951:

...In late June 1951, a fifteen- year- old kid got off a Western Airlines plane in Sheridan and walked hesitatingly to the terminal. His mother had assured him that he would be met, but it was about 10:00 p.m., pitch dark, and the plane was several hours late, a fairly common occurrence for the Sheridan airport. A touch of anxiety swept over him as he thought about no one being there and how he would arrange transportation to the HF Bar Guest Ranch at that hour when there did not appear to be a taxi stand. Completing the worst case scenario, he wondered if someone were there to meet him, how they would recognize the other...

Spotting anyone at the Sheridan airport is not difficult, but *when it is a scared fifteen year old carrying a tennis racket, even the visually impaired could make the connection. A cowboy stepped out of nowhere and said, "Hey, you must be Freddie's boy. I'm Dean Thomas." Those were the only words spoken for the next hour...*

There was a handshake, and I recall a square, rough, very strong hand. That was followed by a wait, in silence, for my luggage and a faintly quizzical look at my tennis racket and, when they came, two large suitcases. I translated the look as, "Real men need no more than a bedroll and a small valise, and they certainly don't play tennis." Talk about intimidation. Here was this trim, forty year old cowboy with movie star looks wearing real cowboy boots, blue jeans, a leather belt with a big silver buckle with "DEAN" carved in the back, and a form fitting snap shirt. I'd never seen a snap shirt before. The hat was set just so, as was the Camel unfiltered cigarette there in the corner of his mouth. He wasn't actually very tall or heavily built; he was compact, extremely strong, and to my eye, without any apparent effort, absolutely radiating power. He might as well have been seven feet tall and weighed three hundred pounds...

We then walked out to the car, where, as I was putting my bags in the back of the huge gray Chevrolet station wagon, I noticed the 16-1 license plate. I was impressed and turned to ask a question of Dean, but he was twenty-feet away, taking a leak against the side of the terminal. I realized that cowboys could even pee with panache...

George was quoted further:

I have few memories that are as sharply etched as these first few minutes with Dean. There are few people I respected more, and none I feared more or whose respect I sought so assiduously. I like to think that somewhere along the line, I was, at least, modestly successful in this last regard..

...When I last saw Dean, perhaps in the late 1980s when I was

fifty something, he still had the power, merely by cocking his head and giving me a sideways glance from under his hat brim, to send me into a total funk. Surely I had said or done something wrong or dumb or had forgotten something. Now that's intimidation...

Dean naturally commanded respect. All with whom he came in contact, from Supreme Court Justices, to United States Senators, to captains of industry to kitchen pot washers—they all wanted to be liked by Dean. They sought his company when they were guests at HF Bar.

So did women. Dean was a man's man, but he was a woman's man, too. He was charming and had enormous sex appeal. He knew it and used it to maximum advantage and was not a shrinking violet when it came to relationships with women. Usually, though, Dean didn't have to make much effort. Women often took the initiative and Dean was most often receptive to their advances. But he did have his standards and had been known to evade aggressive women.

Ed Morsman wrote in *The Postmistress* that:

...Dean was extraordinarily handsome with an engaging personality and ear-to-ear smile. Most women found him extremely attractive and some pursued him relentlessly. The corral is located on a slight elevation so anyone approaching it can be viewed quite easily, especially from horseback. If Dean wanted to avoid someone in hot pursuit, the wranglers had a warning code. "Let's saddle up ole Strawberry" might send Dean off to the barn or up into Wrangler's Roost, the bunkhouse. On the other hand, "Let's bring out ole Wild Flower" might start him preening...

Margi Schroth related a story about Dean being pursued by a

woman. Dean was well along in years, but still virile and attractive to women. One summer, there was a woman who was particularly attracted to Dean and was after him in a most aggressive way. Dean was not especially interested and did his best to avoid her. One evening, when the amorous guest was on the prowl, Dean took refuge in the Horton House. He thought he had avoided her until he left the Horton House and wandered up the path to his cabin, Virtue's Reward. There, sitting in the middle of the path, was the woman with a flashlight. Dean was snared.

The next morning Dean ran into Margi and told her about the encounter. Margi asked him, "Well, what did you do?" Dean answered, with a big grin on his face, "By God, I gave her what she wanted and sent her on her way!"

Dean was a confirmed bachelor. I don't know if he intended it to be that way, but it's the way things turned out. He was deeply in love at one time with the daughter of a dude family, but evidently the family didn't approve of the daughter marrying a cowboy so the marriage was prevented. He had other love interests over the years, and thought about marrying a few times, but in at least one case I know of the object of his affections was divorced and had small children. Dean couldn't quite bring himself to take on that kind of family package.

At times there was some speculation amongst some of his own family members about why Dean didn't marry Hank. There is no doubt that Dean and Hank were fond of each other but whether or not they ever seriously discussed marriage is not known. And while they generally got along, they had been known to have raging arguments. In the end, I believe they probably didn't give the idea of marriage much, if any thought, and even if they did, probably didn't see much merit in the idea. I briefly discussed this with Dean once and he sort of indicated there wasn't much need to marry Hank,

because, as he stated, "I already have the best of both worlds."

Dean was pretty comfortable with his own company, and he had to be. While the summers at HF Bar were busy and there was no end of company for Dean, more, actually than he probably wanted at times, the winters were different.

Wintertime at HF Bar is when reality sets in. There is no hustle and bustle. The place is dead quiet. The leaves are off the trees, the creek is likely iced over, and there is snow on the ground. HF Bar is not nearly as romantic in the wintertime as the dudes think it is in the summer. Dean spent many, many winters at HF Bar alone, save for the company of Lindy Shassetz in the late 1950s and later, Bob Ross, for a few years. Often there was the occasional cook for company.

Dean broke up the lonely winters with an annual thirty day vacation. Most every year he made a circuit of Arizona, California, and often Mexico, when he stopped off to see old friends and family. Often he bemoaned the fact that when he visited old friends and was ready to go out on the town and stay up late, his friends had to get up and go to work the next day. One year he went to Hawaii and stayed with a family who were frequent HF Bar guests. He got involved with an ex-moviestar and had a great time. I can remember vividly a cold February morning after he returned. We were feeding cattle and as Dean told me about the good time he had he ripped off his jacket and shirt to show me his peeling tan.

By the end of his time Dean was seventy-one years old. He had been associated with HF Bar Ranch for fifty years and had attained icon status in the eyes of many. Dean, was, in effect "Mr. HF Bar" and he had seen many changes. He explained some of them in 1978 when he was interviewed for the*Western Horseman* and talked about the differences between the dudes of the 1930s and 1978:

...I see a change in the people who come to the ranch. It used to be that hardly anyone had ridden a horse. Now it's getting so that more and more people own horses and kids have more of a chance to ride than they used to—summer camp and that sort of thing. I think that people are riding more, but I don't think they are quite as rugged as they used to be. They have to have everything a little better...

Dean also described some other changes:

...And I've seen some changes in the ranch...but not many changes as far as buildings are concerned. Electricity is one big change. We used to have our own power plant (Note: The power plant was installed in 1925.) *In those days, Skipper would shut the plant down at 9 p.m. when it was time for everyone to go to bed. Now we have REA lines into the ranch.* (Note: It is difficult to imagine that everyone went to bed just because Skipper pulled the plug on the power. Odds are that that's when the kerosene lanterns and candles came out.)

One thing that did not change over the years was Dean's propensity for accidents and scrapes. Once he got bucked off and put both hands out in front of himself to break the fall. He broke the fall, but also broke both wrists. It took some time for him to heal and have the casts removed from his wrists. During his recovery he found out who his real friends were when it came time to help with some really basic needs.

Another time I was standing right beside him in a narrow alleyway when a mare that had just been bred came charging down the alley. I jumped aside but the mare sideswiped Dean and smashed him into the side of the alleyway. That laid him up for a while, too.

Animal accidents were one thing, but Dean occasionally had trouble with humans. It was in his nature to champion the underdog.

I have vivid memories of one summer evening when Dean and I had been to a family reunion at Ladore Supper Club in Story, Wyoming. We left the party to go home but when we got outside there was a circle of boys taunting another boy in the middle of the circle. I recognized most of them as classmates in high school and former members of the football team.

Apparently, the boy in the middle had done something to offend the other boys and they were taking him to task. One, egged on by the others, was challenging the victim to a fight. Dean, being Dean, stepped into the middle of the circle to find out what was going on. He then proceeded to upbraid the group for picking on someone who, no matter what he had done, was obviously not able to defend himself against the odds. I was standing right beside Dean and prepared to help him out if he got into a scrape, but I hoped beyond hope it wouldn't come to that because these guys were big. Dean, fearless as ever, stared them all down and they dispersed. The next day, the parents of the boy called Dean and asked him if he would testify if they pressed charges against the group of boys. He allowed as how he was not interested and declined.

Dean never went looking for trouble, but often it found him. It definitely found him one night in the Sheridan Elks Club in the late 1950s. According to his account, he was sitting at the bar drinking with some friends and pretty much minding his own business. There was a group of younger folks standing nearby and somehow Dean got in a conversation with one of them who ended up chiding Dean about being an old cowboy. One thing led to another, and Dean and the young guy squared off. Dean got in the first lick and knocked his opponent to the floor. He then let the downed man up, and when he got up he proceeded to knock Dean down. But he didn't let Dean up. Instead, he sat on his chest and proceeded to beat him severely about the head and shoulders.

Dean was a mess. Somehow he stumbled back to Hank's apartment that was just a few blocks from the Elks Club and collapsed on the bed. He was found there next morning by Ax Hill, a New York hand surgeon who, with his parents, Dr. Norm and Libby Hill, had been guests at HF Bar since the 1940s. Ax ministered to his needs and got him moving. Dean then stopped by my parents house where I first saw his injuries. His face looked like a lump of raw meat, but he could still manage a sheepish grin when he described what had happened. I remember that he specifically told me, "By God," Tom, "just remember. If you ever get somebody down, never let the sonofabitch up like I did!"

Dean later ran into the young buck that had done him such injury and told him that he was damned sure ready to go again if the youngster had a mind to. Nothing happened, but, as Dean said, "By God, I was ready!"

Dean was ready then, but in other departments Dean would not be exactly ready for changes at HF Bar that were to come several years later. With the death of Jack Horton, Jr. and the ascension of Margi Schroth as the majority stockholder, the complexion of the HF Bar management scheme was to take on a different hue.

Bob Ross, like Dean, went straight back to HF Bar after the war and worked in the corral in summertime. In the winter he lived in Buffalo but would help put up ice at the ranch, and occasionally filled in for Dean when he went on his annual vacation. However, in 1963, when Lindy Shattetz, the year round man left, Dean asked Bob to work at the ranch year round, which he did until 1972.

Bob Ross became involved in another dude ranch romance in 1967 when he met Linda. Linda grew up on a ranch in Nebraska and when she graduated from college got a high school teaching job in Buffalo. In the summer of 1966 she needed employment until school started. Hank discovered her and offered her the job as dining room hostess.

That was that. Bob met Linda and after dating for awhile they were married in 1967. For the next five years, Bob worked at the ranch year around and Linda taught high school in Buffalo and worked summers at HF Bar. She managed the dining room for two years and ran the chuck wagon for three years.

Bob and Linda had a son, Richard, in 1972. Bob then left HF Bar and went to work for Margie Barker on her place near Buffalo.

Linda continued her teaching and education. She received her master's degree in English from Chadron State College in 1978 and began teaching at Sheridan College in Sheridan, Wyoming. Linda went on to obtain her doctor's degree and eventually retired from Sheridan College. Today, Bob and Linda still live on Margie Barker's place.

Barney McLain continued to be a summer fixture in the HF Bar corral during the 1950s. Barney was like many of his generation of cowboys. He was small, no more than five foot six or seven but he seemed taller with his high crowned hat. Though he was small in stature, he was a giant on horseback. Even late into his sixties, Barney was fearless on horseback. Dean, who had been known to be pretty fearless, and even a bit reckless, himself, marveled at Barney. Once they came back from gathering some horses, and Dean told me how Barney had galloped at full tilt in pursuit of some horses over a dry creek bed littered with large boulders. Dean called him "a wild man."

Ed Morsman had something to say about Barney in *The Postmistress*:

...He wore a tall crowned gray hat that may have been white in the beginning and had a perpetual hand-rolled cigarette dangling from the corner of his mouth. His shirts were always solid colors, usually white, and they were buttoned at the throat to keep out the dust...

...The guests had a great deal of respect for Barney even though he could never seem to remember their names. Cowboys have amazing memories for horses and other livestock. Although they may forget the name of individuals, they can always remember the horse each rode even over the course of decades. Barney frequently called dudes by the name of the horses they rode...

Barney loved little girls because he thought they were most sensible about horses and had a natural affinity for them. A prized possession of many dude children, girls that is, was a picture of themselves with Barney. Barney didn't seem to have much use for little boys.

I have fond memories of working in the corral with Barney. He was pretty stern, but hidden somewhere in that sternness was a sense of humor. If you were willing to learn, and were sensible, he had time for you. If you were a showboat, and thought you knew everything, he didn't like you. Simple as that.

Bronco Jones and I worked together in the corral one summer and became friends with Barney. Barney taught us a few crow Indian phrases. One, which sounded phonetically like "show opie," meant "Give me tobacco." Another, which sounded like "epee cow eke" meant "bullshit."

Once, Barney asked Bronco and me to visit him at his house in Sheridan one Saturday afternoon. He wanted to show us some old photos. When we arrived, he had several boxes of photos. He went through all of them. Most were photos of old time roundups in Montana. I will never forget one photo which Barney described:

...You see that gray horse right there? That sonofabitch had a yellow streak down its shoulder because once you managed to get on the sonofabitch you never wanted to get off 'til you got back to camp...

Late 1950s Corral Crew.
Back row from left: Barney McLain, Dean Thomas,
Whitey (last name unknown), and the author.
Front row left to right: Bob Ross, Bronco Jones and Milt Timar.
(Courtesy of Bronco Jones)

Bronco and I felt privileged to be allowed to spend that time with Barney and gain some insight into the past life of a real old-timer.

When I was attending Sheridan College I would often run into Barney in the winter. He spent a lot of time hanging around the Ritz pool hall and he loved to go to Sheridan College basketball games. Almost every school day, Barney would appear at the entrance to Sheridan College to pick up Ione, who was the librarian.

Barney died on December 27, 1963. Considering the sometimes risky life he had led, Barney had a rather ignominious death. He was driving his car when he had a heart attack and his car crashed into the "Cut and Curl" beauty salon in Sheridan. Ione survived Barney by several years. She returned to the University of Wyoming to work in the library but eventually retired and moved to Dayton, Wyoming, just a few miles north of Sheridan. Ione died in 1972.

It is difficult to describe the nature of the HF Bar workforce over the years. There have been many memorable characters; some more memorable than others. A sample of the types of characters that have drifted through the gates of HF Bar would be Charlie Pancake and Russell Pigg.

Charlie Pancake was the irrigator in the late 1950s. He was a stout, red-faced, scowling German and a man of very few words. Charlie looked like he was born angry. He used his own car, a beat up old Chevrolet sedan, to perform his irrigator duties. It looked like a grapes of wrath outfit with big wads of canvas irrigator dams and poles sticking out of the trunk and the windows all flapping and banging as Charlie drove to his duties in the various fields at a high rate of speed. He never ran over anyone and no one really wanted to tell him to slow down because he might quit and irrigators were hard to find.

Charlie did not like Barney, and the feeling was mutual. To

Barney McLain (left) and Bob Ross (right)
two long-time HF Bar wranglers getting ready to team rope in 1961.
(Photo by Sandy Jacques. Courtesy of the HF Bar Ranch)

Barney, Charlie was that "fat German irrigator." To Charlie, Barney was that "smartass old cowboy." They never missed an opportunity to make snide remarks about the other when the time was right, which was usually at meal time because it was the only time they were in close proximity to each other.

I have a vivid memory of one lunch time when Charlie and Barney got into a scrape. At lunch time we all arrived a few minutes before the dinner bell and sat on a bench outside the kitchen and the employee dining room. In those days, the employee men's washroom was on the second floor over the kitchen and access was gained by external stairs. One day Barney was sitting on the stairs waiting for the dinner bell to ring when Charlie showed up. He started up the stairs to wash up but Barney, who at times could be a bit ornery, was in the way and refused to move. They got into a wrestling match on the stairs which was an amazing sight since Charlie outweighed Barney by at least one hundred pounds and they were both over sixty years old.   The scuffle was short-lived and declared a draw. Charlie trundled on up the stairs and Barney just sat there with a grin on his face.

For the several years that Charlie worked at HF Bar he spent the winters in Sheridan living in a two dollar a day room in the Edwards Hotel. Charlie eventually moved on to a fate unknown.

Russell Pigg was a pot washer in the kitchen who showed up every spring for several years. He was a scruffy little man with few teeth, though he couldn't have been more than thirty-five years old, who hailed from Oklahoma. He always needed a shave and always wore khaki work pants and shirts. When you first met Russell and he told you his name, he always emphasized that it was spelled with two "g's."

Russell moved from kitchen job to kitchen job all over the country and seldom stayed at any of them very long. Along the way he had picked up a taste for vanilla extract. His drink of choice was a bottle of coca-cola half filled with vanilla extract. Russell always had a bottle of coke in his hand and a toothy grin on his face.

Harry the Baker from Midland, Texas, was another fixture for many years. He was known for the lightness of his famous popovers.

Another character drifted in one summer. His name was Oliver and he was French Canadian. He was a likeable and grizzled old hunchbacked guy who signed on as the gardener. He was a good one, too, and was often seen leaning on the garden fence speaking French with guests who had the same ability.

Oliver had an aversion to doing laundry. To avoid the chore, when his overalls got too stiff for even Oliver to wear, he would go to the ranch store and buy a new pair. When he finally left the ranch, there was an impressive pile of dirty overalls stacked in the corner of his cabin.

Oliver's weakness was drink. When he left the ranch he lived in a cheap room in Sheridan and hung around the bars. One cold winter's night he got very drunk and stumbled out the back door of a bar. In his drunkenness he sought refuge from the bitter cold in a mattress carton left for pickup by a furniture store. He was found frozen to death in his flimsy shelter the next morning. Oliver's son from Canada came to take care of matters and visited the ranch. As it turned out, Oliver had been a very successful attorney in Canada at one time but eventually gave up his legal career, as well as his family, because of his addiction to alcohol.

Alcohol was a big problem for many itinerant employees who sought employment at HF Bar. One year Hank hired a family through an out of town employment agency. She was rather desperate because some employees had quit unexpectedly. She was left in the lurch in dire need of a second cook, a cabin woman and a kitchen helper.

An out of town employment agency said they had just what she needed and would send a family, two adults and their grown son, her way. They eventually showed up, but two days late, because along the way they had all gotten drunk and spent a night or two in jail. Annoyed, but with no other choice, Hank put them to work.

It turned out that their normal employment was with carnivals and Howie, the grown son, bragged about how he used to ride a motorcycle in a huge barrel. They had not been at the ranch long before one fated evening when Howie, who wanted to ingratiate himself with the college group, threw his version of a cocktail party in the clubhouse. The group, certainly above the level of Howie's normal social acquaintances, accepted, and as the evening wore on introduced Howie to a drinking game. Howie, being a heavy drinker and an exhibitionist anyway, jumped into the game with enthusiasm.

As the game went on, Howie got very drunk and allowed as how he was such a good drinker he could chug-a-lug a beer can full of gin. Naturally, the other people present didn't think it was possible and bet him he could not perform the feat. Howie did but almost immediately passed out. Some members of the group dragged him to his room and put him on his bed.

The next morning, Howie didn't show up for work. Phillip Long who was a hasher at the time and had attended the party the night before went to look for him and found him dead in his bed. Phillip told Hank, who fetched Dean from the corral. Dean trudged down to Howie's cabin and verified that he was, indeed, dead. It was not a good day at HF Bar Ranch.

Hank and Dean were both upset that this unfortunate episode had occurred, especially because those present encouraged Howie to perform his deadly stunt. Not only did Hank have to deal with law enforcement authorities and the coroner but she also was concerned about the possible damage that such an incident could do to the reputation of HF Bar Ranch. In the end, there was slight mention of the incident in the Buffalo Bulletin but the whole thing blew over.

Hank insisted that those who had encouraged Howie to perform such a stupid feat attend his funeral in Buffalo, which they all did. A sorry epilogue to the sad story is that when Howie's father was informed what had happened, he showed not the slightest sign of remorse, and could only comment "Well, he sure couldn't drink like his old man!" Howie's mother did not seem much affected, either.

The majority of the employees did not come from employment agencies but from other diverse sources such as guest families, friends of ranch guests or friends of the ranch or friends of previous employees either local or otherwise. Jack Horton, in the *Western Horseman* article in 1978 commented:

...This year we have three English students from Cambridge who are working for us in the hayfields. For the corral we employ

high school or early college-age guys who have ridden a lot from local ranches. We find out about them or we hear about hands who are particularly good with horses or good with people. Sometimes we go to them, but often they hear about us and write. About 50-75 percent of the students who work for us return. That applies to the guys who wait on the tables and the girls who work in the cabins...

Many employees were dudes in their youth, employees in their high school and college years and then returned as dudes later in their life. Typical of this bunch are Hoyle Clay "Bronco" Jones and his brother Phillip Long. Bronco worked as a hasher for several years and then became a wrangler. Phillip was a hasher for several years. Both, with their families, have returned as guests for many years. Guests like Bronco and Phillip, of which there are too many to mention here, transcend any categories like "dudes" or "guests." Instead, they have become loyal members of the "extended HF Bar family" whose love of and interest and support of the ranch contribute to its success and institutional memory and consistency.

Many people obtain jobs at HF Bar because their relatives worked there. That's how I got my first job in the summer of 1956. My family had returned to Sheridan from California the previous summer and during the winter Dean asked me if I wanted to work at the ranch as the ice-boy. I had no idea what the ice boy was, and I had never been to the ranch, but as soon as school was over the following spring my parents drove me out and I was introduced to HF Bar. I liked it from the beginning because of the people—Dean, Barney, Bob Ross, Lindy Shassetz and several others.

I arrived before any dudes and was put to work mowing what seemed like acres of grass with a push mower. Soon, however, Dean asked Barney to teach me how to harness Chickadee, the horse that pulled the ice wagon, and hook him to the wagon. Barney also showed me where the icehouse was and how to get the ice out, clean it and deliver it to the cabins. That's what I did, all summer.

The next year Dean gave me the driving job and I spent the summer picking up dudes and supplies in town. Then, toward the end of the summer Dean told me he was going to put me in the corral as a wrangler the next year. I was surprised since I wasn't a "ranch kid" who'd grown up around horses. But, the next spring when I reported for duty, Dean, Bob and Barney all showed me the ropes and I became a full-fledged wrangler. Mind you, I got watched awfully close for a while, I think, but after I proved I was sensible and not going to do anything stupid, and was really eager to learn, they treated me as an equal.

My first summer in the corral was also the first summer in the corral for Bronco Jones. We both still have fond memories of those days and Bronco has pictures of the corral crew that hang prominently in his cabin every year when he returns for his and his wife Botsy's annual pilgrimage. When we worked in the corral we both took pack trips to Willow Park and kind of rotated the duty. Once, which one of us was to take a trip was decided by which one of us played bridge because the trio that was making the trip needed a fourth for bridge. Bronco played so he got the nod.

I continued to work summers at HF Bar through my college years. In the meantime, I experienced what I call the "HF Bar connection phenomenon" which had a major impact on my life.

I attended my first two years of college at Sheridan College, a two-year community college. The summer before I graduated, I met Dave Cole at HF Bar. Dave was the son of William Sterling Cole, at that time the director general of the United Nations Atomic Energy Commission in Vienna, Austria, and a former congressman from New York. Sterling Cole and his wife, Elizabeth, had been guests at HF Bar in the 1930s and had suggested to Dave, who was embarking on a cross-country trip with a friend, that he stop at HF Bar so he could see what it was like, as he himself had fond memories of his time there. Dave did stop to visit. But, the ranch was unexpectedly short of help on the hay crew so Dave and his friend hired on and worked for the rest of the summer on the hay crew.

Dave and I became friends and corresponded. I had been entertaining the thought of transferring to George Washington University in Washington, D.C., because of a suggestion by my uncle, Howard Ringley, who at that time served with the military at the Pentagon. I applied and was accepted. I was in contact with Dave, who was going to work at HF Bar the following summer, and he suggested that I could drive back to Washington, D.C., with him to begin my studies at George Washington. He even suggested that I could live with him in his parents' house in Arlington, Virginia, since his parents were in Vienna and there was plenty of room. I declined as I had already accepted my uncle's offer to live with his family.

In the meantime, I had a great summer at HF and met someone who made it easier for me, financially, to attend George Washington because at the time I hadn't quite figured out how I was going to pay for attendance at an expensive eastern school. United States Senator A. S. "Mike" Monroney (D-Oklahoma) and his wife, Mary Ellen, and their granddaughter were guests at the ranch. I was assigned to take them riding. The Senator did not ride much, so mostly I rode with his wife. During the course of one of our rides, Mary Ellen asked me about myself and I told her that I was going to Washington D.C., to school. She then offered up: "Maybe Mike can give you a job in his office. I'll speak to him." "That would be wonderful I replied," and left it at that, not knowing, really, what to expect. I found out soon after they left when I received a telegram from the Senator's office with a job offer, which of course, I readily accepted.

That fall, I went east for the first time in my life with Dave

Cole. I moved in with him after a short time living with my uncle's family because it was a more workable situation. I enrolled in school and then reported for duty in the Senator's office, which was slightly amusing because the staff had obviously not been told much other than "this kid from Wyoming was going to work in the office." I have often wondered what kind of conversation the Senator and his wife had when he found she had all but offered me a job in his office. At any rate, the staff and the Senator and his family were wonderful to me. They helped make it possible for a green kid from Wyoming to get a great education, not only in academia, but also in the ways of the nation's capitol.

During my stay in Washington, Sterling Cole's appointment to the Atomic Energy Agency expired and he and his wife, Elizabeth, returned to their home in Arlington. I continued to live with them and Dave, who was also a student at George Washington. I will never forget their kind support and friendship.

The HF Bar connection provided other heady and interesting opportunities for me during the time I lived in the Washington D.C., area. For instance, one of the guests at HF Bar the summer before I went to Washington was Supreme Court Justice Potter Stewart and his family. I took them riding and on picnics, as well. On one picnic we got around to discussing my life, and when I told Justice Stewart I was going to school in Washington, he told me that I must call him when I arrived. Undaunted, of course, I did and he invited me to Sunday lunch at his house in Georgetown where his family and I and other invited HF Bar aficionados had a wonderful time reminiscing about "the ranch."

I attended many other social events that centered on the HF Bar connection. Once, Dave Cole and I went to Short Hills, New Jersey, and spent Thanksgiving with Jack and Nancy Gefaell and their sons, Robin and Jay, who were annual guests at HF Bar. One of their sons, Robin, worked at HF Bar as a hasher. Their other son, Jay, and his family are occasional guests at the ranch today. Many other students with the HF Bar Ranch connections who were attending college in the East were present at the Gefaell family Thanksgiving. Then we all went to New York where we joined up with even more of the HF Bar family and continued the reunion at yet another level. It was there that I was introduced to whiskey sour cocktails in the bar of the Commodore Hotel. That was pretty heady stuff for a Wyoming kid.

Hank often visited the Washington area and Dottie Davis, who was then a major stockholder in HF Bar, would host a cocktail party in her Georgetown home. It would be filled with dozens of people bonded by the HF Bar connection. It was an experience to be a part of these gatherings and meet HF Bar people in their "other" element.

The HF Bar connection phenomenon would continue when I graduated from George Washington University. I spent the summer working at the HF Bar Ranch and pondered my career. The Vietnam War helped with the decision making process as I was faced with the decision to either volunteer for the service of my choice or get drafted. In the end, I joined the United States Air Force and began what was to be a twenty-seven year career.

In 1963, I received my commission as a second lieutenant and since I had some time before reporting to a technical course at Chanute AFB in Rantoul, Illinois, I went to HF Bar for a month's leave. It was then that I met my future wife, Georgina Mackie, from Stow-on-the-Wold near Broadwell, Gloucestershire, England. Georgina was working at HF Bar because of an HF Bar connection, as well.

The year before she had met a family in England who offered her a job as a nanny for their children in Maine. She lived with them for almost a year. When it was time for her to return to England, her employer, Judy Davis, who was a friend of Hank's, allowed as how it would be a shame for Georgina to return to England without first seeing the West. So, Judy Davis contacted Hank and arranged a job for

Georgina. When I showed up on the scene we became acquainted and interested in each other. Since I had to leave soon and report for duty in Illinois, I invited Georgina to stop and see me on her way to New York, where she had a scheduled departure date to return to England by boat.

The long and the short of it was, that Georgina did come to see me, and we got married, having known each other for only three weeks. As soon as we married, she had to catch the boat and return to England to face the music, as we told no one we were going to get married. There wasn't time.

Over the years of our marriage and involvement with my Air Force career which took us to parts near and far, we would have three children: Jamie, Tommy and Kate. My first regular Air Force assignment was to Ellsworth AFB, South Dakota, a mere five hour drive in those days from the HF Bar Ranch, so we had the opportunity to visit the ranch often for a year or two. In later years, from other widespread locations, we would visit the ranch whenever we could arrange military leave. Little did we know, that in future years, Jamie's exposure to the HF Bar Ranch would cause him to follow in the footsteps of his great uncle, Dean Thomas, and embark upon what has become, so far, a lifetime career at the HF Bar Ranch.

The Dudes

Two guests became so enamored of the ranch that they bought major portions of stock in the corporation. They were Dorothy (Dotty) Mondell Davis and Frederica (Freddie) White.

Dotty Davis was the daughter of Franklin Wheeler Mondell. Frank Mondell was born in St. Louis, Missouri in 1860, settled in Wyoming in 1887 and proceeded to become a prominent figure with a long list of accomplishments. Among them was the fact that he took an active part in the establishment and building of the town of Newcastle, Wyoming. He was elected as the first mayor of the town and later became a member of the first Wyoming State senate and then was elected as a Republican to the Fifty-fourth Congress. He lost his bid for a second term and served in Washington in various appointments until he was elected to the Fifty-sixth Congress and served in the House of Representatives, with various important committee assignments from 1899 until 1922 when he did not seek renomination. He did, however, run for the Senate, but unsuccessfully. He later became a director of the War Finance Corporation in 1923 for two years and then studied law and was admitted to the bar in 1924 and commenced practice in Washington, D.C.. In this capacity, Frank did some legal leg work for Skipper and Warren Gorrell when they were trying to establish HF Bar West in the late 1920s. Frank Mondell remained active in Republican politics and at one time served as chairman of the Republican National Committee before he died in Washington, D.C., on August 6, 1939.

His daughter, Dotty, worked in the newspaper business in Washington, D.C., and married Sherlock Davis, who was in the sugar business. The history of how Dottie became associated with the HF Bar Ranch is, unfortunately, dim, but there was probably an association between her father and Skipper over the years.

At any rate, Dottie became an aficionado of HF Bar and eventually a major stockholder in 1949, when she bought some stock from Bobby Horton, who had by this time figured out that he did not have any kind of future with HF Bar. Initially, he sold about half of his stock to Dottie and most of the remainder only a few years later. Dottie also bought a significant amount of stock from Jack O. Horton, Senior, in the mid-1950s.

Dottie was active in the annual stockholders meetings and did her part to promote HF Bar Ranch on the east coast. When she made her annual pilgrimage to HF Bar she resided in Farthest West. Dottie's husband, Sherry, was to die and after a time Dottie married a man named Wes Frame.

Dottie died in 1975. Her estate contained provisions that gave Jack Horton Jr. the option to buy the major share of her stock, which he did in 1979. Jack's acquisition of Dottie's stock cemented his position as the major stockholder in HF Bar Ranch.

Another significant stockholder was Frederica (Freddie) White. When Freddie graduated from Vassar in 1933, she somehow got word of the fact that Skipper was looking for a ranch secretary. Freddie interviewed with Skipper and got the job. She then began a cycle of working at HF Bar in the summer and another dude ranch in Arizona in the winter.

In the fall of 1940, while visiting her sister in Summit New Jersey, Freddie met George White. George was a widower with two children, George, Jr. and Mary Carolyn. George and Freddie fell in love and married in the spring of 1941. Freddie was supposed to work at HF Bar that summer, but since she wasn't able to do that she recruited Marjorie Brown to work in her place. That was the summer that Margi met Tom Barker, a wrangler. Their story was told earlier.

Some years later, in 1949, Freddie prevailed upon George to visit HF Bar. When they arrived, George was horrified by what he thought was excessive drinking. He wanted to turn around and leave right then. Freddie, however, implored George to please give the ranch a twenty-four hour chance. George reluctantly agreed.

Freddie took George on a very long ride over Stone Mountain

from which he returned saddle sore and weary. He was miserable. Freddie took him to their cabin where George got into the bathtub to ease his bleeding knees. While he was soaking, Freddie plied him with an abundance of martinis, for medicinal purposes, of course. Freddie's caring nursing technique provided the balm needed to mellow George out. He became a true HF Bar aficionado and he and Freddie returned to HF Bar every summer for the next thirty-five years.

During one of their vacations, George accomplished a first at HF Bar. He purchased a king size bed and installed it in their cabin, Roundup. George's daughter, Mary Carolyn, jokingly muses about whether George was lecherous or whether George and Freddie, who were both very tall, just got fed up with the small ranch beds. She suspects it was the latter!

Freddie loved HF Bar so much that, over time, she acquired a significant amount of HF Bar stock, most of it from Jack O. Horton, Sr. Jack probably sold the stock because he needed the money, but, most likely, he also had realized that he was not destined to play a part in the ranch operation and so had no particular reason to hold on to the stock. The shares certainly did not pay dividends.

Freddie did more than just vacation at HF Bar every year. She owned enough stock to have a say in ranch matters and was an active participant. She also took an active part in promoting HF Bar at every opportunity and for a few years wrote an amusing newsletter, *Hosstalgia* which I mentioned before. Freddie's newsletter did much to record some HF Bar guest history and provides an inkling about the HF Bar family. A typical example is found in the 1961 edition:

...An awful lot of old timers came back to the ranch—Doris and Tucker Ames were there from Nyack, and Joan Aitken was back for the first time since 1940 when she was Joan Brown and just a teenager. And of course the George Brooks were back—George first came in 1929 and he and Polly have been coming for twelve straight years. It wouldn't be the same without them and "Danny" and

"Charley" (Note: Their horses) *would be sad sacks if they didn't come back. Mrs. King D. Brown was back, too, with her son, Grover. She started coming in 1935. And Elise Cooper was here for a few days—she and her family have moved to Quogue which is on some long island (sic) near New York. Mr. Wendell Fentress was back with David, and then of course the Fultons all came. Betsy worked in the chuck wagon again, scrambling eggs and mashing milkshakes, and Penny came with her and spent the whole summer. The rest of the Fulton clan wandered in at various times and finally all wound up being there at once—in East Meets West cabin, natch!*

Dede Gray was here for the first time, but her mother, Betty Baldwin, was here way back in 1927, and the Greers from Washington were back, and did Kay ever cotton to my little black and white Pinto pal named "Thunder". It was sure mutual, and Kay could really handle that horse! Ann Gardner came with the twins, Lynn and Tom, and we were sorry that Bob couldn't get here— especially "Jonesie" for Jonesie and Bob seem to have a great deal to discuss on the trails—though Jonesie says it is kind of one-sided and he can't get a word in edgewise. Bill, their other son, was a hasher. Mary Lou Hackenburg came for the first time but her father was here in 1928 and 1929. Bob and Louise Heartt were back, and so were Roy and Hazelle Hoffman, and I think they covered the whole darn state of Wyoming. And of course the Hickoks were here with Fred, and their pals from Casper, the Carl Jenkins. ...John and Nellie Kelly were back,—he first started coming in the 1920s. You ought to see the saddlebags John made—all by himself. ..Serge and Helen Klotz shellacked everybody at some game called bridge—I'm not exactly sure what it is, as we horses mainly stick to stud poker. Serge and George White spent a heck of a lot of time trying to open up an old, old trail to the Middlefork...Jimmy Jacques was back, and she started to come in 1929. Hugh and Phyllis Long were here, with Margie and Elsa, and we sure missed Bronco who has been wrangling us horses around for a good many years. That tall guy in the red and

Saddlestring

white striped pants got Bronc into the army, but I guess that means
we can all relax about the world situation. Phillip, Phyllis Long's
other son has gotten so darn good at hashing he didn't spill a single
bowl of soup down anybody's neck...

...Jane and Jeannie Lee were here from San Francisco—sorry
Ivy couldn't make it...And Jimmy Lagae came back with Ina—and
she is really pretty, even from horse standards—and their cute little
trick of a cowgirl named Susie was with them. Jimmy first came in
1932. Truman and Sis Morsman were there, of course, covering all
the territory. This year "Long Tom," one of my closest buddies, took
Truman up to Seven Brothers Lakes, and figured when he got there
he'd HAD it, so he took off for home, hell bent for election! He got
kind of mixed up on the trail and finally found a forest ranger and got
him to call up Dean Thomas, my boss, to come and get him. When
he got back to the ranch Truman came up to ride him, and darned if
those wranglers didn't have him tied to every post in the corral, and
they even had a cowbell latched to his neck! It was sure funny.

George McElroy was there and he used to be a hasher back in
1936. This year he bought his wife, Elvira, and Candee and Tim, and
all of them took to the ranch like a calf takes to its ma, so we're
hoping they'll be back this summer. The Jim Orrs came, and Hattie
and Stuart Pollard brought Art and the new baby, and Jack and
Eleanor Horton came over a time or two from Salt Lake. Lolly Espy
Parkhurst was back with her new husband, Bill—Lolly started
coming in 1947. Mrs Lawrence Stabler was here with her husband
and she first came in 1922. And Andy and Potter Stewart (Note:
Associate United States Supreme Court Justice.) were here, too—
Andy first came in 1937. One day when Potter was out fishing a
little late Andy got really worried about him. "Think of it," she said,
"if anything should happen to Potter—all those FOUR-FOUR
DECISIONS in the Supreme Court. Harriet and young Potter and
David were there, too, of course, and Potter was really hauling in
the fish. So were the Schroeders and the Shafors. The Shafors first

started coming in 1937, and if Marian and Shafe can't catch fish,
there aren't any to catch. Pete and Jean Taylor were back with Susie
and Ann and you ought to see Ann ride "Peanuts."
  Susie takes after her old man all right, for she can throw a lot of
mean horseshoe ringers in the pits...

For several summers George's son, George Jr., worked at HF
Bar in several capacities: hasher, driver and hay crew member. He also
served in the U. S. Army and attended ranger and airborne schools
where he developed parachuting skills. When George left the Army in
1961 he and his wife, Josephine worked at HF Bar before they began
the rest of their lives. Freddie wrote, in her newsletter, how George
put his parachuting skills to use that summer. George prevailed upon
Wales Wolfe, a good friend of HF Bar and accomplished pilot, to
take George up in his Piper Cub airplane (which he used to land
regularly on a hayfield in back of the Horton House) so George could
give a demonstration jump over HF Bar. Freddie's description of the
event was:

  Guess what George White did? He took to scaring the dudes
out of their wits...by jumping out of airplanes into the ranch pastures.
Some people are nuts, don't you think?

George's daughter, Mary Carolyn (MC) worked in the store
when she was a teenager. She eventually married Stebbins Chandor,
a physician. Mary Carolyn and Steb have been faithful HF Bar guests
since 1964 as have their children and grandchildren.
  Freddie White cared immensely about HF Bar and in 1967 she
sold her stock to Jack Horton, Jr., because she wanted him to be able
to carry on with the ranch. After he bought the stock, Jack Jr. must
have written Freddie a letter outlining his plans for the ranch. In a

Saddlestring

letter written on October 25, (Note: Year unknown but most likely 1967.) Freddie wrote:

> *...To get on to your letter: It is exciting. Just what we wanted to have happen—and we knew we could never do it ourselves—largely through ignorance of what SHOULD be done, and how to do it—partly because we are too far from the scene and 3 weeks there constitutes our only vacation. It is so gratifying to have you have our stock, and I am pleased that the results of the appraisal show that the ranch is worth $450,000 at least, and therefore your stock is already worth over twice what you paid. I KNEW Jackie, that if we had held we could have made a very substantial amount on our stock—but that would have missed the point entirely. We didn't buy that ranch to make money. We bought it to save it for you and young George to run together. It didn't work out that way—but half of that dream worked out, and it is nice that the "half" is a HORTON!*

Freddie then reveals her thoughts about the other major stockholder, Dottie Davis and gives Jack Jr. some advice:

> *...Your future plans for the rancho sound exceedingly good, and we are glad you are "making haste slowly." You say several times in your letter, "Dottie and I plan..." I beg of you to be careful on this score. It is not that we don't like Dottie, it is that she is easily persuaded and the last person who sees her before a decision, is likely to sway her to that person's side. ...You pretty much know where you stand with Hank and Dean—and therefore the person to worry about is Dottie. Doubtless this is none of my business— nothing about HF Bar is any of my business anymore—but I want YOU to succeed so much, both personally and for the ranch that I'm daring to say this to you. I hope that George and I can mess out of things..*

Freddie closed her letter with almost an entire single spaced typewritten page that described the last mountain trip that she made with her husband George. She began that part of the letter with:

...I think of all the things you plan to do, the thing which appeals so personally to us is the use of the mountains...

Unfortunately, Freddie died unexpectedly in January of 1975. George remarried Elizabeth "Betty" Washburn, a widow, in 1976 and introduced Betty and her children and grandchildren to HF Bar. They continued to spend their summer vacations at the ranch for about the next ten years. George White died in October, 1988.

Often HF Bar and its guests made the society columns. Betty Beale, the noted Washington society columnist was a good friend of Dottie Davis. I do not know if she ever visited HF Bar, but she must have had an inside track to write about HF Bar in a column published in *The Hartford Times* on August 14, 1968. The column read:

...Out at HF Bar Ranch near Sheridan, Wyo., the working and dude ranch where 150 horses roam the most beautiful terrain in the country, people poured in as the convention (Note: Democratic National Convention.) *began and spent all their time riding and fishing. They brought their transistors, but static in the mountains doesn't encourage listening.*

They arrived as the more politically curious departed, including two former Life Magazine *beauties. One was Sally McLaglen, wife of filmdom's director, Andrew McLaglen. About 15 years ago she was picked by* Life *as one of the 10 most beautiful women in America. The other was former diplomat Francis Spalding's German born wife Sigrid, whose calm, brunette beauty once adorned the cover of the magazine.*

Saddlestring

The director of the new Devil's Brigade, *starring Bill Holden, and* Bandalero, *with Jimmy Stewart, Raquel Welch and Dean Martin sat taller in the saddle than his favorite western star John Wayne. Andy, a bigger man even than his late father, Victor McLaglen, is 6 feet 7! When he had a birthday party at the ranch of oil tycoon Jack Love and his wife bought a pair of stilts for Sally.*

The most unusual thing in the West this summer was the Gourmet Pack Trip.

The Charles Galeys, former Philadelphia Mainliners of the Galey & Lord textile fortune who now have a ranch at Sheridan; Alada Robinson Sage of the Sage Foundation; Montana cattle baron Albert (Buster) Brown were four of the adventurous sixsome who annually camp out for a week by the snowy peaks of the Black Tooth. When they took their first pack trip the women complained bitterly of the dullness of the daily fare; so thenceforth a fifth pack horse carried delicacies Daniel Boone never dreamed of.

They slept in sleeping bags under tents but they began their evening meals with Mai Tai cocktails prepared at the Outrigger Canoe Club in Honolulu and flown in dry ice to Sheridan. (Note: Apparently they were then delivered to the ranch and a wrangler was dispatched to make the final leg of the trip to deliver the precious cargo.) *The cocktails were ordered by Marine Corps Gen "Buck" Schmuck, who with New York orthopedic surgeon Dr. Ax Hill, completed the group.*

Life among the Camp Fire Girls was never like this!

Yours, B.B.

Thousands of other interesting guests passed through the main entrance of the HF Bar Ranch during this period. For some, it was only a one-off experience. For others, the experience was repeated many times. For yet others, an annual visit to HF Bar has become a perpetual routine that if broken, for some reason, leaves an indelible hole in their year. One thing is for sure; even only one visit gives most people a plethora of memories and usually a yearning to return that can last a lifetime.

A laundry list of all the wonderful people that have become part of the HF Bar family would serve no purpose for this book. A collection of all their tales could be the subject of yet another book. Edgar Morsman did a valiant job of collecting some and publishing them in *The Postmistress of Saddlestring*. There are many more out there.

HF Bar has survived because of its loyal fan base. And the souls of the fans are salved when they make their pilgrimage to HF Bar. It's an incredible and mutually complementary cycle. It might be called the HF Bar Experience.

Part V

A Work in Progress

1981—Present

Chapter 10

The Transition
1981-1989

Challenges

Hank and Dean were the symbols of the HF Bar Ranch. Over the years they had acquired an extensive fan club comprised of hundreds of HF Bar loyalists who made annual, or at least periodic, pilgrimages to HF Bar.

Margi, on the other hand, was the new kid on the block. She had no ranch management credentials and certainly no management experience in the dude ranching business. And since she and Jack had never married, Margi didn't even have marital status or the Horton name to hang her hat on. That is not to say, though, that Margi did not have a following, even from the beginning. In her first year at HF, while Jack was still alive, Margi made many fast friendships that endure today.

But what Margi really had going for her was a legacy. Jack left her his interest in the ranch because he believed she had the stuff required to insure that the place his grandfather had started seventy years before would survive intact. Margi took that charge seriously. To carry it out would not be easy. Many challenges lay ahead.

Margi had a healthy respect and fondness for Dean and Hank and all the contributions they had made to HF Bar in their many combined decades of service. But they were getting old. She also had a respect for Jack's wishes, so she set about to gently insert herself into the management equation and learn the business. It didn't take her long to get her feet wet.

Margi's first initiative was to save the Clubhouse. The Clubhouse is a massive log structure built in 1924 by a traveling Swedish builder. (Note: He was also employed to construct the log recreation building at Paradise Ranch at the same time.) The Clubhouse is built into a hillside and at the time was the first building encountered on the right hand side of the then main road as one entered the HF Bar. (Note: Margi has since changed the entrance to the ranch so that one enters from either a north or south route which keeps the very center of the ranch complex traffic free, safer and quieter.)

The Clubhouse has always been the ranch social center and the scene for various gatherings, especially weekly dances, over the years. Unfortunately, over the same period of time, the structure had seriously deteriorated. Water leakage from the irrigation ditch above the Clubhouse had taken its toll and rotted the logs on the bottom of the structure. Just how serious the problem was finally came to light when the man who called the weekly square dances refused to work because the floor was so shaky he feared the building would collapse.

Margi launched into the building recovery job with gusto and, at the same time, much trepidation. She engaged a contractor who jacked the enormous structure up so the lower logs could be replaced. The whole operation made Margi very nervous. She had the sinking feeling that the jacked up structure would collapse and they would "end up with a pile of Lincoln Logs" in the swimming pool which was just across the road and down the hill from the Clubhouse. Fortunately, the operation went as planned and the Clubhouse was successfully stabilized. Today, bands willingly play for dances in the Clubhouse with no safety fears.

Margi, in the beginning, received very welcome moral support and practical advice from a neighbor, Christy Love, who at the time owned the neighboring UM Ranch. Christy gave Margi the resolve and confidence to continue. Margi said that Christy told her words to the effect of "If I can do it then so can you."

And continue on she did. The next priority project was the replacement of the swimming pool that was built in 1931. One of the first jobs that Dean had when he went to work for the HF Bar Ranch was to lug thousands of old horseshoes to the pool construction site. The horseshoes were used to reinforce the concrete. Dean once told Bob Platt that the pool, which at the time was heated with a wood stove, was the first outdoor heated swimming pool in the United States. Dean's assertion is debatable and cannot be verified—but it makes a good story.

Over the years the pool had developed cracks that allowed untreated water from Rock Creek to invade the pool. This eventually resulted in what one observer declared to be a new coat of green paint. Actually, on closer examination it proved to be green algae that caused its condemnation by the health department. Obviously a new one was in order. Margi, sensitive to the fact that Dean had a long association with the pool, not only because of the fact that he helped build it but had also maintained it over the many years, asked Dean if he would mind if they replaced it. Apparently his answer was, "Well, hell no. Let's get rid of the goddamned thing!" So much for sentimentality at the HF Bar Ranch!

Margi remembers, however, that as the old pool was being demolished she observed both Dean and Hank standing together, hands in pockets, on the porch of the office watching the operation. For them it must have been a moment of mixed emotions. Margi also recalls that when the construction crew tore down a large patch of shrubbery to make way for the new pool, they discovered literally thousands of champagne corks littering the ground beneath. History does not relate how they came to be there.

While these two projects had to be done, others did not, at least as far as Hank and Dean were concerned. Hank had a bittersweet feeling about the whole situation. She was relieved when she realized the ranch was going to continue, but she hated to see any improvements. How she rationalized that the ranch could successfully continue without needed improvements is unknown. Dean, on the other hand, according to Margi, was more accepting. But there was still some resistance on his part—sometimes quite a lot.

As Margi began to get her feet on the ground she became more confident. Her awareness of the extent of deterioration that had occurred over the years prompted her to conclude some improvements in operations and management were sorely needed. Many of them had been called to her attention by Jack when he was still alive. Some items had been discussed many times at annual meetings but the discussions were not followed up by action. Margi knew that action was required if the ranch was to remain a credible operation.

In spite of some resistance, Margi charged ahead and worked her way through her initial critical "to do" list. When she got through the end of the list in 1985, she compiled, for the record, a list of projects completed from 1981 to 1985 and the results. Margi prefaced the record with the statement:

Examples of negative attitudes and opposition 1981—1985:
All of the following projects have been carried out and were greeted

with disapproval. Note that several of these were mentioned in Ranch Corporation Minutes dating back to the 60s, but were never carried out.

The list read as follows:

Project 1
Trimmed over 200 trees.
Result
Haven't lost a roof since.

Project 2
Water Filtration Plant—guests were getting sick and had been advised by the Johnson County Health Clinic to drink bottled water.
Result
Provides safe drinking water—Easier on plumbing, washing machines, etc.

Project 3
Saddles rebuilt
Result
Reduced liability risk—Safer, more comfortable for guests and horses—easier to use.

Project 4
South Fork Ditch—we were not able to flood irrigate 2 new fields—Grimm and South Fork—Had to be irrigated using aluminum pipe costing $50 per day in diesel fuel in addition to pump repair and employee time.

Result

At approx. cost of $5,000 we are now able to irrigate 4 fields—completely eliminating pump/pipe use.

Project 5

Field Fertilization, Plowing, Replanting—Can find no record of last fertilization.

Result

In one year, hay tonnage went from 126 tons (1981) to 326 tons and has remained at that level. Much field improvement, i.e. rocks, ditches.

Project 6

Main Water Line—by own admittance, put in in the 1920s with second hand pipe.

Result

Where pipeline is new, problems have been virtually eliminated. Easier for more than one person to know system to turn on and off.

Project 7

Roofing—almost all roofs are in ill-repair. A systematic replacing had to and has been undertaken.

Results

Eliminates continual expensive patching and internal damage to buildings.

Project 8

Guests staying for shorter periods of time...need riding instruction...many mention it...not as experienced as long-term dudes.

Result

Adds to enjoyment of stay...Eliminates many liability problems and lessens risks of serious injury to riders and horses.

Project 9

Bakery Bin—Garbage cans were unsanitary, difficult to clean around, inconvenient. Wooden table was illegal.

Result

Adds convenience for baker. Easier to clean around. At $800 cost was much more economic than commercial types offered by Nobel and Northern Supply for $1200.

Project 10

Pack trips—have gotten sloppy. Wranglers taking turns has completely eliminated any consistency. Pack equipment had been arranged to be re-furbished. Against a direct order to Red Rideout, this was not accomplished.

Result

Much interest from guests. Potential income producer if given proper attention.

Neither Hank, Dean nor Margi were shrinking violets. Rather, they were strong, opinionated people. Hank and Dean were old, tired and in ill health. Margi was young, energetic and full of ideas. She also believed that if she kept the ranch intact it was a way of keeping Jack alive. While they all usually did their best to be amicable to each other, there were occasional flare-ups generated by frustration on both sides.

Often the conversations were spirited. Some of it has been recorded. In a fit of pique, Dean was reported to have said:

...You just want to get rid of Hank and me...

To which Margi replied:

...Not so...but can no longer tolerate this constant erosion

with negative criticism and nasty remarks...

And, Dean retorted:

> *...You'll lose lots of guests if Hank and I aren't here...*

And Margi replied again:

> *...#1 I do not want you to leave; #2, Perhaps that would be the case. However, there is a very healthy percentage of new guests and we will lose them ALL if the situation remains the same...*

Dean is also reported to have said:

> *...In another couple of years, she'll have gone through all of the money...some things need to be done, but she's gone overboard...I used to be able to talk Jack out of these hair-brained schemes, but she just gets mad...*

And Margi's reaction was that it was:

> *...Frustration more than anger; I'm taking the rap for trying to put back together something that has been neglected for years...*

And, so it went for several years. But it wasn't always like that. Margi enjoyed Dean's company. Often Dean would take Margi out to dinner in town and always took the trouble to introduce her to his many local friends. In fact, it was Dean who introduced Margi to her future husband, Dave Bliss, in the local feed store. Dean, in Margi's opinion, was "quite a guy" and she was very fond of him.

Margi is also quick to point out that in spite of the challenges, she, Dean, and Hank had some good times together. She still

During the transition there were challenges but also some good times.
From left, Margi Schroth, Dean Thomas, and Hank Horton.
(Courtesy of the HF Bar Ranch)

remembers, fondly, some of the Christmas celebrations they had at HF Bar, often with Margi's father, Ray Schroth, and other members of her family present.

While most of the transition discussions occurred behind closed doors, some of the discussion spilled over into the dude arena. Hank and Dean were not too reticent about expressing their opinions to their longtime friends and guests. Many things got said at cocktail parties.

Some guests, particularly some of the old time guests, were prone to take sides though not always in an overt way. Mostly it only took the form of expressing their opinions at cocktails. Margi had to prove herself to them, and in some cases it was "damned if she didn't and damned if she did." I distinctly remember that one time when I was there Margi had instructed one of the groundskeepers to mow the weeds around the saddle barn to "tidy things up a bit." One of the old-timers, sitting on the bench at the saddle barn groused that she shouldn't do that because the weeds kept the dust down!

While some grumbled, everyone enjoyed the benefits of the improvements—like improved water quality! Most people adjusted. But in a rare instance the opposition to Margi manifested itself in more than grumbles at cocktail parties.

Dr. Norman A. (Ax) Hill was a noted New York hand surgeon. He had been a regular at HF Bar since his parents, Dr. Norman and Libba Hill of Cincinnati, became regulars at the ranch in the 1940s. Ax was a gregarious guy and a gracious host and was a very good friend of mine. In the later years of his career he would spend two or three months at HF each summer. He had visiting privileges at the local hospitals in Sheridan and Buffalo and did a fair amount of surgery while on his summer vacation.

Ax's problem was that he had an excessive fondness for HF Bar; but under Hank and Dean, not Margi. Ax also was a self-styled expert on everything at the ranch and at times assumed the mantle of third in command. His opinion was not always sought and, when received, not always welcome. He was noted for standing around the corral when it was time for the morning ride. He had acquired a couple of Missouri Fox Trotter horses that could walk the legs off of most ordinary horses. Ax would wait for unsuspecting new guests and present himself to them as the resident wrangler who would be glad to take them on their introductory ride and tour of the ranch.

Most new guests aren't hardened to the saddle and it is customary to take them on relatively short rides until they get used to the experience. Ax, undaunted, would line them out and go on a long first ride. If that weren't bad enough, he would put his Missouri Fox trotter into high gear and then chide his bouncing and saddle weary retinue: "by God you've got to keep up if you're going to get anywhere." The result was shaken, sore and weary guests that survived a really awful ordeal. Ax spoiled the first ride for many new ranch guests which annoyed Dean. He would mention it to Ax and he would desist for a while, but not for long.

In later years, in the late 1980s and early 1990s, Ax presented a real problem for the ranch. He had trouble adjusting to Margi's management of the ranch and was very vocal in expressing his views. In addition, his excessive drinking, his interference with the operation, and his actions around other guests created difficulties, and Ax was asked to leave.

Ax tried his hand at a few other dude ranches in the area but had unfortunate experiences at them as well. In his last years, some of Ax's personal problems, and probably his loneliness, became too much for him and he chose to depart the world under his own terms. It was a sad ending. But Ax, in the end, left a positive legacy for the area he loved so much. Ax had a considerable estate, and, in addition to several bequests to eastern establishments, gave very sizeable financial gifts to the Sheridan Memorial Hospital in Sheridan and the Johnson County Healthcare Center in Buffalo.

During the transition, Margi looked for ways to ease some of Dean's managerial burden so he would have an easier time of it. She didn't want Dean to go; she just thought he should be a bit freer with more time to enjoy himself. So, she hired a local man who had a wealth of experience to take some of the load. The concept was right, but the idea didn't work because Dean didn't slack off; he just kept on doing what he had always done. He did not know how to ease up. It wasn't in his nature. In the end, Dean's designated replacement moved on because there were just too many bosses around HF Bar.

Margi would try other management schemes with various other players over the next few years, some of which didn't work. Some years after the transition period, however, Margi would light on the right management equation and personnel that would allow HF Bar to continue as a successful operation.

Family

While the Horton family had become just Hank and her two step-grandchildren, Anne and Will Dixon, and Bill Horton's daughter, Suzanne Timken, Margi began a family of her own.

In 1987, Margi married Dave Bliss, a cattle rancher from Otter, Montana. Each operated their own ranch and did a lot of commuting to be with each other. Their daughter, Lily, was born on June 5, 1988. With her marriage Margi also acquired an extended family as well. Dave had three step-children: Lindy Burgess and Steve and Charlie Pattison, and a son, Scott Bliss, with his wife, Linen, all of whom live in the Sheridan area.

In 1992, after five years together, Margi and Dave decided to dissolve their marriage. While they had many things in common, they did not share a desire to have more children and the rift in their relationship grew too great. The divorce was amicable, however, and Margi and Dave, and all the other family members, remain good friends. In fact, Charlie Pattison, an accomplished silversmith, displays his beautifully crafted western silver jewelry and buckles on the porch of the HF Bar Ranch house every summer and sells it to appreciative guests. Repeat guests are adorned with a lot of Charlie's works of art.

Beginnings and Endings

In 1984, my son, Jamie Ringley, was introduced to the HF Bar Ranch scene as an employee. Although he had visited the ranch when he was young, he did not really "know" it. So the family decided he must be given the opportunity to experience HF Bar as an employee and arranged a job for him in the summer after he completed his first year of college at Auburn University at Montgomery, Alabama. We lived in Virginia at the time, so when Jamie finished school I picked him up and we went to the ranch.

Jamie had a wonderful summer. He was able to work alongside his great-uncle Dean, as I had, and to get acquainted with Margi and Hank. Jamie loved the experience and worked several other summers in various capacities during the transition. Little did I know, nor did he, that it was the beginning of what has become, so far, a life long career.

It was when I took Jamie to the ranch that Dean was diagnosed with lung cancer. He had been feeling ill and his doctor in Sheridan referred him to doctors in Denver for further diagnosis. I took Dean to the airport early one morning. He flew to Denver and was met by an old army buddy who took him to the doctor where he was examined and received the dreaded news. Dean flew back to Sheridan that night and I met him at the airport. I asked him about the diagnosis. He told me it was not so good.

When we returned to the ranch it was late, but the lights were still on in the Horton House so Dean and I stopped by. Hank and Ax Hill were talking and Dean and I fixed drinks for ourselves and settled in. Dean then told Hank and Ax the bad news.

Dean acknowledged the grim reality of the situation and toward the end of the conversation declared, "By God, if it gets too bad I know how to take care of it!"

With Dean's inference that he might take his own life, if he thought it necessary, Ax looked alarmed and as we were all leaving invited me to his cabin for yet another drink to discuss the matter. He allowed as how he thought we should do something to prevent Dean from doing anything that drastic. I told Ax that I didn't think he really meant it and that even if he did I thought we should respect his right to do whatever he thought best. After all, it was his life and he had to deal with it. Ax finally agreed. Years later, when Ax took his own life, I remembered that ironic conversation.

Dean underwent surgery and, typically, the day after he arrived back at the ranch he was up at the corral roping horses. Eventually, however, the illness took its toll. Dean died aged 77, on October 27, 1987.

The day Dean died, Dave and Margi had driven Dean up to look at the Sawmill pasture. At the time, it was clear to Margi that Dean was dying. But Dave still chuckles when he recalls that Dean, even though sick and frail and dying, noticed that someone had left a garden hose unrolled and grumbled about it. He was the HF Bar foreman to the last drop.

When they returned to the Horton House, Dean was so weak that Dave had to carry him upstairs and put him in bed. Later, Margi went in to see him. He was laying there peacefully on his side with his head resting on his hands. He told Margi that he was going to die. Margi responded, as we all would in a similar situation, "Oh, of course you're not," to reassure him.

Margi then went to the telephone and called me—at that time I was stationed in England—to tell me that Dean was dying. She also asked me if I wanted to talk to him. For some reason that I still do not understand, I declined. Possibly, I subconsciously wanted to remember him in a certain way, not as a detached feeble voice from a deathbed. Soon after, Dean died.

Dean died during hunting season. At the time a party of hunters was staying at the ranch. The evening that Dean died, the hunters were still dining in the Ranch House just opposite the Horton

House. Margi knew if an ambulance arrived to take Dean away the hunters would notice and naturally assemble to find out what was happening. Margi didn't want a commotion. She wanted it to be quiet and dignified for Dean. So she and Dave covered Dean up and he lay there peacefully until late in the evening when the hunters finally returned to their cabins. Then she called the ambulance and Dean was quietly removed from HF Bar after fifty-six years of service. HF Bar had, indeed, lost an icon.

Dean would have been highly amused by the scene of Margi and Dave waiting for the hunters to finish dining so the ambulance could be summoned. If he had been able to watch from above, he would most likely have had a wry smile and a mischievous twinkle in his eye as he drank a bourbon and branch water while he waited for the hunters to leave.

When Dean died, Hank was eighty-four years old, sick and fragile. For years she had painfully suffered from what she would call "wonky" hips, and had had several replacements. Not only was advancing age taking its toll, Hank was somewhat embittered. Though she had become inured to death, one cannot help but think that being witness to the passing not only of her own children so long ago, but also to the principal members of the Horton family, must have been a heavy emotional burden to bear. And now Dean was gone, the last link with anything to do with the past and HF Bar. Of course, Hank being Hank, she would never have shared her innermost emotional state with anyone.

Hank was also bitter about the ranch. Though, as I said before, she was glad the ranch was to survive, she took no truck with the changes that were being made. Hank must have thought it was time to go, and she eventually did. On March 20, 1989, Hank died. The last HF Bar icon was gone.

Through it all, Margi had been there for Hank, regardless of their tenuous relationship. Margi believed that she owed it to Jack to look after Hank as well as the ranch. And she did that with compassion and understanding. Margi was present when Hank died at Sheridan Memorial Hospital in Sheridan. According to Margi, Hank was comatose for the last three days of her life; yet, she murmured non-stop as if she were reviewing her entire life.

Oh, that her review could have been understood and captured to possibly explain this enigmatic woman who charmed so many and mystified others. Ed Morsman told me that his uncle Truman, who was devoted to Hank, once said, in the presence of his wife, that Hank was the "most fascinating woman he had ever met."

The disposition of Hank's estate was interesting. Skipper's holistic will had passed his estate into Hank's estate. Skipper's estate, of course, included the HF Bar brand. For years after Skipper's death in 1948 everyone—Hank, Dean and Margi— used the HF Bar brand in livestock transactions. It was common practice for any of them to sign papers for F. O. Horton; for instance, "Margi Schroth for F. O. Horton."

In the process of executing Hank's estate, her attorneys tidied up Skipper's holographic will and estate so Hank's estate could be properly executed. The end result was that Hank's estate, which included her minority share position and the HF Bar livestock brand, was placed in a trust for Will and Anne Dixon. So today the ranch does not use the HF Bar livestock brand but does have complete use of the HF Bar name in all other matters relating to the ranch. Margi acquired the Broken Spear Brand which is now used to brand livestock.

Henriette "Hank" Horton in her final years at the HF Bar Ranch.
(Courtesy of the HF Bar Ranch)

Chapter 11

HF Bar—1989-2005

The Family

Margi and Dave had divorced because of Margi's absolute determination to have a larger family. Margi continued her bent in this direction by working hard to learn the adoption process. She was successful and over a period of years found four beautiful children to join her and Lily at the HF Bar Ranch. The oldest is Margi's daughter Cara, who is twelve. Another daughter, Turner, is ten as is a son, Gus. The latest addition to the family is a baby boy, Avery, who at this writing is two years old.

Margi has kept close contact with the biological realitives of her adopted children. She is very respectful of the fact that her children have the right to be associated with other biological family members who have often been invited to HF Bar. As a result, the situation is honest, open and healthy for all.

Margi has modeled the very successful HF Bar youth activity program, which will be discussed later, based on the needs of all her own children, as they grow up. So, even in their youth, Margi's children have a definite influence on the success of the HF Bar Ranch operation.

As the HF Bar Ranch approaches its one hundredth anniversary in 2011, Margi's family is growing up. Lily will soon begin her college career. For her entire life Lily has been exposed to the hard work required of everyone who helps to make HF Bar successful. Margi has provided Lily with every opportunity to learn the business from the ground up. As a result, Lily has gained a wealth of experience and is able to multi-task and be productive in many areas of the dynamic HF Bar operation. Lily has definite views about her upbringing and future, for she stated:

>   ...*Growing up on the ranch has been so great nothing can compare! I have met so many interesting people, guests and employees. I appreciate the ranch so much and I am very that happy I have gotten the privilege to live here...Right now, I am just thinking about getting into college and doing my own thing. I can totally see*

Each year Margi sends 2,500 Christmas cards with a family photo to friends of HF Bar. Pictured in the 2005 photo are, left to right, Jigger, Cara, age 12; Margi, Gus, age 9; Donut, Lily, age 17; Avery, age 20 months; and Turner, age 9.   *(Courtesy of the HF Bar Ranch)*

myself coming back to the ranch but before I do, I want to have a life apart from it...

Cara, Gus, Turner and Avery, all of whom are much younger, will have the same opportunity as Lily. As they mature and develop in the HF Bar environment, and progress through their high school and college years, it will be interesting to watch how each of them, with their individual personalities and interests, will figure in the future of the HF Bar Ranch. Opportunity awaits the children and the future of the HF Bar Ranch hangs in the balance.

The Team

When Margi arrived on the scene in 1979 HF Bar had a lean workforce; one year round employee, Dean Thomas, and twenty-eight full time summer employees. That size workforce was all that Hank figured was needed to keep the HF Bar doors open because the high guest population was never over eighty at any one time. Since then, the size of the staff has grown.

As the staff has grown, so has the staff concept changed. In past years, it was common practice to refer to the employees as "the help." Margi eschews that term, because today the staff at HF Bar is more than "help" by several magnitudes. To Margi, the "staff is everything."

The days have passed when, in addition to the usual complement of college students and children of guests who worked in the hayfields and dining room, the ranch procured employees wherever they could find them, often from employment agencies. Today, HF Bar has a recruiting program with many major colleges and universities. This program, plus word of mouth from trusted employees, guests and friends, results in over three hundred applications each year for only sixty positions. Thus, Margi and Jamie are able to be selective and form quality staff relationships that last years.

Margi takes care to nurture the staff at the very beginning of the season. She conducts orientations to insure that staff members understand how important they are to the operation and also what is expected of them. They are made to understand how they will be working in an atmosphere of "studied chaos" and that they must be "incredibly flexible." Margi is able to tell, in about two days, if a new employee is going to be successful in the HF Bar environment. The majority are successful and become part of the HF Bar culture for life. Even though most move on to other careers, HF Bar remains an anchor for them and a basis for many lasting relationships. A limited number of employees, about seven, are year around members of the team and many others return every season for many years.

One who has learned to be flexible and cope with the studied chaos is Jamie Ringley, the Resort Manager. When Jamie graduated from Auburn University in 1988, he came to visit us in Hawaii while he explored his career options. After a short time working at part time jobs while he pondered his future and pulled the slivers out of his hands from working in a lumber yard, he suddenly announced in the spring of 1988, "I guess I'll go to HF Bar." He did, and has been there ever since.

Jamie has probably worked at every job available at HF Bar except the corral, and so has learned the job of office manager from ground up. Like his great uncle Dean Thomas, Jamie has developed a loyalty to HF Bar that transcends mere "employment." Jamie has been at Margi's side as she has restructured, expanded and reinvigorated HF Bar.

Like me, Jamie met his future wife at HF Bar. Frannie Payson first arrived at HF Bar with her parents, Bill and Harriet, when she was twelve years old in 1984, which was, incidentally, the first year Jamie worked at HF Bar. Frannie then vacationed at HF Bar every summer until 1991 when she worked as a cabin girl. The next summer, she came as a guest but stayed on to work in the kitchen and did so every subsequent year until 1995 when she was the dining room hostess.

Over the years, Jamie and Frannie became very good friends. Their friendship led to romance and they were married at HF Bar in September 1995. They had a glorious wedding outside, with family members and HF Bar guests in attendance. Following the wedding, Jamie and Frannie were delivered to the reception at the Ranch House in the horse drawn ice wagon. As a backdrop to the conclusion of the ceremony, the entire HF Bar horse herd was released from the corral to charge down the lane and signal the beginning of a new life for the newlyweds.

Jamie and Frannie have had two children; Charlie and Georgina. Since Jamie and Frannie were married at HF Bar, they thought it appropriate that their children should be baptized in the same place. And so they were dipped in Rock Creek in ceremonies attended by family and friends of HF Bar. For Charlie's baptismal ceremony, a special song was written by Pat Kelley and sung by his wife Melody Kelley. Both Pat and Melody are long time ranch guests and friends.

Jamie and Frannie Ringley with their children
Charlie (age 7) and Georgina (age 4).
(Courtesy of the author)

Richard Platt is another long time employee who has a special relationship with HF Bar for, as has been mentioned before, he is the fourth generation of the Platt family to be associated with the HF Bar Ranch. Richard was born in 1967 and has spent at least a part of each year of his life since then at the HF Ranch. In 1985 he transitioned from a guest to a summer employee. After he graduated from the University of Vermont in 1989, he spent a large part of each year as an employee and in 1996 became a year round permanent employee.

Richard is instrumental to the success of the HF Bar Ranch. His interests lay in outdoor activity and hunting. He developed the very successful sporting clay shooting program, which was designed by world-renowned shooters, John Cochran and Jack Mitchell, and manages the hunting program which is a large part of the HF Bar operation. Richard also is responsible for the HF Bar Ranch water quality. It is Richard who insures that the water meets all standards mandated by the Environmental Protection Agency. As a result of Richard's efforts, the drinking water at the ranch is of the highest quality and has received numerous awards from the Environmental Protection Agency.

Richard is the only staff member who lives year around on the ranch. (Note: During the winter Margi and her family reside in Buffalo. Jamie Ringley and his family live in Sheridan and Jamie commutes, although during the busy summer season he frequently spends days at a time on duty at the ranch.) Richard's continuous presence and general knowledge of the ranch operation, in addition to his involvement in the hunting program, make him a valuable asset. Richard totally understands the need for flexibility at HF Bar and is capable of performing whatever task is at hand, whether it be making an emergency repair on the plumbing system or filling in as a hasher in the dining room.

While Jamie Ringley and Richard Platt are, at present, the longest serving permanent members of the staff, there is the current longstanding team of year-rounders made up of corral boss Jared

Richard Platt, the fourth generation of his family
to be involved with the HF Bar Ranch.
(Courtesy of Richard Platt)

Gagliano and Paul Scherf who feed and manage all of the cattle and horses throughout the year. There is also the "maintenance and construction" crew headed up, currently, by brothers Eric and Michael Leis. This group of workers has captured the old-style architecture and design in adding to and building new cabins with hardly a hint that these buildings have not all been standing since the 1920s. According to Margi:

> ...These are people who go the distance to match an old stain color, find an old window or door and build a porch slightly slanted so that the ranch maintains its old rustic charm in spite of modern amenities...

There are many others, too numerous to mention here, who return each year as well. They all contribute to the success of the HF Bar Ranch operation and are loyal and valuable members of the team.

The Dudes

When HF Bar guests are asked why they return year after year, in some cases generation after generation, they cite many reasons. One long time guest, Elinor Constable, said it is because the HF Bar Ranch has a unique "soul" that draws her family like a magnet. Another said they return because HF Bar has a special "essence" not found elsewhere. Whatever the appropriate term is to describe the gravitational tug of HF Bar, there is no doubt that to many, many people, the thought of HF Bar evokes cherished emotions and sentiments that bring them back.

One guest, Dick Balsiger, believes that HF Bar, over time, becomes an embedded part of the family heritage. To go somewhere else on the family vacation would be unthinkable! HF Bar has even been used as a yardstick to determine the suitability of potential new family members. Elinor Constable delights in explaining that her children wanted to insure that their intended spouses were compatible with HF Bar so they vacationed with their intended spouses at the ranch before the marriage deals were sealed. Kind of like a trial by fire.

HF Bar devotees have an endless fascination in everything to do with HF Bar. Any change is noticed and can become the subject of discussions for many years. A case in point is Castle Rock.

Castle Rock stands as the sentinel for HF Bar. North of the ranch lies a long ridge that runs east from the Big Horn Mountains. Embedded in the ridge are massive sandstone cliffs that overlook the ranch. The cluster of cliffs was named Castle Rock long ago but the name of the originator has been lost to the ages. As one enters the ranch gate about two miles from the main ranch, Castle Rock is the geological feature that is a sight for the sore eyes of returning guests.

Geologically, Castle Rock is part of the Kingsbury Conglomerate formation. In fact, Castle Rock is an old river bottom whose side banks have eroded away over millions of years.

Castle Rock was further altered by nature in 1959. The moment was unobserved but heard by Dean Thomas on the night of the Alaskan earthquake on August 17th. Margi described Dean's description of the event:

...He was sitting in the Middle Ranch house and he heard this roaring sound. He thought an airplane had hit Castle Rock.

The next morning Dean went out to find fissures in the structure of the westernmost cliff face and gravity had joined forces, no doubt due to the northern tremors, to act as a giant cleaver. The face of the cliff fell as though it had been cleanly sliced away. It became rubble at the bottom of the cliff. Imagine the surprise of returning guests when they discovered that nature had made such a drastic alteration to the ranch sentinel. The aberration is still discussed today.

One long time guest likes to share his love of the ranch and experiences with others and add to the corporate body of HF Bar lore. Ed Morsman wrote *The Postmistress of Saddlestring*, Wyoming which I have quoted extensively in this book. Thanks to his efforts many treasured anecdotal jewels have been recorded for posterity.

Ed and other friends and members of his family engaged themselves in another effort to describe their Big Horn Mountain experiences. In one of three booklets produced, *The Fire Trail*, Ed writes about the background and substance of the effort:

...The HF Bar is smack in the middle of this beautiful and interesting country. Truman Morsman was attracted to the Big Horns in the 1940s and rode through much of the mountains with packers such as Harry Huson who ran the corral in the 1920s and into

Castle Rock in wintertime.
Note how the face of the formation on the left appears to have been sheared off.
(Photo Courtesy of HF Bar Ranch)

the 1930s.   Truman and his friend George White knew most of the trails better than anyone in the area, although they often disagreed with each other. Truman occasionally referred to a trail connecting Penrose and Hunter ranger stations as the Fire Trail because it was designed to assist firefighters in crossing the foothills. Ironically, we recently talked to a volunteer firefighter who had never heard of the trail, which raises a number of interesting questions the Forest Service might address.

Discovering the Fire Trail became somewhat of a quest, although the term discovery is a bit hyperbolic. Some or all of the trail was known to the occasional elk guide, but it was unknown on the ranch.   In 1998, Ed Morsman waded the North Fork just downstream from the Piney Creek diversion ditch, sat down to reboot, and discovered he was sitting on the Fire Trail.   As frequently happens, the solution is easier than stating the problem.

In July, 1999, Robert Constable and Ed Morsman backpacked up the Fire Trail to the Middle Fork and back to the ranch by way of Ginger's cabin. This trip is recounted in The North Fork Revisited. In July, 2000, Robert and Phillip Constable and Ed Morsman decided to finish the Fire Trail quest by walking from Paradise to the Middle Fork, thus completing the Fire Trail from another direction and in different years. Unfortunately, they were seduced by a Circe called Trail 401 which promised splendid scenery, easy walking, and other pleasures. The short cut made Humphrey Bogart's travails in the African Queen look like a stroll in the park. This trip was recounted in The Trail Less Traveled. It was time to do the whole damn trail or know the reason why. We can hear Truman chuckling over a martini. Our first assault on the Fire Trail consisted of two hikers, the second had three, and in some form of faux logarithmic progression, the third attempt was carried out by six survivors ranging in age from 25 to 62. Robert Constable and Ed Morsman were the constants on all three trips. The role of Phillip Constable was played by his understudy and brother-in-law, David Allen, as

Phillip was detained by urgent familial issues. David had a constant smile as he was avoiding the same sort of issues. The remaining three were Ed's sons Jim and Tim Morsman and Jim's fiancée, Angela Peyton....

The three booklets provide a humorous recount of the travails of good friends in their mountainous quests; they also give the reader some pithy insight into some local history, all done with a sparkling and irreverent sense of humor. All of this adds to the HF Bar lore and serves to remind others of the fun and comradeship that can be found at HF Bar Ranch.

HF Bar is also a spawning ground for lasting friendships among the guests. Most inveterate guests vacation at HF Bar at the same time every year and look forward to the annual reunion with their friends. One guest told me that it is hard to get through the first meal after arrival at the ranch because "you have to hug everyone you have not seen for a year."

Guest loyalty to HF Bar takes many different forms but in all cases it is steadfast. In the Hank and Dean era, toward the end, when the ranch was in a physical decline, guests coped. They never considered not going to HF Bar. Instead, some of them took small home repair tool kits as part of their luggage so they could make minor repairs to their cabins.

When Dean and Hank were gone, the guests naturally transferred their loyalty to Margi. They admired her for her determination to preserve the HF Bar Ranch for them and they supported her efforts. But in some cases the transfer of loyalty was not without sadness. One guest lamented that:

...Sadness has prevailed with a change at HF Bar with me

with the loss of our leaders—Dean, Hank and Ax Hill and what used to be a ranch style. Now we have more of a family recreational place which we need to survive. Margi is doing a great job here at HF Bar. I still feel sad but I will deal with this loss...

Guests discover HF Bar in many interesting ways and often find surprising connections. An illustrative case in point involves Bob Montgomery. Bob is a West Point graduate and Vietnam veteran who practiced law in Washington, D.C., for thirty-five years before retiring to northern California.

Bob's first introduction to HF Bar occurred on a ship. Bob was selected as a Rhodes Scholar at Oxford University, England and in 1960 boarded a ship to take him to England. On board, he met another Rhodes Scholar, Jack Horton, Jr.

Bob and Jack became good friends at Oxford. After one year, Jack left Oxford to fulfill his obligation to the United States Navy incurred as a result of his Naval Reserve Officers Training Corps scholarship to Princeton. Bob stayed on to complete the last year of his studies and then married. Bob then takes up the story:

...My wife, Sandy, and I were introduced to the HF Bar by Oxford classmate, Jack Horton, while we were driving across the country on our honeymoon in June, 1962. As we were passing through eastern Montana, it suddenly occurred to me that we might not be too far from the ranch Jack was always carrying on about, at which he had generously invited me to stop and spend the night "whenever I was in the area." Reaching him at the ranch (Note: Jack just happened to be on leave from the Navy.) *from a pay phone in Billings, we were virtually ordered to alter course and head south "taking care not to be ambushed while crossing the Crow Reservation." We spent three wonderful days in the Horton House, and departed vowing to return as soon as time and resources permitted.*

Saddlestring

By the early seventies we had settled just outside Washington, D.C., were raising three children, and I was playing tennis with Jack at least once a week. My mother had also passed away, and my father had remarried a lovely lady named Isabel (Nelson) Carlson, and taken up residence in New York City. In 1975, at Jack's urging, Sandy and I began our annual visits to the ranch with our children, which have continued with only a couple of exceptions for the past thirty years.

At some point in the late seventies, my father and Isabel were at our home for the Thanksgiving holidays, and the conversation turned to the subject of our previous summer vacation at a Wyoming dude ranch. After listening for a few moments, Isabel inquired: "Where in Wyoming is this ranch?" I said: "Eastern Wyoming, at the foot of the Big Horns." She said: "Near what town?" I said: "Sheridan, and an even smaller town named Buffalo." She said: "What is the name of this ranch? "The HF Bar," I replied. After a long pause, Isabel said: "My dad was foreman of the HF Bar, and I was born there!"

This precipitated an extended discussion of the "old-timers" she had known as a child, which included a particularly memorable wrangler named Dean Thomas. We immediately proposed that my father and Isabel join us at the ranch the following summer, but Isabel strongly demurred, explaining that she would love to see the ranch again, but "could never go back there as a dude." It required many months of cajoling, and an extremely warm letter from Dean, to convince Isabel that whatever the barrier had been between the dudes and the "hands" many years ago were no longer in effect, and that she would be warmly welcomed by Hank and Dean, and she and my father joined us at the ranch almost every summer thereafter until my father passed away in 1996.

One of the highlights of each of these vacations for Isabel, which continued until she was almost 80 years old, was a horseback ride over the saddle to a neighboring ranch that Isabel always

referred to as "the TAT" (now known, I believe, as the Rafter Y)...
(Note: The Rafter Y and TAT brands are registered to various members of the Goodwin family. The TAT brand is registered to Ralph Goodwin, Jr. As discussed earlier, the TAT brand originally belonged to Mr. Tathwell, who sold his place—now known as "the lower place"—to the HF Bar Ranch but retained the TAT brand.)

The story is reinforced by Isabel Nelson's daughter, Karen Carlson, who shared a passage that her mother wrote:

...When he (Edward Berger Nelson, born April 6, 1889 in Charlton, Iowa) was 19, he moved to Buffalo, Wyoming with his brother Emil. He drove freight wagons to the fort near Buffalo, and did well enough to buy a snappy team and buggy. This he drove while courting my mother, Margery Elizabeth Frame, who had grown up in Buffalo. Margery and Ed were married June 11, 1913, when she was 17 and he just 24. John Raymond was born the next spring, and Margery Isabel on April 1, 1916. By that time, Ed was foreman at a dude ranch called the HF Bar in Saddlestring, Wyoming, (Note: The name "Saddlestring" did not really exist at that time.) *at the foot of the Big Horn Mountains. There he met Ferry William (Bill) Leach, the delicate son of a Wall Street "Bear" and they decided to start a dude ranch of their own. In 1918, the Nelsons and Bill moved to the TAT Ranch...Bill bought the land; Edward was a partner in buildings, livestock, and all phases of the business as it grew. And grow it did. Bill went East every winter and signed up dudes for the coming summer. Ed ran the ranch. Soon an adjoining ranch was leased, and our family lived there for a number of years...*(Note: And that's yet another story, similar, of course, to the HF Bar story—local boy with the ranch "know-how" backed by Eastern capital.)

Bob Montgomery's story is yet another instance, and there are many others, of a tantalizing interconnectivity. It is often discovered, in the strangest ways, and in the most unexpected places, by those

thousands of souls that have passed through the portals of HF Bar.

Another dear friend and Interior Department colleague of Jack Horton, Jr., became a staunch supporter of Margi and the HF Bar Ranch. Margi describes Chris Farrand:

...Chris Farrand loved Wyoming and, specifically, loved the HF Bar. An avid hunter, fisherman and outdoorsman, Chris made sure he was always available as an ear for me during those early years of running the ranch. Eventually, he sat on the ranch Board of Directors. Chris, his wife, Christa, and sons Stephan and Alex came out for family vacations, and both boys worked at the ranch in the 1980s. In time, they brought their wives and families to stay.

Chris was a vice president with the Peabody Energy Company and for several years the company has brought important clients to the ranch to hunt. Whenever Chris came out to look at a mine or other company holding, he always said, "If I'm within 100 miles of the ranch, I need to stop by to visit."

On September 11, 2000, he came with a business group to ride in the afternoon, have dinner and stay the night. He was in the lead of the group with the wrangler bringing up the rear when something went terribly wrong. Although no one saw it clearly, Chris's horse took off down a hill within a mile of the corral and he was pitched off over the top of the horse's head. He landed on a rock with such an impact that despite forty-five minutes of CPR by the ranch staff and paramedics on the site as fast as possible from town, his injuries were fatal. The horse stood grazing three feet away from where Chris fell.

I, as well as all of the ranch staff members who had known Chris for so long, was devastated. Nothing like this had ever happened. (Note: Margi means during her tenure at HF Bar. She is fully aware of a similar tragic horse accident that killed Bill Horton's wife, Sis, in 1935). *Lily and I traveled back to St. Louis, where Chris lived, to a memorial service bringing his cremated ashes back with us. Later, there was a memorial service at the ranch where a plaque inscribed in his memory was placed on a rock near the site of his death. His sons, Stephan and Alex, his colleagues at Peabody Energy, many of his old Interior Department friends and people from the ranch attended this service.*

One other ironic note that is so typical of the ranch is that Chris was wearing Jack Horton's boots at the time of his accident. When Jack died, I gave Chris all of Jack's good cowboy boots. He had worn them for years. His sons scattered a portion of his ashes on the ranch near where Jack's were placed.

Ranch Operations

Since the HF Bar Ranch was established ninety-four years ago by Skipper Horton and Warren Gorrell, it has been operated continuously for fifty-seven years since Skipper's death by two people with no Horton blood: One, Hank, was a Horton wife; one, Margi, a Horton fiancé.

Hank had ten years of on-the-job-training when she found herself, in 1948, shouldered with the awesome responsibility to insure the survival of the HF Bar Ranch. She shouldered the burden admirably and made sure the ranch endured for the next thirty-three years.

In 1981 Margi found her self thrust into the same situation that Hank had faced thirty-three years before. Margi had been given the same legacy—the stewardship of HF Bar. But the circumstances were different. First, Margi had absolutely no experience to fall back on. What she did have, however, was a charter from Jack and a strong sense of responsibility to carry on for him. Hank and Dean were there to provide continuity but it was up to Margi to use her energy, drive and desire to carry the HF Bar into the future as had the other stewards before her.

Anyone who has ever had anything to do with ranch operations of any kind knows the learning curve is never complete. And it's not complete for Margi either. But when Hank died, Margi had enough experience that she felt comfortable in her own skin and prepared to march on with the preservation and future development of HF Bar.

From the beginning, Margi was not interested in change for change sake. She was determined to hang onto those features of the HF Bar operation that worked; to keep the constants that brought faithful guests back year after year and generation after generation. But, she was also obliged to ferret out what needed to be changed or improved. This process would require experience and experimentation.

One program that did not require analysis was the horseback riding program. It was an obvious keeper.

Horseback riding has always been the core activity and greatest attraction of the HF Bar Ranch. People still ride after breakfast in the morning, and in the evening after supper. People still must sign up for evening riding on a yellow pad posted on the dining room door. And Saturday afternoon is always "horse holiday." It gives the horses a break and the corral crew a chance to rest as well.

The complexion of the riding program has changed, however. In previous decades, guests were more adventurous and were prone to make lengthy forays into the mountains, often on pack trips that lasted for days and sometimes weeks. Today, trips to Willow Park are available and well worth doing because of the excellent fishing, the amazing scenery and the back-to-basics kind of camp life seldom found today. However, fewer people elect this option than in previous years and content themselves with riding over the many trails in the more immediate vicinity of the ranch. (Note: It is interesting to contrast this 2005 observation with the 1930 observation made by Gertrude Horton that less people seemed to take advantage of the mountains than in the very early days. It's all a matter of degree.)

Keeping relatively close to home can prevent some challenges for the ranch and the wranglers. Elinor Constable, whose parents Admiral and Kay Greer were annual fixtures at the ranch for many years, as were Elinor and her husband Peter and their children, for many more, has described one such incident:

It was in the late 1970s that a group of about eight or nine people, including Elinor and Peter, decided it would be a great adventure to ride to Ginger's meadow on the top of Stone Mountain and spend the night. It was really to be just kind of an overnight picnic. They took no packhorses, but simply loaded their horses up with saddlebags filled to the brim with food and liquid refreshment, tied bedrolls on the back of their saddles and took off in the

company of a wrangler named Jim Roach.

They had a wonderful trip up through South Fork canyon. When they reached their destination, Jim Roach, a young, but capable, wrangler tied up the horses while the group unloaded their gear and made camp. Jim then hobbled the horses so they could graze in the meadow but not range too far. After a camp supper, several drinks and many stories around the campfire they all turned in for a pleasant night under the stars.

Unfortunately, when the stars disappeared and the sun came up, the horses were nowhere to be found. The stranded party searched everywhere, they thought, but to no avail. Jim Roach, the hapless wrangler but an extremely conscientious one, was chagrined that the horses had managed to somehow disappear, even though hobbled. The only honorable thing for him to do was to return to the ranch for more horses. Jim recalls that he literally ran the whole way back to the ranch which was no mean feat considering the terrain. Jim explained the situation to Dean, who, as Jim recalls, was not too pleased about the situation, and eventually returned to his charges with fresh mounts. The party saddled up, loaded their gear, and set off for the ranch only to discover, just a few minutes away, some of the lost horses peacefully grazing.

Jim couldn't find three or four of the horses so gathered up what he found and took them back to the ranch. In the next two days all but one of the missing horses straggled into the ranch. Yet one small gray pony named Mouse was still missing.

Two weeks passed and Mouse had not been found in spite of numerous search parties. Everyone was about to give up and feared the worst for Mouse. But one morning, one of the wranglers was gathering horses in Red Canyon. She found some horses and was moving them down the canyon when she heard a horse whinny behind her. She looked up on the side of a hill and saw a horse limping along as though it had a broken leg. Closer inspection revealed it was the missing Mouse, still hobbled. At that point,

Mouse managed to slip his hobbles and sped off to join the other horses. Mouse was none the worse for wear, other than he had probably lost a hundred pounds. People still marvel when they speculate what that little horse must have gone through for two weeks.

Those kind of horsy experiences are challenging and humbling when they occur and HF Bar history is replete with many other similar episodes. They make great fodder for stories years later, as evidenced by the fact that even today, twenty-five years later, Elinor Constable still delights in recounting the story of the missing horses.

There are some other differences in the riding operation, not so much between today and the Hank and Dean era, but between today and the 1930s. John Gordon, who first visited HF Bar in 1925 and then for several years in the 1930s, recalls that in the old days guests were responsible for bridling and saddling their own horse and unsaddling when they returned from their ride. He believes that in those days the guests were encouraged to develop an affinity with their assigned mount. Guests, usually young girls, were known to visit the corral even during non-riding hours and groom their horses.

For the past forty or fifty years the horses have been saddled by the corral crew and then await the arrival of their riders. That is not to say that guests do not develop a relationship with their mounts. Some guests expect to be assigned the same horse year after year. Some horses have even been passed from generation to generation.

Over time, the HF Bar Ranch has had to change the focus of the riding program. Not as many people now keep horses on farms which no longer exist back home and therefore the experience level of guests is lower. Now, instruction and supervision require more emphasis.

But for many years people flocked to HF Bar to become imbued with the western way of life on a true working ranch. John Gordon, who has vivid memories of the 1920s and 1930s when guests were given the opportunity, indeed, sometimes the charge, to help out with ranch work, including branding livestock. And he remembers that sometimes the corral crew gave demonstrations on livestock branding and asked guests to participate.

To support the riding program today, the ranch maintains a herd of approximately two hundred forty horses in order to insure a suitable mount for everyone from the beginner to the most experienced horseperson. Not all of the horses are owned by HF Bar. Some of them are leased from Dave Bliss and John and Marsha Christian. And good dude horses are hard to find. For years, Bob Douglas has found and bought horses for HF Bar. It's a difficult proposition. In addition to being scarce, suitable horses range in price from $1,250.00 to over $1,700.00. In the old days it was not that difficult to pick up an ex-ranch horse for $100 to $175.

The HF Bar dude horses are considered the hardest working employees on the ranch and are therefore treated very well. Their teeth are floated when necessary and they are wormed once a year and, of course, they are shod every spring and the shoes removed in the fall when they are turned out to pasture. In addition, old horses are no longer "canned" (Note: Sold for dog food.) as they used to be. Nowadays, when they have outlived their usefulness in the dude string, they are turned out to pasture to live out their days until it is necessary to euthanize them.

Riders are not left on their own unless they want to be and are qualified to ride alone. Riding lessons are available for those that need them and experienced wranglers are on call to guide guests over the trails as well as answer questions regarding safety and horse riding techniques.

For safety reasons, children under five cannot ride out of the corral. But, during the morning and evening rides some ponies and horses are kept in the corral for the children so they can pet, lead or ride them around the corral under supervision. This practice lets the children become familiar with horses and gives them the confidence so they will be ready to ride when they are old enough.

The atmosphere around the corral has not changed. It is the place to be in the morning and after dinner. Guests love to stand around and lean on the fence rail, or sit on a long bench and watch the corral activity. The corral area still looks as it did in the 1920s. The only differences are a couple of new gates in the corral and a wooden sun guard that covers the area where guests assemble before and after riding.

Another constant is the Dining Room. The Dining Room is in its original location—just off what is now called the Little Dining Room which was, in the beginning the sole one room residence on the ranch. It was there, in 1911, that Skipper built a small addition to the original Ranch House so he would have a place to feed his first guests. Then later, the existing ranch house was virtually built around the original residence.

The Ranch House is an imposing white two story wooden structure that has, over the years, received a myriad of external modifications—mainly the addition and deletion of a number of porches. In the last few years a porch was enclosed on one end of the building to house an HF Bar museum, and yet another porch was built on the front. In 2003, a large addition was made to the kitchen which has been remodeled countless times over the years. In 2005 a further Dining Room and outside porch wing was added.

But the Dining Room has remained relatively unchanged. It is still the social focus of the ranch. Three times a day guests converge on the large, airy room to eat, family style, whatever fare the kitchen has to offer. Families actually eat together, which is an increasingly rare phenomenon in this day and age, at long wooden tables that have seen decades of service. Most often, two or three families who have sat together for years, will mingle with new families that Margi has carefully assigned to their tables. Margi

oversees the Dining Room seating chart vigilantly every day, sometimes by the meal, to assure that the guests are pleased with their tablemates. Often these sensitive seating arrangements are the basis of lasting friendships.

The atmosphere is boisterous and informal. This informality has not always been to everyone's liking. Long ago, one newcomer left in a huff after only one evening meal when he was chagrined to discover that no one "dressed for dinner." He was one of the very few who has ever had that problem at HF Bar. This, by the way, was the same gentleman who arrived at the corral for his first ride dressed to the nines in his formal eastern riding attire. He proclaimed to all within hearing distance that he was a very experienced rider and demanded one of the finest horses on the ranch. Of course, Barney gave him a suitable mount which promptly dumped the pompous rider in a glorious pile of horse manure in the middle of the corral.

Central to the Dining Room are the hashers who Ed Morsman described in his book:

...The servers have always been called hashers, a decades-old term that belies the quality of the food. Hashers typically have been, and are, prep school or college students who are children of guests and have been guests themselves. While solving a particular labor problem in tight markets, this choice of employee presents its own unique management issues. While generally cheerful and reasonably efficient, the young hashers tend to be hyperactive, free spirited, daring, unmotivated by the usual economic considerations, and highly hormonal. For years, the male hashers lived in a small cabin aptly named the Passion Pit that served as a social center for gathering, drinking, singing, and other activities that when discovered, tend to shorten a parent's life expectancy.

The Dining Room under Margi's guidance has also become a photo gallery. The walls are adorned with countless photos.

Some are individual photos of old time employees, like Barney McLain and Dean Thomas, family members and guests. There are also hundreds of guest Christmas card photos that have been assembled into busy collages.

Flora Westin was an inveterate amateur photographer from New York and equally inveterate guest who spent summers at HF Bar for several decades and took hundreds of the photos. Flora's legacy to the ranch, for all to enjoy, is a series of photo albums that span five decades.

The physical set up and atmosphere are not the only elements that have remained the same in the Dining Room. Not one to tinker with proven tradition, Margi still serves a few dishes that have been on the menu for forty or fifty years and serves them on china with the Blue Willow pattern that has been used ever since HF Bar served its first guest in 1911.

That is not to say that all things are sacred. Margi has made many changes in the Dining Room, one of which had to do with wine. According to Dick Balsiger, who has been a guest since 1969, Hank had an aversion to wine bottles on the table in the dining room and therefore, paying guests, to avoid a raised eyebrow from Hank, would bring their wine to the dining room, pour the wine into a water glass, and then keep the bottle hidden under the table.

One day Dick's wife, Bobbie, declared that the people at her table were going to drink wine from wine glasses and so she brought wine glasses to the dining room and used them. But the bottle stayed under the table!

Margi has scrapped the unusual requirement for wine bottles to be stashed under the table and today offers a varied selection of wine for the dining room. The bottles are welcome on the table tops.

HF Bar's main calling card has always been that it is a natural venue for outdoor activity that can renew the spirits of its guests.

Skipper sent this very message in a 1923 brochure when he stated:

> *...A vacation doesn't mean just slumping. It means, if you are to get the most out of it, working hard at something entirely different; it means putting into play a different set of muscles that within a few days you actually live the new life to the utter exclusion of the old and when the time comes to go home, though the return will be with regret, you will find yourself going back with an eagerness for the old job and a zest for the old life that could only come as a result of a renewed mental and physical condition brought about by a refreshing and complete change. Years will have dropped from your shoulders like feathers from a molting hen. And you will come back again...*

Skipper also took the theme further when he wrote:

> *...if you, the tired businessman, are looking for a place to spend a vacation with your family where you can really get acquainted with your children again by doing with them every day those things you have been wanting to do with them; or you, the mother, are looking for a place not made complicated by modern social conditions where boys and girls, and dads, are kids again, where the day's fun or work has left all so refreshingly tired that an hour or two in the Clubhouse in the evening tops off a full day and sends them to the feathers at 10:00 p.m., to sleep the clock around— if it weren't for the cursed rising bell, then, oh well, you'd better just be writing to the ranch this booklet is telling you about...*

Margi has rejuvenated this theme which languished for many years. Where Skipper was energetic and sometimes, at least until the 1940s, almost cajoled the guests to get involved with ranch life and take advantage of all it had to offer, Hank was more phlegmatic about the idea. Hank believed that the basic opportunities to ride, fish and hike were available; it was up to the guests to take advantage of them if they wished. True, Hank did have scheduled activities, but they were mostly in the nature of the occasional gymkhana, barbeque and weekly square dances.

Often, the fun was generated by the guests themselves in what Ed Morsman describes as "the made at home variety of fun." In the 1940s era, and later in Hank's as well, impromptu activities were dreamt up at cocktail parties when guests were being silly and simply having fun. One such typical instance involved Ed Morsman's parents, Julia and Ed Morsman. A group of guests decided to dress up in costumes to amuse themselves. They adorned themselves in outlandish outfits obtained from Hank's magic trunks which contained an ample supply of suitable attire. Ed's mother gathered up a supply of horsehair from the corral and made a wig to complement her costume as an Indian maiden. When they had a sufficiently good time at HF Bar, the merrymakers retired to a bar in either Sheridan or Buffalo, where the bartender refused entry to Ed's mother, the Indian maiden.

An overriding difference that Margi has made in the activity area is the accent she has placed on youth. This element was missing during Hank's stewardship, but is not new to HF Bar.

Many old time guests remember previous years when there were many children at HF Bar. In those days, however, they were attended by governesses and looked after separately. All the children, for instance, would eat in the small dining room.

Hank did not really encourage the presence of small children at HF Bar. There were some, for sure, and they were accommodated to a degree. For instance, there was always a "mosquito fleet," which the name was given to the group of children sent out to ride under the supervision of one of the wranglers. I speak from personal experience when I say that in previous years mosquito fleet duty was to be avoided if possible. This attitude has changed, for as Margi states it was:

...definitely an attitude we have tried to erase over the past twenty-six years...

Mostly, parents were responsible for their children's entertainment. The ranch did not provide that kind of service.

For the most part, activities at HF Bar under Hank were oriented toward adults and usually centered on alcohol. This was not a new phenomenon at HF Bar. Throughout its history HF Bar has always been known as a place for great merrymaking. Indeed, at times in its history, HF Bar has had the reputation for being a "wild place." In fact, John Gordon remembers that in the 1930s the perception among many was that all the wild party people assembled at HF Bar, while the more sedate folks went to neighboring Eaton's ranch. (Note: I'm sure there are HF Bar and Eaton alumni who would disagree with that perception).

Margi has not erased any of the traditional activities that have made HF Bar successful, but she has carefully redirected the emphasis on many. For instance, social drinking is still an enjoyable part of the social fabric at HF Bar but the days of hard core ranch-wide wild drinking parties have diminished. However, cocktail parties—both ranch-wide and individual—still abound. At nighttime, people have fun and if you wander around the cabins you will hear gales of laughter from the cabins as guests play games of charades, Dictionary and other brain teasers as well as poker.

The Gin and Tonic Classic has been held at Salt Creek (Note: A series of old houses obtained in the 1930s from the Salt Creek Oil fields and used to house employees.) every August for over twenty years. The event was instigated by two hashers, Steve Platt and Hoddy Klein, according to Steve's father, Bob Platt. Many ranch employee alumni return each year to attend this popular ranch-wide party.

Other activities have been expanded. For instance, fly fishing on the fifteen mile stretch of Rock Creek has always been a main attraction. In the past, the fishing was there if one wanted to fish and it was up to the individual to provide their own equipment and figure out where to go to catch the wily trout. Now, HF Bar offers the services of the Rock Creek Anglers, an exclusive Orvis fly fishing outfitter, to the guests. Rock Creek Angler guides not only take guests fishing on Rock Creek, but make arrangements for them to fish on other popular Wyoming streams where they have secured private waters for the guests of the HF Bar Ranch. The guides also teach novices how to fish, sell equipment and offer professional advice on current fishing conditions. A major change to the fishing program is that all fishing on HF Bar is under catch and release rules which will insure enjoyable fishing at HF Bar for generations to come.

The HF Bar website describes the fly fishing on HF Bar as follows:

...For many, an outing on Rock Creek evokes fond memories; you might wade into your grandfather's favorite pool, and find memories of his remarkable talent suddenly being refreshed; or perhaps you recall your daughter's excited smile after releasing her first rainbow. Of course, you'll always mark the spot where the legendary "one that got away" really did get away.

Truly, the HF Bar Ranch never seems to change. Come with friends and family to practice the art of angling in the way it is meant to be; in fine places, with fine people...

As with the fishing program, the shooting program has been given new dimension. Previously, there was a site down at the Middle Place, where one could shoot skeet. It was not used much except by those guests that had a true interest in shooting.

Rock Creek Shooting was formed to expand the shooting program and six sporting clay courses were designed by longtime ranch guest John Cochran and Englishman Jack Mitchell. Under the

management of Richard Platt the facility has become a world class destination for the sporting clay enthusiast. The courses offer the setting and variety of shooting situations that satisfy shooters of every skill level. And for those who don't shoot, and want to learn shooting and gun safety, professional instruction is available. The shooting program has also been expanded to include bird hunting on the ranch which is a private game bird reserve. Shooters now have the chance to hunt released pheasants, chukars and wild Hungarian partridges.

Margi has maintained the momentum that Jack Jr. started with the fall hunting program. In the fall, HF Bar offers superb guided deer and elk hunting. Some of the parties that hunt each year have hunted at HF Bar for over twenty years. Like with the summer guests, they know what to expect at HF Bar and it's why they return year after year.

Margi's emphasis on youth has evolved into the children's program. Margi sums up the program as follows:

...The HF Bar Ranch is a magical place for kids. The very nature of the ranch compels children to explore, discover, and participate in all of what's happening around them.

Nature hikes, Frisbee golf, scavenger hunts, overnight camping trips, face painting, and arts and craft classes are just a sampling of activities available to kids through our children's program.

The HF Bar employs a director for the children's program and a staff to provide organized activities for children each day. Of course, the kids are free to "just be kids" and they are not required to do any of the activities. The focus of the programs is to encourage the kids to make the most of their vacation, to meet each other, and add fun options to the long list of possibilities for them on the HF Bar Ranch...

Margi's welcoming environment for children has caused many longtime HF Bar aficionados to delight in bringing their grandchildren to experience the place they have come to know and love. In fact, the introduction of the children's program has developed into a successful niche market for HF Bar.

To keep guests apprised of the available activities for any given day, the HF Bar Ranch puts out a newsletter called *Saddlestrings*. Margi personally prepares and issues the publication each day to keep all activities up to the minute and to keep the schedule flexible. On a typical day the newsletter offered the following fare in the "What's Goin On" section:

At 9:00 a.m. meet at the Clubhouse (and we'll round up as we see you, too!) and we'll go on a nature walk...maybe go check out those baby pigs down the road and see if apples are growing yet on the apple trees.

Pool Cookout for everyone. Meet at 12:30 for some tasty vittles and an easy day by the pool. Kids—bring your bathing suits and work up an appetite with a pool party. We'll have a Skip 'n Slide, sidewalk chalk and frosty lemonade. Let's play in the sun (with sun block!!) all day!

1:30—Family Tie Dye—Get a t-shirt or bandanna from us or bring your own and come COLOR your world. This is a great family outing so that you can all have that perfect photo taken in your brightly colored new duds!

YOGA with MIMI will follow at 4:00 in the clubhouse.

SOCCER GAME —on the field below the Big Barn—4:00 p.m.

Pony Rides for all you young cowboys and cowgirls who are (almost) ready to ride the wide open range! Meet at the corral at 7:30 p.m.

STORY TIME at 8:00 p.m.—Come gather at the Chiminea with milk and cookies—wear your Jammies if you want—and hear a story or two!!

The newsletter also announced, among other things, that:

At the Ranch office front desk you will find an HF Bar Ranch Bird Sightings book. We invite you to report all feathered-friend encounters, whether they be of beauty or enchanting melody. For instance, you can hear the trill of a veery behind the cabin we call "Outlaw" and right in the horse land below Margi's or as you leave or come back from a ride. They nest there yearly. Please stop by and record your name, date and the bird species you spotted...our Ranch count is over 100 which is a world class number...

The goal of the HF Bar activity program is not to over organize people. It is, rather, to offer opportunities and adventure.

Margi approached the deteriorating infrastructure of the ranch with the same philosophy she used in evaluating the activity program. Her creed was: "If it has worked for years, why change it?"

Unfortunately, there were things that were broken or at least so seriously outdated that they were about to break or were unsafe. People expected HF Bar to be rustic but they also liked functional plumbing and electricity. To ignore the problem would eventually drive guests away. So Margi set about to remedy the situation The improvements did not happen overnight, but working within her available budget, Margi eventually managed to get the HF Bar electrical and plumbing systems up to snuff. It was not easy, and help was needed. Margi made several local professional contractors a part of the staff. Jay Walker from Buffalo and Ken Evans from Sheridan did excavation work for years. John Terry, who Margi describes as "Buffalo's premier plumber," retired in 1986 and then joined the HF Bar staff as the resident plumber for many years. John died in August, 2005.

Carl Waugh and Wilbur Robbins of Buffalo and stonemason,

Ralph Burger, worked for years, well into their seventies, building and remodeling. Today's stellar crew of workmen have carried on the tradition of "keeping things old, making it all work."

The cabin improvement program extended well beyond the replacement of the electrical and plumbing systems. Most of the cabins had porches and many of them extended over Rock Creek as it meandered its way through the cabins sprinkled along the creek. The porches were decades old and crumbling. Most needed to be replaced and while she was about it, Margi had many of them redesigned and enlarged to make them more functional.

This technique was extended to the cabins as well. Over the seventy or eighty years that most of the cabins had been in existence they had been remodeled and renovated countless times. Occasionally, additional rooms had been added to some of the cabins which resulted in some very unique floorplans. But Margi embarked on an ambitious plan to expand the capacity of HF Bar by adding bedrooms to existing cabins where it made sense as well as to install a second bathroom in most of the cabins.

All of the modifications were accomplished without changing the look of the cabins. They might be bigger, but they basically look the same. Needless to say, the additions made some of the cabin floorplans almost mazelike, which the guests believe add to the charm if not their confusion when they first walk into the cabin.

Margi has added five new cabins since she has been at HF Bar and they all fit in nicely with the established ranch setting. They look like they have been there forever. The added cabins have made a difference in the ranch guest capacity, but Margi's growth plans are limited. She is very aware of the need to keep HF Bar within itself. Too much growth could spoil the look and feel of HF Bar.

HF Bar must also house the employees. Some wranglers live on the second floor of the saddle barn, but nowadays people prefer more privacy. Other employees have, over the years, lived in a row of rooms, affectionately called "Coney Island," which was directly in back of the ranch house kitchen. Another row of small one room cabins was located near Coney Island but across the creek. That row was called "The Plunge." These units were demolished because they were unsightly and firetraps. (Note: In 2005, Margi built two new cabins where The Plunge was located. The name of one of the cabins is, appropriately, The Plunge.)

Today most of the employees live up in the area behind the horse barn. To date, sixty-one rooms with shared bathrooms are provided for the employees. These are located in a "Village" behind the barns where employees can congregate for fun as well as for living. It is a very collegiate atmosphere.

Some structures have remained relatively unchanged. One is the Horton House built in 1920. The Horton House is maintained for guests and is still used by long time guests to gather as they did in Hank's time and regale each other with memorable ranch stories. It still has the relatively same look and feel as before, but gatherings are not quite the same without Hank.

Other structures, like Farthest West, at the end of the lane leading from the corral, have been changed rather extensively. Farthest West has been lived in by a succession of Hortons, including Jack, Jr. and Dottie Davis. Margi has made many structural and cosmetic changes to create a home for her family and it is where they live from late spring to late fall. Margi also uses the comfortable and informal setting to host parties for guests and local friends.

The ranch store building remains unchanged since it was built sometime between 1911 and 1920 except that the front porch has been modified and another door installed. Inside, there have been a few physical modifications, but basically it remains the same except for the contents. The store used to have a very modest inventory— some western clothing, a few postcards and snacks. Margi has expanded the operation a great deal. Now the visitor to the store is presented with many more purchasing opportunities. The ranch newsletter *Saddlestrings* advertises the store as follows:

FOR SALE AT THE TRADING POST

Drop by the Ranch store and check the array of items from local merchants and artisans. Did you see those kids' T-shirts with Gordy, the pig's, photo on the back! Pick up an HF Bar T-shirt or a polar fleece jacket or vest specially made for us. The sweatshirts are "hot" for a chilly night! The new vests and jackets for adults and kids come in a variety of styles from very casual to (almost) Seventh Avenue.

There is beautiful ceramic ware from some of the potters in Buffalo. The Ranch store carries a wide assortment of beverages, chips, snacks, candy, bottled water and sundries. There's everything for all of your needs, and if we don't have it, we can get it. There are at least, two trips to town each day. Just ask the office people and they'll place your order for delivery (most of the time) the same day.

In addition to the ranch store inventory, selected vendors have always been a part of the operation and they still are. For example, Paul and Argyro Michelsen of Powder River Imports periodically show their contemporary and southwest sterling silver jewelry and Zapotec Indian rugs on the front deck of the ranch store. The Michelsens have been a fixture at HF Bar for over nineteen years.

It used to be that if you were a guest at HF Bar you were essentially cut off from the outside world. There was a telephone in the office which you could use but you had to be sure and ask the operator to report the charges so they could be put on your bill. Then, not too many years ago, the first pay telephone was installed in the little dining room. This was a great breakthrough. I remember one long time guest, when he discovered the new pay phone, immediately called his office back in New York to get updated on his business. On completion of his call, he exclaimed: "It was just like going to heaven." Eventually, four pay phones were installed

including one in The Village which is exclusively for the use of the employees.

Naturally, many people still go to HF Bar to get away from the outside world. But if they want to communicate they can, for the office in the store offers free high speed internet and easily accessed telephones. And, there are some spots on the ranch where a cell phone can be used to contact the outside world.

One aspect of the HF Bar Ranch operation that has changed is the emphasis on agriculture and livestock production. In the old days, these endeavors presented an opportunity to add profit to the bottom line of the HF Bar balance sheet. But, there were disastrous years as well, caused by drought and the state of the national economy, when agriculture was not profitable and financial solvency was bolstered by the resort end of the business.

Hank and Dean engaged in agricultural production to some extent. They raised hay, oats and barley and in most years bought yearling steers or heifers to feed during the winter and sell the next fall. But toward the end of their time, their efforts had declined.

Margi has taken the agricultural aspect of HF Bar Ranch in a different direction. Partly because of the scarcity of agricultural workers and the increased cost of farming equipment, Margi decided that it is a far better use of the ranch these days to set aside some parts of the Ranch as riparian areas for conservation purposes and other parts for winter pasture for the horses and the registered Angus cattle that Lily runs in partnership with her father, Dave. All fields are irrigated. A very intricate system of gated irrigation pipe now carries water to areas never before irrigated and an extensive stock watering system has all been installed throughout the ranch. Today, it can be said, that agriculturally, the HF Bar Ranch is being put to its best use.

Philosophy For The Future

With twenty-four years of experience under her belt, a natural inclination toward excellence and a love of people, Margi has evolved a philosophical model to carry the HF Bar into the twenty-first century. She has long been inspired by the Disney Company who she believes "seeks excellence in their work." The Disney Company, which according to Margi, is only happy with occupancy rates well above the industry standard of 88%. Margi is proud of the fact that HF Bar maintains a 100-104% occupancy rate and that of those, 75% are returning guests.

The year 2005 was the best year on record for the HF Bar Ranch. But that success did not come easy. It was, according to Jamie Ringley, "bloody hard work." But, both Margi and Jamie take pride in the fact that the hard work by the HF Bar team was behind the scenes and invisible to the guests. To the guests, the operation appears seamless and effortless most of the time.

In spite of the successes, Margi maintains a vigilant guard against complacency and instills this same attitude in the staff. She is aware that success can be fleeting. "We must make sure," she maintains, that "we don't get complacent. There is always more we can do."

Margi's ultimate objective is that people who visit HF Bar should be happy. She is happiest, she maintains, when she hears "gales and gales of laughter" and often rejoins staff members with the outcry, "Look how happy we are making these people!"

Margi also believes that HF Bar should be involved in the community. This aspect was evident in the early days of HF Bar, less so when Hank was in charge. But, Margi has revived community relationships with Buffalo and Sheridan, Wyoming. For example, HF Bar has become a popular destination for local school trips when children can participate in a variety of activities, including popular

hayrides. Senior citizens are also welcome. Many local senior groups take advantage of HF Bar to have a "day out" when they have a nice lunch and perhaps a lecture and a tour

Local citizens may also book HF Bar facilities for other events. Because of the magical setting, the HF Bar Ranch has become a popular place for weddings. Margi estimates that approximately 35-45 weddings, not all local, have been conducted at HF Bar. Not only is the setting wonderful, but the HF Bar staff provides excellent catering for the reception afterward as well as accommodations for attending guests, if needed.

Special groups have also discovered HF Bar and have been welcomed. HF Bar provides a great environment for a range of groups from the physically and mentally challenged to corporate gatherings. Margi and the staff are sensitive to the needs of all groups and take great care to insure that all special needs are fully satisfied.

Margi's sense of social involvement extends to charity causes as well. Locally, an HF Bar donation package which might include dinner for eight, or a few days stay at the ranch, is a very popular charity auction item and always brings a substantial winning bid to benefit the charity involved. HF Bar auction packages are popular in other parts of the country as well. For instance, the HF Bar Ranch donated a five day stay at the ranch to the Red and White Ball in Greenwich, Connecticut, to benefit the Red Cross. The winning bid was $28,000! The person who made the winning bid was a guest at HF Bar and has been a return guest since.

And so, the HF Bar story continues into the twenty-first century. Soon, a one hundredth anniversary celebration will be in order. Margi Schroth, during her last twenty-four years at the helm, has taken the measures needed to rejuvenate HF Bar so it can successfully continue for the foreseeable future. When asked what she sees as the future of HF Bar, Margi gets a faraway look in her eyes and muses that she is not certain, but of one thing; she is emphatic that as long as she is there, and she doesn't plan on leaving anytime soon, she will continue to act as a responsible steward as have those before her. She feels a weighty responsibility to preserve such a special place.

In reflecting on past stewards, one cannot help but wonder what Skipper, and Warren for that matter, would think about HF Bar today. How would it measure up to their original vision? I believe they would be pleased. They would be pleased that HF Bar has been kept intact by its stewards—Hank, Dean, Jack Jr. and Margi. No doubt they would also be pleased that after ninety-four years it still provides pleasure for so many. And they would be pleased that the stewards have kept faith with the original Articles of Incorporation of June 21, 1913, which state that:

...the principal object of said company is and shall be to engage in the general business of conducting pleasure resorts...

HF
VOLCANO
OF
JOY

RANCH HOME
HF BAR RANCH
BUFFALO
WYO.

Acknowledgments

This book was made possible because of the support I received from Margi Schroth, owner of the HF Bar Ranch. The project would have been impossible had she not placed an abundance of original source material and photographs at my disposal. In addition, she took time, at her busiest time of the year, to arrange interviews and group discussions with HF Bar guests. Thank you Margi.

I am also grateful to Jamie Ringley, the office manager, who was equally supportive.

Several HF Bar guest families provided a wealth of information about HF Bar and kept me honest with the manuscript. Ed Morsman, who thankfully wrote *The Postmistress of Saddlestring Wyoming*, and his wife, Beth, were enormously helpful as were Bob and Pam Platt, who have the longest generational association with the HF Bar Ranch.

Several copies of the draft manuscript in various stages of work were passed around to guests for review and comment. For their interest and assistance I am grateful to Phillip Long; Hoyle Clay "Bronco" Jones; Bob Montgomery; Mary Carolyn Chandor; Peter Eaton; and Mildred Good. To others who have read a version of the manuscript and are not known to me, I appreciate your interest.

I conducted individual interviews, in person and by email, and group interviews with several people who, directly and indirectly, provided invaluable information which enriched the text. I am very thankful to: Bev Hiza; Richard Platt; Pam and Willard Dixon; Anne Dixon; Will Dixon; John Brockway; Charles Brockway; Leila Javitch; Bob and Linda Ross; Thomas L. "Tee" Barker; Suzanne Timken; Jim Niner; Shirley, Watty, Lila, Jay, Peter and Kirby Taylor; Elinor Constable; John Gordon; Terry and Peter Stead; Nancy Duble; Dick Balsiger; Lou Castaldi; Russell Huson; Harry Huson; Karen Carlson; George White, Jr.; Vesta Ringley; Bob Balkenbush and Lynn McCleary

Others who provided source material were Martin McCarty; Steve Smith; Shorty Smith; and Jim Hamilton. Thank you.

Several institutions were of great assistance in my research. I would like to thank the staff of the Johnson County Public Library in Buffalo, Wyoming, and, in particular, the director, Cynthia Twing; the Sheridan County Fulmer Public Library and the Wyoming Room staff in Sheridan, Wyoming; the Salt Lake City Public Library in Salt Lake City, Utah; the University of Chicago Registrar's Office in Chicago, Illinois; the Montana State Prison Public Affairs Office in Deer Lodge, Montana; the Wellesley College Registrar's Office in Wellesley, Massachusetts; and the Rowland Hall/St. Mark's School Registrar in Salt Lake City.

The pen and ink drawings used throughout the book are by E. W. "Bill" Gollings, an HF Bar employee in the 1920s, who produced the drawings to illustrate HF Bar Ranch marketing brochures. Drawings were provided courtesy of the HF Bar Ranch.

I am also indebted to Henry Stewart who, as an advocate for his grandparents, Warren and Demia Gorrell, whom he never knew but nevertheless reveres, helped me provide balance to the book and

credit to his grandparents.

A thank you goes out to proofreader Sarah de Souza for her sharp eyes and knowledge of the arcane intricacies of style and to Computer wizard John Belobraidic who can work miracles with old and less than perfect photos.

This is my second collaboration with Annette Chaudet of Pronghorn Press. As usual, she offered enthusiasm and total support. In addition to her moral support, I am grateful to Annette for again leading me through the mysteries of publishing and for formatting, editing and publishing this book.